Praise for
Catholic Women Confront Their Church

"The courageous Catholic women profiled in this timely book have issued a clear call for the transformation of the institutional church. Their faith is profound; their voices are strong. Their message has the power to change hearts, minds, and hierarchies."
—Joan Connell, former editor of *Religion News Service*

"In Celia Wexler's meticulously assembled inquiry into the state of mind of contemporary Catholic women, we hear from ten different subjects, each as riveting and articulate as the next, calling for compassionate and heartfelt change. The result is a stunning choral effect, worthy of being heard in the sacristy and in the streets, by men and women alike. Wexler's prose reads with the clarity and conviction of a beautiful prayer."
—Madeleine Blais, Pulitzer Prize–winning journalist, University of Massachusetts Amherst

"For most of modern history, Americans have been religious outliers—we're the rare society that's both prosperous and devout. In recent decades, however, a growing number of Americans, especially the young, have drifted away from organized religion. This is a complex phenomenon with multiple roots. Celia Wexler has summoned her impressive journalistic skills to tell one aspect of this story with great insight, empathy, and humanity."
—Paul Taylor, Pew Research Center, author of *The Next America: Boomers, Millennials and the Looming Generational Showdown*

CATHOLIC WOMEN CONFRONT THEIR CHURCH

Stories of Hurt and Hope

Celia Viggo Wexler

ROWMAN & LITTLEFIELD
Lanham • Boulder • New York • London

Published by Rowman & Littlefield
A wholly owned subsidiary of
The Rowman & Littlefield Publishing Group, Inc.
4501 Forbes Boulevard, Suite 200, Lanham, Maryland 20706
www.rowman.com

Unit A, Whitacre Mews, 26-34 Stannary Street, London SE11 4AB,
United Kingdom

British Library Cataloguing in Publication Information Available

Library of Congress Cataloging-in-Publication Data
Names: Wexler, Celia Viggo, 1948– author.
Title: Catholic women confront their church : stories of hurt and hope / Celia
    Viggo Wexler.
Description: Lanham : Rowman & Littlefield, 2016. | Includes bibliographical
    references and index.
Identifiers: LCCN 2016005014 (print) | LCCN 2016020403 (ebook) | ISBN
    9781442254138 (cloth : alk. paper) | ISBN 9781442254145 (electronic)
Subjects: LCSH: Women in the Catholic Church.
Classification: LCC BX2347.8.W6 W49 2016 (print) | LCC BX2347.8.W6
    (ebook) | DDC 282.082—dc23
LC record available at http://lccn.loc.gov/2016005014

∞ ™ The paper used in this publication meets the minimum requirements of
American National Standard for Information Sciences Permanence of Paper
for Printed Library Materials, ANSI/NISO Z39.48-1992.

Printed in the United States of America

CONTENTS

Acknowledgments   vii

1 Introduction: Catholic Women Confront Their Church   1
2 My Story   13
3 Frances Kissling: Abortion's Moralist   25
4 Sharon MacIsaac McKenna: From Convent to Commune   39
5 Sister Simone Campbell: God's Lobbyist   55
6 Marianne Duddy-Burke: Beyond Catholic Incorporated   71
7 Diana L. Hayes: The Thorn in the Church's Side   87
8 Teresa Delgado: Trauma and Faith   105
9 Barbara Blaine: Still Seeking Justice   123
10 Gretchen Reydams-Schils: Breaking Through the Silence   141
11 Joshunda Sanders: Coming Home   159

Afterword: For Our Daughters   177
Resources   181
Notes   185
Bibliography   199
Index   203
About the Author   207

ACKNOWLEDGMENTS

This book began in earnest after I participated in a memoir workshop at the Key West Writers' Workshop Program in January 2014. I submitted my first chapter, terrified of what my colleagues would think. I received a very positive critique and enough encouragement to move on with this book. My teacher, Madeleine Blais, and my fellow students helped to launch me.

My agent, Kathi Paton, believed in the book and found a good home for it. She encouraged me over many months of writing and rewriting and helped me shape an effective book proposal. Sarah Stanton, my editor at Rowman & Littlefield, offered patient and constructive criticism that I deeply appreciated.

My boss, Andrew Rosenberg, director of the Center for Science and Democracy at the Union of Concerned Scientists, where I worked as a public-interest lobbyist until April 2016, permitted me to work part time for ten months in 2014 and to take "book leave" in August 2015. That time was invaluable.

The nine women you will meet in this book were incredibly generous with their time and insights. They were willing to share their deepest thoughts about their faith, and their own life stories. I hope that this book captures some of their depth, intelligence, courage, and idealism. My dream is that someday all of my subjects will get to meet one another at a dinner party. I am sure we would find a lot to talk about!

This book was difficult to write because it touches a facet of my own life—my Catholic faith—that I have struggled with for many, many years. My wonderful spouse, Richard Wexler, is a Jewish atheist. Yet whenever I was tempted to quit writing, he bucked me up and supported me. He believed in me—and in this book. We met when we were journalists, and he is a very good editor. His incisive critiques of each chapter improved this book. He has been patient, when I've been "absent" every Saturday for more than a year, writing away. He's also put up with my grumpiness. My daughter, Valerie, has become an extremely keen and sharp-eyed editor, whose careful research and final reviews of chapters always led to better writing.

Valerie is the real reason for this book. I wrote this book for all our daughters. They need to understand our struggles with Catholicism and why they matter.

1

INTRODUCTION

Catholic Women Confront Their Church

There is a reason that I called this book *Catholic Women Confront Their Church* and not *Catholic Women Confront Their Faith*. To me, faith embodies both a personal experience of God, and an adherence to principles guided by that experience, which inform my life. Church is very different: It is the institution that in theory is supposed to help me develop and participate in my faith. But often the institutional church has been a barrier to that faith.

The problems that have dogged the church's approach to women are both centuries old and persistent. As Catholic historian Margaret Harvey observed, "Women have no effective role in church government, cannot be priests, rarely study theology, and are limited in what they can do when they have. Those who control church government are men, and, what is more, men who cannot marry and who are seldom intimate with women." Harvey wrote that in 1976.[1] While other institutions and churches have made dramatic progress on women's rights since the 1970s, the Catholic Church has not.

I began this book in late 2012, just months before Pope Benedict XVI broke a six-hundred-year tradition and stepped down from his office. One Vatican expert termed the resignation the "only great reform of Benedict."[2] A month after the stern, judgmental Benedict stepped down, the church's cardinals chose, on the fifth ballot, the first Latin American to head the papacy, Argentinian Jesuit Jorge Mario

Bergoglio. Greeting 1.2 billion Catholics for the first time, he talked of "working together in the Church of Rome . . . part of the governance of love, of trust."[3]

The sunny and tolerant Pope Francis has shaken up the church and displayed a more tolerant tone when discussing sexual ethics. Pope Francis has spoken about the need for equality between men and women and calls for a new theology of women. He has advised women religious that if they're looking for a good spiritual director, they should look to wise women in their own communities.[4]

But he has closed the door on any reconsideration of the ordination of women to the priesthood. And he can wax poetic about women in ways that can irritate feminists. "The qualities of delicacy, peculiar sensitivity, and tenderness . . . are abundant in the female soul," the pope said in 2015, suiting them for an "irreplaceable role" in family life. That role should be central, he said, even if they aspire to do other things.[5]

As I complete this book, there are few indications that the church's approach to women has fundamentally changed. Since 1965, popes have been advised by a group of bishops from around the world, called a *synod*. Pope Francis convened the Synod of Bishops in 2014 to begin a discussion on Catholic families and how to respond to their needs. That discussion was continued in October 2015 when the synod met again.[6]

On April 8, 2016, Pope Francis released his long-awaited response to the synod deliberations. The document, termed an apostolic exhortation, offers hope to divorced and re-married Catholics wishing to receive Holy Communion. The Pope suggests that full participation in the church may be permitted to such couples by a priest on a case-by-case basis.

While its tone is warm, nonjudgmental, and respectful of the role of conscience in moral discernment, the document does not signal any dramatic departure in church doctrine. It defines same-sex marriage as not "even remotely analogous to God's plan for marriage,"[7] and shows no softening of the church's official stance even on artificial birth control.

The document does speak out against the oppression of women, and affirms the "equal dignity"[8] of both sexes. But it is not a rousing call for women's empowerment in the church. "I certainly value feminism,"

Pope Francis wrote, "but one that does not demand uniformity or negate motherhood."[9]

While the Pope urges priests to more fully understand family life, he does not consider whether a married priesthood or women's ordination might help priests better understand the problems of families. Instead, he suggests drawing on the "broad oriental tradition of a married clergy"[10] and involving more women in the training of priests to inform priestly perspectives.[11]

It is not surprising that the Pope's response to the synod largely ignored the role of women in the church. Not one woman had a vote in a synod whose focus was the family. Thirty-two women joined the 270 bishops and cardinals as auditors or other nonvoting participants. While women were able to chat with the men and express their views, the experience wasn't always pleasant, said auditor and attorney Sister Maureen Kelleher. The prelates share the same seminary training and have a vision of the church that often differs from that of the laity, Kelleher told the *National Catholic Reporter*. There were times, she said, "I've felt the condescension so heavy, you could cut it with a knife. . . . Some of it is, 'Oh, here comes the bleeding heart. Well, she's a woman—what else would you expect?' kind of thing."[12]

Indeed, while Pope Francis has cheered the progressive wing of Catholicism, his ascendancy has sharpened the battle between those who would address the reality of living as a Catholic in the twenty-first century and those who want to preserve the church's authority at all costs.

For women in the United States, many issues are fraught with political as well as moral significance. Social issues appear to dominate the 2016 presidential campaign more viscerally than they did in 2012. Abortion, homosexuality, and even contraception remain controversial and part of the debate. Several Republican candidates would ban abortion without even exceptions for rape or incest.[13]

The Catholic Church has not been immune from these political battles, and they've appeared to open up a fissure divided by gender. Women religious, concerned about social justice and addressing poverty, are more likely to stand with Democrats. The United States Conference of Catholic Bishops, on the other hand, often joins with religious conservatives to support the moral positions of Republican candidates.

(On other issues, such as the treatment of immigrants and refugees, the sisters and the bishops often stand together.)

When I sought women to profile, I did not have an agenda. I wasn't looking for an affirmation of faith; nor was I looking for resistance to it. I just wanted to discover whether the struggles I felt were shared by others. I was on a quest, seeking the answer to a very personal question: Was it possible to be a woman who was an independent thinker, a professional in the workplace, who firmly believed in women's equality, and still be a Catholic?

This was not an academic exercise for me. I felt that I had reached a fork in the road. Either I would find a way to stay Catholic that made sense to me and respected my intellect and feminism, or I would have to leave the church. I knew that the journey would be difficult. I knew it would have to start with one crucial piece of unfinished business: I had never directly confronted the scars of my Catholic childhood. Until I had the courage to tell my own story, I concluded, I could not tell anyone else's. For that reason, the next chapter in this book is my story.

I've arranged the nine profiles of Catholic women that follow my own story in roughly chronological order, based on the date of a seminal incident in their lives, to track their experiences with the history of the last half century of the institutional church, beginning just before Vatican II and concluding after the ascension of Pope Francis to the papacy.

Frances Kissling rose to national prominence as an outspoken Catholic who opposed church teachings on abortion and contraception. Despite her often-acerbic sound bites aimed at the Vatican and church leaders, Kissling also has been thoughtful about abortion and its ethical dimensions. For twenty-five years, she headed Catholics for a Free Choice, now called Catholics for Choice. She is currently president of the Center for Health, Ethics and Social Policy, a small nonprofit that works to improve the status of women throughout the world, focusing on sexual and reproductive health, women's rights, civil conversation, and other issues. She continues to write and speak about church policies affecting women.

Sharon MacIsaac McKenna is a former nun who lived in a commune in Toronto, Ontario, where she underwent intensive psychotherapy, eventually training to be a therapist. In her book, *Freud and Original Sin*, MacIsaac McKenna challenged her church's long-held interpretation of the biblical story of original sin, using Sigmund Freud's insights to make her point. Married to a former priest, she is the mother of one daughter and grandmother of two girls. Although she made her peace with the institutional church long ago, its sexist policies still can anger and frustrate her.

Sister Simone Campbell, executive director of NETWORK, the Catholic social-justice lobby, saw an opportunity in the very public censure of women religious by the Vatican in 2012. Taking advantage of the media attention, she launched the Nuns on the Bus tour across America, which focused on the needs of the poor and critiqued Republican proposals to cut federal funds for domestic programs. The media-savvy nun has appeared on *The Colbert Report, 60 Minutes,* and *The Daily Show* and wrote her memoir, *A Nun on the Bus: How All of Us Can Create Hope, Change and Community.*

Marianne Duddy-Burke is the executive director of DignityUSA, which represents thousands of gay, lesbian, bisexual and transgender Catholics throughout the country. Dignity believes that LGBT Catholics are "beloved persons of God" with the right to "participate fully in all aspects of life within the Church and Society."[14] Duddy-Burke is married to a former nun and has two daughters. She writes regularly for the *Huffington Post.*

Diana L. Hayes was a lawyer in her thirties when she converted to Catholicism. The former attorney went on to become the first African American woman to earn a pontifical doctorate in sacred theology, a degree she received from the Catholic University of Louvain, Belgium. In 1988 she joined the theology faculty of Georgetown University. Now retired, the emerita professor of systematic theology continues to lecture and write about the African American experience in Catholicism and about womanist theology. Her ninth book, *No Crystal Stair: Womanist Spirituality,* was published in August 2016.

Teresa Delgado's embrace of her Puerto Rican heritage and her efforts to come to terms with her rape as a teenager informs her work as associate professor of theology and ethics at Iona College, New Rochelle, where she also directs Iona's Peace and Justice Studies program. A married mother of four, Delgado has written about Catholicism's contribution to a Latin American culture that encourages women to be submissive. In her sexual-ethics classes, Delgado helps her students think about sexuality in a Catholic ethical context.

As a young teen, Barbara Blaine was repeatedly sexually abused by her parish priest. That experience eventually led her to found the Survivors Network of those Abused by Priests (SNAP). Blaine's tireless work to prod the church to do more to protect the vulnerable from sexual predators and to help survivors heal earned her a national award from *Ms.* magazine in 2002. Married, with graduate degrees in law, social work, and theology, Blaine in 2014 marked the twenty-fifth anniversary of her organization, which now has more than twenty-two thousand members.

Gretchen Reydams-Schils chairs the Program of Liberal Studies at the University of Notre Dame. Born and raised in Belgium, married, and the mother of three, Reydams-Schils found that her European Catholicism often has been considered suspect at Notre Dame. She's been frustrated by her inability to break through the silence, feeling increasingly marginalized as the campus has grown more politically and doctrinally conservative. Author and editor of several books in her specialty, ancient philosophy, Reydams-Schils also wrote *An Anthology of Snakebites: On Women, Love, and Philosophy*, which uses a series of fictional conversations between two friends to offer a feminist commentary on the masterworks that inform the Western academic tradition.

Joshunda Victoria Sanders was raised by a mentally ill Catholic mother and grew up in poverty in New York City. Talented and resourceful, Sanders found mentors who helped her escape the homeless shelters and subsidized housing of the Bronx for boarding school and eventually Vassar College. She broke from the obsessive faith of her mother only to discover—after experiencing deep loss and years of wandering seeking God—a Catholic community that welcomed and nurtured her. Sanders has been a successful journalist and speechwriter. Her work has appeared in *Kirkus Reviews, Gawker, Publishers Weekly, The Root*, and the *UTNE Reader*.

Over the course of meeting these women, one factor became clear: All were shaped by the legacy of Vatican II, whether or not they were even born when Pope John XXIII convened the council in 1962. Vatican II was, in some ways, the Arab Spring of Catholicism. It ushered in a brief window of hope and transparency when it looked like democracy might prevail over rigid institutions, when collegiality—between pope and bishops, bishops and priests, and priests and laity—might become the norm.

Vatican II did result in some changes. Encouraged to modernize, women religious gave up their floor-length medieval habits and assumed more freedom to work in the world in a variety of occupations. The Mass could be said in the languages of the countries where Catholics worshipped, and the priest would face the congregation, not have his back to it. Music at Mass began to include guitars and folk songs adapted for worship. A new spirit of ecumenism meant that Catholics now could pray with non-Catholics and attend Protestant weddings.[15]

There was more receptivity to theologians, including young theologians with new ideas, and women and laymen were permitted to study theology. That was a new development, said theologian and former priest Gregory Baum, who played an influential role at Vatican II, only to be sanctioned by the church in later years. "We have theologians who are not priests," he said. "This did not happen in the nineteenth century. Lay people have made an enormous contribution."[16]

Two major changes in how the church approached the world also emerged from Vatican II. The church no longer considered the Jewish people enemies of Catholicism, acknowledging that all mankind was culpable for the death of Christ.[17] And the Vatican recognized that Catholics make moral decisions based on the promptings of their own conscience, as informed by the church. That recognition was based on church teachings that had been ignored for hundreds of years.[18]

But the larger promise of Vatican II—that the church would adjust to the modern world, liberalize the priesthood, opening it both to married men and women, revise its teachings on sexual morality, and become less authoritarian—was the victim of a huge backlash, one that reverberates to this day, although certainly tempered by Pope Francis's more compassionate tone.

Pope John XXIII had created a commission of clergy and lay people to consider the question of artificial birth control, a commission continued by his successor, Pope Paul VI, and even expanded to include more lay people. But the commission's recommendation—its members reportedly voting fifty-two to four to permit artificial birth control for married couples—was ignored by the pope.[19] Instead, he issued an encyclical, *Humanae Vitae*, which left unchanged the teaching that artificial contraception was "intrinsically wrong."[20] The encyclical shocked Catholic laity and created huge fissures in the church.

The papal intransigence had long-term implications. Writing on the twenty-fifth anniversary of the encyclical, the late Jesuit moral theologian Richard A. McCormick lamented some of those effects: "For some years now acceptance of *Humanae Vitae* has become one of the litmus tests for episcopal appointment. . . . Theologians who question it are excluded from speaking in some dioceses and seminaries, and are regularly denounced by the right-wing press as 'dissidents' and 'disloyal.' . . . Great numbers of Catholics no longer look to the church for enlightenment in the area of sexual morality."[21]

As the church hierarchy shut the windows that John XXIII had pried open, it continued to elect popes with rigid belief systems. Pope John Paul II, for all his charisma, and Pope Benedict XVI both disdained a world they felt was immoral and corrupt. The increasing rigidity of the church, particularly as church leaders focused on sexual morality and the reproductive rights of women, is part of the stories of the women I profile.

These women also inherit another very different legacy—that of liberation theology. Articulated by Latin American bishops in the late 1960s, liberation theology emerged as Catholic clergy and laity tried to address the oppression of the poor by repressive governments—governments that often had been allied with the church hierarchy. Liberation theology taught that the gospel requires that we do more than pray for the oppressed. Christians must be actively engaged in making the world more just, and must perceive that the structures that permit poverty and injustice are themselves sinful. As Fordham University theologian Michael Lee put it, "A liberation spirituality invites us to look at the crucified people of our world and ask them . . . 'What do I need to do to bring you down from the cross?'"[22]

Pope John Paul II did all he could to suppress liberation theology, concerned that its approach was too close to Marxism and strayed too far from church orthodoxy.[23] Pope Benedict also was cool to it. The movement is having a rebirth under Pope Francis, who invited Rev. Gustavo Gutiérrez, one of the founders of liberation theology, to meet with him. Pope Francis also moved to beatify Archbishop Oscar Romero, who defied the oppressive regime in El Salvador and was murdered while he was saying Mass. Romero's cause for canonization had stalled because of the opposition of conservative church leaders.[24]

Finally, the women of color I interviewed have been influenced by womanist theology. Pulitzer Prize–winning writer and novelist Alice Walker is considered the mother of the term *womanist*, defining it in her book *In Search of Our Mothers' Gardens: Womanist Prose*. Her description is broad, but at its heart it "affirmed connectedness to the entire community and to the world" and a "concern" by women of color, for the well-being of black men as well as women "in a culture that oppresses all black people."[25] At its core, says theologian Diana Hayes, womanist theology is a critique both of black theology, which had viewed the black experience solely through the eyes of black men, and of feminism, which was not expansive enough, addressing sexism but not classism or racism or other forms of oppression.

Out of all these influences and trends, certain themes emerge in this book:

> *The primacy of conscience:* In its *Declaration on Religious Liberty*, Vatican II affirmed that "the human person sees and recognizes the demands of the divine law through conscience."[26] These women strongly believe that the individual, informed by the church's teachings, makes choices based on the dictates of his or her own moral compass. This doesn't mean that anything goes. Rather, it demands more of us, because we have to commit to a set of values thoughtfully and prayerfully considered. Blind obedience to church mandates is not enough.
>
> *The importance of social justice:* These women strongly espouse the notion that the gospel compels us to serve others, make the world more just, and reduce oppression. But when they look critically at the institutional church and its priorities, they see many failures. Some address those failures within church structures, challenging the church to do better. Others fight for social justice through their engagement and service in secular institutions. Either way, it is a core part of their faith lives.
>
> *Rejection of the church's opposition to women priests:* These women, well-read in the history of the church, think the church doesn't have a leg to stand on when it comes to justifying the exclusion of women from the priesthood, challenging the premise that, since only males were present at the Last Supper, Christ intended ordination to be restricted to one gender. MacIsaac McKenna questioned the logic of that argument by asking whether all

priests had to be Jews, since only Jewish men attended the Last Supper, calling it "so stupid, you can hardly believe it." There is a profound sense of loss, a regret that the church's denial of ordination to women deprives it of the talent and commitment that the church badly needs.

Doubt that ordination is enough: Many of these women feel that opening up ordination, while a positive development, would not be sufficient. They contend that the church requires a more fundamental structural change, a recognition of the priestly power of all Catholics—lay, religious, and priests. They don't believe that the ordination of women would be the magic bullet to radically reform the church. And while agreeing that ordination should be open to women, some suspect that women in the priesthood, without any other reforms, would not significantly change the top-down power dynamic in the church.

Appreciation of Pope Francis but skepticism about what he can do: These women are generally happy that the new pope has changed the tone, but they're not waiting for radical change to happen. Most believe he hasn't done enough to expand women's power in the church. Even those who strongly welcome his approach do not expect miracles. Reydams-Schils advised Pope Francis to do all he can for his successor, because "one pope is not going to make the difference to turn this tide."

A faith that transcends the institutional church: These are women of faith, but their belief system is far deeper than allegiance to Catholicism per se. It largely is propelled by a commitment to the gospel message of serving one's neighbor and the larger world. As Sister Simone Campbell put it, "Faith is so much more than the church, so that's a big comfort—that Jesus is bigger than the institution."

One final note: I am a journalist. I do not claim to be either a theologian or historian. I do not presume to be an expert on the Catholic Church. Nor does this book aspire to be a definitive examination of the views of Catholic women on the church. But I do believe that this book will speak to Catholic women like me, torn between the faith they love and the institutional church that often sets their teeth on edge. This is the conversation that Catholic women are not having with one another, and should be. I hope they will find some comfort in these stories. I know I did.

2

MY STORY

I can hear my father now, reciting the Nicene Creed. *I believe in one God, the Father almighty, maker of heaven and earth*, the words intoned gravely by him and hundreds of other worshippers, heavy words falling like stones. I would wince as the creed continued, recited loudly like a battle cry against the world of non-Catholics outside the plain wooden doors of Saint Cecilia Church in suburban Rochester, New York. I was sure one of those heavy words was aimed directly at me.

The faith of my father was not a warm and fuzzy faith. The picture of the Sacred Heart that hung in our living room, the crucified Christ in my bedroom, even the Madonna bookended with bronze baby shoes: all looked down on us with sorrow. It didn't help that the cross that held the dying Christ was incongruously pink to match the color of my bedroom walls. They were reminders of my sinfulness.

My Catholic childhood was no grimmer, and likely far less grim, than that of many other Catholic children of that era. But I had a soul that soaked up Catholicism directly and vividly. From a very young age, I also experienced a keen awareness of my body and my senses. The collision of Catholic guilt with heightened sensuality does not make for a comfortable life.

Not until I read Mary McCarthy's *Memoir of a Catholic Girlhood* did I realize that other Catholic seven-year-olds believed they had committed a sin serious enough to exile them from the Eucharist right before making their First Communion. McCarthy had broken her fast with an unthinking sip of water.

But the prospect of not participating in the ceremony, and wearing her veil and dress, as well as the ire of her guardians, overcame her conviction that doing so would be an unforgivable mortal sin. She brazened it out. "God would never forgive me; it would be a fatal beginning," McCarthy wrote. "I went through a ferocious struggle with my conscience, and, all the while, I think, I knew the devil was going to prevail: I was going to take Communion, and only God and I would know the real facts."[1]

My sin was more complicated. I had touched my genitals—briefly, fleetingly—while thinking about my favorite uncle's upcoming wedding. That produced a sensation of pleasure that I couldn't name. I couldn't describe what I had done, even to my mother. When I tried to tell her that I had committed a mortal sin, she told me she'd take the blame for it. Guilty of a sin I couldn't even define in words, I participated in my First Communion with the same sense of doom and damnation that McCarthy had experienced, but without her bravado.

Things didn't get better after that trauma. The neurotic women religious who taught us continually dramatized a war within and a war without. They wore the full habit of the Sisters of Mercy, their long black skirts rustling as they nervously patrolled the parking lot that served as our playground. Sister Mary David was principal when I entered kindergarten. She was under five feet tall but stocky, with the bearing of a warrior. We all cringed at the thwack her steel ruler made as it sliced the air and landed on the knuckles of a miscreant.

I had the bad luck to have been born left-handed. I remember being closeted away with Sister Mary David and another sister for hours. They would take the pencil I was holding in my left hand and move it to my right. I don't remember any anger, just persistence. Totally puzzled, I would switch it back to my left hand. They finally gave up. To this day, I don't understand why I refused to capitulate and why they caved.

But the nuns rarely gave in when the issues were bigger. The war without was waged against the godless Communists who pounded nails into the skulls of brave Christians who would not renounce their faith. They described the threat of World War III and the new evils coming from Red China, warning that Chinese guerillas could soon be taking over our little suburb. (What made things worse was my fear of Chinese *gorillas* marching down Culver Road, at the end of my street.)

The war within, if possible, was even scarier. We were taught that our own minds and bodies were ready to pounce on us if we let up our vigilance even for a few seconds. We were taught to avoid any "occasions of sin"—any person, place, or thing that might lead us into sin. I took that command quite literally, terrified that I might accidentally read something in the newspaper or hear something on television that could corrupt me.

My soul, according to the nuns, was a fat oval, almost in the shape of a heart. Sister Mary Florian drew it on the blackboard and filled it in with white chalk. When we sinned, Sister took the eraser and wiped away the white. Sin made our souls black, disgusting to God and all good people. Only confession, and a perfect act of contrition, could restore us.

In fifth grade, my teacher, a menopausal nun barely on the right side of sanity, asked me to read the definition of *flesh* from the huge dictionary at the front of the classroom. I was mortified. She then taught us to how the worst sins were sins of the flesh.

The war between mind and body and the ceaseless vigilance against "impure" thoughts grew worse with the arrival of puberty. I wore my hair in a high ponytail. I would shake my head to literally shake off any thoughts I deemed unseemly, and the ponytail would swish up and down and around. It got so bad, Sister Jeanette, my twenty-something seventh-grade teacher who was rational and had a sense of humor, actually asked the parish priest to counsel me. He tried, but I remained unconvinced. The ponytail continued to move. (Twenty years later, we had a chance meeting when I was working as a journalist. By then, she'd left the convent and was working as a fitness teacher, I believe.)

But with all the pain, the rituals of Catholicism brought great beauty into my life. I loved the recurring drama of the Mass, the liturgical symbols, the musky, heady smell of incense on High Holy Days, the music. For some reason, our small family library contained a slim volume of Renaissance Madonnas. I was entranced by the reproductions of paintings by Raphael, Leonardo da Vinci, and Fra Angelico, etched in gold leaf. I would turn the pages slowly, drinking in the beauty of the images. The gospels gave me a vision of the power of language. "*In the beginning was the Word, and the Word was with God, and the Word was God.*"

That facet of Catholicism became even more pronounced when I attended Catholic high school. Unlike the squat, no-frills structure of my grammar school in the blue-collar Rochester suburb of East Irondequoit, Our Lady of Mercy was in the tony suburb of Brighton. Looking like a cross between a castle and a fortress, the three-story sprawling brick structure had been designed by noted architect J. Foster Warner and erected in 1928. Over the years, it had been enlarged to include a junior college for postulants, sisters in training. In 2002 the building was designated a Brighton landmark. I remember its stairs and marble and professional-grade auditorium with blue velvet seats and a balcony. I got lost nearly every day traveling from class to class.[2]

The scary nuns of my childhood were replaced by worldly and wise nuns, who seemed not to breathe the same air as my grammar-school teachers. The church was changing, and they had lost the white wimples that had hidden their necks and part of their faces. They had legs! And they showed bits of hair under shorter veils. These were women, some with doctorates, who decided that, as the sixties were coming to an end, it was up to them to ensure that the female students in their care were not let loose on the world like a bunch of naked chicks.

They snuck in unconventional lessons. Our earth-science teacher pointed out helpfully that a house of prostitution reportedly operated in the Blossom Road area near our school; she then explained prostitution to us. Those considered the brightest among us got to take some classes in the junior college.

Our English teacher let her best students read anything they liked. I chose André Malraux's *Man's Fate*. We discussed Camus and existentialism. I read *Madame Bovary* in French; of course, what my teachers did not realize is that I so feared wandering into "an occasion of sin" that I would skip all the passages referring to sex.

This fear of sin led me to be likely the only young woman in my graduating class of 240 girls to actually learn new information from the film shown to us at the end of senior year by a Catholic team of husband and wife medical professionals. They explained, aided by a filmstrip, the mysteries of sexual intercourse. I was floored and, I must confess, initially quite repulsed.

By the time I graduated from high school, the sexual revolution was in full swing. Pope John XXIII had opened the doors of a fusty old church and let in light and air. The unrest reached into the University of Saint Michael's College, a Catholic college in Toronto, Ontario. It was part of the University of Toronto, whose downtown campus then included six affiliated colleges, with a total enrollment of roughly forty thousand students. Marshall McLuhan was thinking about the medium being the message in a modest building next to my dorm. The priest who taught me sophomore theology spent a semester debating with us the pros and cons of his abandoning his vocation. He left and married a former nun.

Theologian Rev. Gregory Baum and philosopher Leslie Dewart were on campus, stirring things up with a progressivism that respected the integrity of other faiths and explored new interpretations of scripture, even new definitions of divinity. And a few blocks away, a British psychoanalyst with the improbable name of Mrs. Smith was running a commune to which priests and religious flocked. No one was quite sure what went on there.

The revolution went on without me. My biggest act of rebellion was to attend Mass at the Newman Center and receive Communion as both bread and wine, something not yet approved by church hierarchy. We also said the Lord's Prayer, concluding with what I had always been taught was the "Protestant" ending: *For thine is the kingdom, and the power and the glory, forever.*

But that doesn't mean I believed mindlessly. I have always been skeptical about life after death and the existence of heaven and hell. On the other hand, I believe something continues after we die. It would be too cruel if the billions of people who lived on this planet and endured slavery and torture, poverty, imprisonment, and disease, were cheated of a better existence. If there is a god, and an order to the universe, how could these suffering billions not have a better future?

Likewise, I developed my own definition of *transubstantiation*, the belief that at Mass, bread and wine become Christ's body and blood. To me, transubstantiation is an everyday occurrence. It's the miracle that turns notes on a page into music, words into the alternative reality of novels, or streaks of paint on a canvas into art so vivid it creates new worlds. If I had my way, the host that the priest holds before the congregation would be a mirror, and we would perceive God living in each of us.

I always thought that Mary, the Mother of God, was misunderstood. The few words Scripture attributes to her reveal a woman whose notion of social justice would make her a suitable blogger for *The Nation*, and whose only request for a miracle was to ask her divine son to spare a wedding couple the embarrassment of running out of wine. Her words don't comport with the pious, passive woman extolled in church literature.

I always wondered, too, whether Mary was the first young woman approached by an angel and offered the opportunity to bear Christ. It seemed to me it would take someone with a lot of imagination and faith in herself to have acquiesced, to have believed the impossible was possible. I couldn't understand why Catholic dogma so harped on Mary's being a virgin. Why wouldn't she have had a normal married life and given birth to other children? Would that make her story less admirable?

And I never had much respect for Catholic hierarchy—or for any hierarchical organization, for that matter. Journalism, the profession I dreamed of joining, and then did join, gave me a way to challenge the establishment without breaking the rules. It would be my escape. The irony is that the first journalism outlet to offer me a job was a Catholic newspaper in Upstate New York. The paper was fat with ads, with a healthy weekly circulation. I liked my bosses, who were old-time newspapermen who happened to be Catholic.

I recall that early in my tenure, one of the senior editors told me with some relish about a former editor of the paper, a priest who had been murdered some years before. The case had never been solved, but there were rumors that the editor had had a gay lover and the killing was a crime of passion. The man whom they suspected had worked at the paper, although what he did there seemed sketchy, and he disappeared after the murder. In that not-so-distant past, such crimes and potential scandals seldom made the newspapers.

I remember a high-ranking, respected cleric stood behind me and wrapped his arms around my neck while I was covering a news event at the headquarters of Catholic Charities. It did not feel fatherly. I also recall the stories of rectory housekeepers who were regarded as friends with benefits by the priests for whom they toiled.

But what really intensified my struggles with the Catholic Church was *Roe v. Wade*. The church was obsessed with the 1973 Supreme Court decision that legalized abortion. I blush to think I was dragooned into narrating an anti-abortion video that the diocese put together.

What bothered me was that opposition to abortion was paired with opposition to contraception. How could the church have it both ways? If abortion meant killing babies, wouldn't you be glad to have a way to prevent conception in the first place?

If there was a moment when I grew cynical about the church, it was the day a "pro-life" volunteer, a woman of means who'd likely not experienced a moment of struggle in her life, proudly recalled manning an anti-abortion hotline and giving advice to a mother of four of limited means in a shaky marriage who discovered she was pregnant. She knew her husband was not the father. She had obtained some form of a morning-after pill to end the pregnancy and was considering taking it. "I told her to flush that pill right down the toilet," the volunteer beamed. I wondered if she ever considered what hell that caller might face because of that glib response.

A few years later, when I had a job in mainstream journalism in another city, I visited a clinic staffed by nuns working in a low-income neighborhood. The nuns fitted their impoverished clients with diaphragms. I knew the story would have been my ticket out of journalism's minor leagues. But I didn't bust the sisters. I couldn't. They were serving the gospel I believed in.

Still, the warnings of my grammar-school nuns remained alive in my scrupulous soul. Intellectually, I had no problem with premarital sex. But emotionally, I knew that if I slept with someone and then he left me, it would destroy me. I would not be able to recover from the guilt combined with the blow to my self-esteem. Having deep unfulfilled sexual needs and a hyperactive conscience did not make my twenties any picnic. I remember dating a somewhat older editor I really liked. He had blue eyes and a red beard, great taste in restaurants, and a great love for James Joyce. We would take long lunches in a fancy place with white tablecloths, and he always ordered wine and dessert.

On Valentine's Day he gave me a silver paperweight in the shape of Robert Indiana's pop *LOVE* sculpture. But when we went to an office party, he got pretty drunk and picked up a male hitchhiker on the way back to my house. And later he confided to me that he'd been expelled from Catholic seminary because he'd been caught holding hands with another seminarian. "Do you understand?" he asked me. I said I did, but really didn't. How could he be gay and act as if he were my boyfriend? With that confession, he ended the relationship.

I concluded that marriage was not in my future. Any man who would want to marry a virgin, I figured, would be a self-righteous prig who wouldn't share my liberal views. And a man who shared my politics would never be able to understand why I was so sexually inexperienced. What I hadn't reckoned with was meeting a man who accepted me, Catholic baggage and all. The fact that he is a Jewish atheist is proof to me that God has a sense of humor.

As my wedding day approached, I figured I needed advice about birth control. I remember asking a journalist colleague and good friend how he and his wife planned their family. He made clear that they had no problem with contraception. "We may be Catholics, but we're not idiots," he told me. I sought the counsel of a priest as well. When I explained my problems with scrupulosity, he listened carefully and advised that I would be a nervous wreck with the rhythm method, "natural" family planning that regulates family size by scheduling intercourse when the woman isn't fertile, the only system the church officially permits. He suggested trying something more conventional.

That's not unusual. There's a silent cadre of priests, theologians, and intellectuals who in their counseling work privately are quite progressive when it comes to sexual matters. But in most cases they live comfortable lives and don't make waves. They don't take on the institutional church. They shut their eyes to the struggles of millions of Catholics who accept the institutional church's word as God's word and who suffer from it.

We have a new, more progressive pope, but that hasn't dramatically changed how the American hierarchy operates. Our bishops continue to be obsessed with the unborn, gay marriage, and the contraception mandate in the Affordable Care Act. They organize right-to-life rallies, speak about the White House encroaching on "religious liberty," and perceive women only as mothers and teachers. The American church had been an institution that shut its eyes to pedophilia among its ranks and when discovered, tried to cover it up and shush its victims. It is an institution that even today, condemns abortion more loudly than it ever did priestly sexual abuse.

My conflicted feelings about the church grew more pronounced when I moved to Northern Virginia in 1996. Walking into a Catholic church in Alexandria, Virginia, was like walking into the 1950s. This is a region that includes the nation's Super Zips—enclaves of some of the nation's wealthiest and best-educated Americans.[3] My neighbors have doctorates and work in the highest echelons of government. Yet the Diocese of Arlington is known for its conservatism and was the second-to-last diocese in the country to permit girls to be altar servers.[4]

In 2012, the diocese began to ask its volunteer Sunday-school teachers to formally declare their allegiance to the teachings of the Catholic bishops, including the bishops' strong opposition to the Affordable Care Act's insurance requirements on contraception.[5]

My parish church by and large reflected the conservative views of the Arlington diocese. It even hosted a lecture on the Spanish Inquisition, which described a kinder, gentler persecution of the Jews than history presents.[6]

There have been a few reprieves from Masses that failed to nurture. One summer an older priest was a guest of the parish and gave inspired sermons. I still remember his reference to theologian Frederick Buechner and his advice: "Your vocation in life is where your greatest joy meets the world's greatest need." For a few months, a priest visiting from Poland treated us to simple expressions of what it means to love God and one's neighbor. When he left, I told him how much I had appreciated his sermons.

"That's not me," he said modestly. "That's the Holy Spirit working."

"The Holy Spirit doesn't come here very often," was my sharp retort.

I'm not sure how I would have handled my growing discomfort with Catholicism, Northern Virginia–style, were it not for my friendship with Deb, a divorced Catholic neighbor and government contractor, with both a security clearance and a knack for making friends. My teenage daughter, who took care of her cats, told me about the lady who transformed her condo into a showplace, her walls bright with sunny Caribbean colors, and her cabinets and tabletops adorned with exquisite mosaics of her own creation. After we had become friends, Deb suggested I attend 9 a.m. Mass with her and her daughters, when the parish folk choir made the preaching more bearable.

Deb left Northern Virginia for Colorado and the chance to pursue her mosaic art. But I was so taken by the choir that I joined it. Catholic churches often are not friendly places. Even the kiss of peace—the greeting Mass participants are supposed to extend to one another—tends to be a pro forma handshake. I never attended the parish coffee-

and-doughnuts events after Mass. I don't eat doughnuts, and I never thought my views would be in sync with most practicing Catholics.

Choir changed that. My group includes a psychiatrist, several lawyers, teachers, scientists—even a researcher with the Government Accountability Office. Our director is a disciplined and talented musician with an acerbic and irreverent wit. We know one another and have created a fellowship that I value. After choir practice, we hold hands and ask for prayers for a husband or wife undergoing a surgery, a troubled student who committed suicide, a daughter taking a college-entrance exam, a neighbor with terminal cancer. We say a brief Our Father or Hail Mary. To me, those moments of prayer with people I know and respect feels like community, feels like church.

I haven't discussed my views with other choir members, but I get glimpses of kindred spirits. A few years ago, one of the priests urged the congregation to oppose the decision to move a teen-wellness center from its location in a trailer near a shopping center to the local public high school. The wellness center would provide a range of health services, including mental-health and substance-abuse counseling and immunizations.[7] But the priest was only concerned that the move would make it easier for teens to get access to contraceptives. Another choir member, the mother of teens, shook her head. "That's exactly where it should be," she muttered under her breath. Tight smiles, rolled eyes, grimaces (especially in my alto section)—to me they all betray discomfort that may not be as deep as mine but is present nevertheless.

A few scientists have theorized that there is a gene that prompts some of us to seek out religion.[8] I don't know whether that is true, but I do know that I need God. I need to believe in a power greater than myself who watches over me and the rest of the world. I need to appreciate nature and my own good fortune, as well as my troubles, in the context of that faith. And, for me, faith cannot be solely personal. The Catholic Church, for all its flaws and for the narrowness of the vision of its leaders, has sunk its roots deep into my bones and flesh.

There is no doubt that my life has been enriched by the gospel, the stories of the saints, the world's cathedrals, and the solemn and spiritual liturgy of the church. I don't want to appreciate the church's music, art, and history as a disinterested spectator; I want more. But that's where the struggle comes in: I cannot reconcile my conflicted feelings for the church I cannot bear to leave.

My hope is that this book will contribute to the larger conversation about the future of the church and its approach to women. But this book also has a more personal goal for me. Writing it offers me a way to resolve some of the unanswered questions in my own soul: Has my struggle for so many decades been worth it? Or is the chasm between me and the institutional church just too large to bridge?

Pulitzer Prize–winning journalist Madeleine Blais once wrote that journalism often is a "frightening and perilous and delicate" process that allows you as the author "to go through someone else's truth to get to your own."[9] This book is my perilous journey.

3

FRANCES KISSLING

Abortion's Moralist

Blonde and energetic, Frances Kissling has a clear, authoritative voice and booming laugh that fills her sunny condo in one of Washington's best neighborhoods. Its white sofas and walls are offset by brilliant flashes of color from her almost-wall-sized abstract paintings. The living space is accented by two wooden figures from Mexico—an angel and a Madonna. The purity of the folk art complements rather than conflicts with the sophisticated urbanity of the setting; the contradictions work. That may be an apt summary of Kissling's own history: One year out of high school, Kissling entered the convent. A decade later, she was running an abortion clinic. Both decisions, she says, were motivated by a desire to serve.

When Frances Romanski was born in 1943, few could have predicted her exceptional life. A childhood spent in a working-class neighborhood in Queens, a divorced mother whose second husband adopted her, and the Catholic Church, which permeated every facet of her world—all these elements would contribute to the making of a rebel and intellectual.

Her mother's two failed marriages led Frances to decide she was not interested in becoming either a wife or mother. Early on, too, she adopted views that would place her in opposition to the policies of the institutional church—supporting a woman's right to both contraception and abortion.

But Catholicism had an equal role in her formation. It led her first to the convent and ultimately to the helm of Catholics for a Free Choice, CFFC—now known as Catholics for Choice—which speaks for Catholics who disagree with the church's rigid stance on the reproductive rights of women. For more than two decades, Kissling was the group's highly visible spokesperson, taking the fight on abortion directly to the church hierarchy, to the doors of the Vatican itself.

She was, she concedes, the queen of sharp sound bites. Among her favorites: "I spent the first twenty years of my adult life looking for a government I could overthrow that could not put me in jail, and I found it in the Catholic church."[1] Today she is less likely to jibe and more willing to listen, trying to understand the logic underlying official church positions on a variety of issues, while continuing to believe that the church's stance often is wrong. "It's kind of like your parents," she says. "They have some ideas that are off the wall from where you sit, but you know them, and you have affection for them, and you cut them a certain slack. You try to understand where it comes from in the most generous way possible." That tolerance, she says, is also a part of her "continued identification with Catholicism."

One of the nation's better-known Catholics, Kissling spent fifteen years living entirely without Catholicism—and not missing it. "I was a young, sexually active single woman with no desire for marriage. What in God's name did this church have to offer me?"

But that was Kissling in her twenties and early thirties. Things were far different when she was a child. She was a product of Catholic elementary and secondary schools, a good student who didn't get into trouble. She admired the priests and nuns, who encouraged her and advised her.

As the daughter of working-class parents growing up in the 1950s, she faced limited career options, and religious life seemed to offer more opportunities for study and advancement. "So for me, the convent was that thing that resembled a professional life." In Catholic school, students were taught about the three states of life, and the religious life was considered the highest calling. "I was an ambitious person. . . . Why should I aspire to anything other than the highest state of life?" she says with a laugh.

Her mother's history had always complicated her Catholic experience. Her Catholic mother had divorced and remarried a Protestant, the man who gave Kissling her last name. At school, Kissling learned that divorce and remarriage was forbidden to Catholics. This bothered her so much that she confided her worries to her confessor. The priest told her, "Well, have your mother come and see me, and we'll see what we can do for her."

At her prodding, Kissling's mother agreed to go, to be told that rapprochement with the church was possible only if she ended her sexual relationship with her husband, and agreed to take Communion either in the rectory or at a nearby parish. Secrecy was necessary to avoid the scandal of a divorced woman receiving the sacraments.

Kissling's mother shrugged off the offer. "To her this was totally absurd." As a preteen, Kissling didn't grasp the full implications of a married couple living as brother and sister, but the notion that her mother "had to sneak around" to receive the sacraments was "very disturbing."

Kissling was finding a number of issues—mostly on sexual ethics—where her views differed from those of the institutional church. But that didn't seem to be a big thing back then. Since Catholics rarely publicly challenged church teachings, if you were a practicing Catholic it was just taken for granted that you believed what everybody else did. "Orthodoxy was assumed on one hand, but on the other hand nobody was really asking you very much."

The convent still seemed a viable option. "My story to myself was, 'The church actually needs people like you. Because things do need to change, and if would be good if there were people who were nuns and priests who were not so rigid and crazy about this stuff.'"

After completing Catholic high school, and a year at Saint John's University in Queens, Kissling entered the convent. But that's when her mother's history again intervened. At the time she joined the convent, some religious orders still had policies denying entry to illegitimate children. When Kissling submitted the required papers, it became clear that she'd been conceived a few months before her parents were married. Her mother had gotten involved with a soldier. When she discovered she was pregnant, she told the army chaplain. He intervened, and the couple married. Nevertheless, Kissling was reluctantly accepted into religious life because two priests who knew her "went to bat for me."

Life in the convent was pleasant, she recalls. There was time to think and a sense of order, peace, and community. The new entrants, called *postulants*, took college classes, even music appreciation. The sense of shared rituals—everyone wearing the same habit, following the same schedule, going to chapel together—were "bonding experiences. They connected you both with the other people, but with something outside of yourself. It was all part of a spiritual life. That part of me that is a heart, as opposed to a head, found those things good. . . . People cared about each other."

But the Sisters of Saint Joseph of Brentwood, Long Island, were not so caring when it came to Kissling. The illegitimacy still rankled. "I didn't do anything out of the ordinary while I was there, but it was clear they were watching for the moment when they could urge me to leave." At a routine weekly meeting with the mistress of postulants, she was asked, "Would you like to go home?" And she found herself answering, "Yes."

The nuns didn't suggest that she think it over. Her mother was called, and she was packed off. But not without one final cruel word. She was taken to the attic of the motherhouse, a tidy space furnished with two straight-backed chairs. Sitting in one was the Mother Superior. Kissling was asked to sit in the other chair. "This is my exit interview. The only thing I remember from that interview was her saying to me, 'Well, you know, we never really wanted you.'

"I was just sort of numb, as you sometimes walk through an experience." Her mother picked her up, reassuring her that she had "so much to offer," suggesting she join the Peace Corps.

"For me, that was the end of Catholicism. As far as I was concerned, that period of my life was over. I just closed the door and went about, in essence, a secular life from that moment on. I had no interest in Catholicism anymore."

She finished her college studies at The New School for Social Research, now called The New School, about as far from Catholicism as you could get. Based in Greenwich Village, The New School was founded in 1919 by a group of intellectuals unhappy with the "intellectual timidity of traditional colleges." It aimed to be a place of learning where "faculty and students would be free to address honestly and directly the problems facing societies in the twentieth century."[2] It has long been a hotbed for leftist, liberal culture. Kissling hadn't earned high marks in theology, and the admissions officer joked, "Given that you got a C in theology, we'll definitely take you."

This was the sixties. Student activists were opposing the war in Vietnam, and campuses across the country were the focal points of sit-ins, teach-ins, and demonstrations around the war and other issues. The sexual revolution was in full swing. Kissling was in the thick of things. She helped found a campus chapter of Students for a Democratic Society, whose youthful adherents wanted to fundamentally challenge the status quo. "I got arrested for the first time in my life" while participating in one of the early demonstrations against the war at the United Nations. "I always wanted to change the world."

Just how she would change it, wasn't clear to her. After graduation, she held a series of administrative jobs and landed at a trade group, the American Association of Psychiatric Clinics for Children. It was 1970, and abortion was legal in New York State. Two physicians who knew her and her background were opening an abortion clinic in Pelham, New York. "They asked me if I would run it. That sounded like a great thing to do to me. I had no qualms about it." She had no "Catholic feeling" that abortion was a sin. On the contrary, as a single woman who was sexually active, although personally careful to use contraception, she thought women needed access to safe abortions. She was prompted by the same instinct that had made the convent attractive: the desire to serve. "I would have a responsible job, and I would help women."

New York legalized abortion three years before *Roe v. Wade* made it legal throughout the country.[3] Kissling recalls that the typical client "drives up fourteen hours from Kentucky, in a beat-up old car with her boyfriend. Arrives at the clinic at 4 a.m." They are waiting when she opens the clinic several hours later. "They're sitting in their car in the parking lot, scared to death." They tell their story. The woman has questions: "What's going to happen to my fetus? Is my fetus going to feel pain? Am I going to go to hell? Where is my fetus going to go? Will God punish me? Am I doing the right thing?"

Those women asked "all the big questions," Kissling says. They had thought about what they were doing and felt that they didn't have an option except abortion. "I wish I didn't have to do this, but I have to do this," they would say. Most women, Kissling found, "take this thing seriously. . . . They want to do the right thing. They're not like, 'Ah, a medical procedure, unwanted tissue, bye-bye.' That's not how women look at it."

Kissling "learned about Catholic guilt because of lot of people came in with Catholic guilt." She ran the administrative side of the clinic and was not a counselor on staff. But she would help out. To answer some of the women's questions, she had to read up on Catholic theology and "get a more sophisticated understanding of sin." But also, she says, there is "that part of Catholicism which is just simple. 'No, God is not going to punish you. God is not about punishing people. God loves you. Jesus is compassionate'—just very simple things you say to people to reassure them."

"You're not doing a bad thing," she would tell them. "You're doing the best thing you can do."

The staff would not perform abortions on women who were uncertain. They'd be asked to come back after they'd thought about their decision, and the staff might refer them to counselors outside the clinic. In other situations, she says, it was clear that a boyfriend or a parent wanted the abortion but the woman did not. Those women, too, would be sent away. "If you want to have a baby, your parents don't get to decide this."

In her experience, Kissling says, parents are more likely to push a child to have an abortion rather than have the baby. Even those who oppose abortion, she says, change their tune when confronted with a pregnant daughter. "It was, 'Oh, my God, she can't go through with this. She's in college. I think in her case—her case—she made a mistake, but she shouldn't have to live with that mistake forever. She's really a good girl. She wasn't out being a tramp like the others.' Because there's always that: Abortion is justified for three reasons—rape, incest, and me. And everybody else is a slut."

Between 1970 and 1980, Kissling ran the day-to-day operation of two abortion clinics, then did some international work on abortion, and went on to serve as the first executive director of a membership association for abortion providers, the National Abortion Federation. She left that job to work with feminist author Ellen Frankfort on a book tackling an issue about which she felt strongly: the denial of Medicaid funds for abortion to poor women. *Rosie: The Investigation of a Wrongful Death* told the story of Rosie Jimenez, who died from an illegal abortion because she was too poor to obtain a safe, legal one. The book gave

Kissling a chance to address her concern that the abortion movement was not "as attentive to the issues of poverty as I felt it should be."

Just as Kissling was becoming immersed in the abortion world, a few Catholic women formed a small nonprofit, Catholics for a Free Choice, to represent Catholics who opposed the church's increasingly rigid stance on contraception and abortion. In 1978 Patricia McMahon, then–executive director of the five-year-old group, approached Kissling and asked her to join CFFC's board.

The request needed a little time to process. Kissling knew she did not agree with the institutional church on many issues. But she saw the possibilities for this new group and its mission. "Abortion is very serious for me. It *is* a moral issue," she says. "And for most people I work with, it's a political issue. It is a medical issue. It's a women's-rights issue. But it is not a moral issue. So even though I had been working in abortion close to ten years, I felt that there was this enormous absence of a space for moral consideration about abortion, and Catholics for a Free Choice was clearly a place where you could do that."

But *was* she a Catholic? The woman whom *Boston Globe* columnist Ellen Goodman would call the "longtime philosopher for the pro-choice community" had to seriously consider that question.[4] Rollo May wrote about the "will to love," Kissling says, and Kant the "will to power." She wondered whether there might be such a thing as the will to believe. That tallied with the advice the church gave to those struggling with their faith. The answer for those with doubts was to behave as if they had faith, and that faith would come, she says. "Not in a superficial way," she adds, but to explore, read, and pray over it. She knew she would not be returning to the Catholicism she had known as a child growing up in the 1950s and later as a young woman. But she knew the church had been changing since then. She concluded that she would join the board of CFFC and that her "personal project of exploration" would be to determine how and whether she could be a Catholic.

To Kissling, Catholicism is partly a matter of upbringing—what formed you in your earliest years. It is tied to your ethnicity and class and geography. It's also a definition confined less to strict adherence to a certain set of beliefs than to the way you view the world. And with that framework, she qualified.

"The early formative years from two years to twenty years are dominated by Catholicism in every single way. Nuns who taught me. Priests who befriended me. Camp I went to. The schools, the whole thing. My life was a Catholic life." Being raised Catholic in an outer borough of New York City with a stepfather who was "a tradesman, who worked a craft, who got up at five o'clock in the morning and went out and did a construction job and came home dirty" is a part of her DNA, and part of the DNA of many of the women who organized and ran CFFC, she says. They had a visceral understanding of the demands motherhood placed on working women.

Kissling saw that firsthand when her stepfather abandoned the family and her mother was forced to take the only job she could find, working the night shift as a telephone operator. "She probably made forty dollars a week and tried to support four children on that kind of money. A very hard life."

And Kissling's mind always worked like a Catholic's. Even when she was doing abortion work, she sensed the difference in the way she perceived abortion from other pro-choice activists. While the institutional church pronounced abortion a crime against the unborn, and pro-choice activists felt that abortion was solely a matter of a woman's right to control her body, Kissling saw that abortion was "very nuanced. It involves more than one value."

The institutional church, she contends, has focused the entire question on the fetus, while pro-choice groups ignore the morality question altogether. "I'm the one that's stuck, thinking of both issues." That raised some suspicions in the pro-choice movement. "There's a lot of respect for me, but there's also a certain amount of 'What is this love that Frances has for the fetus?'"

In 1982 Kissling took over as president of CFFC, a job she held for the next twenty-five years. One early goal was to beef up the group's Catholic bona fides. "The people on the board were Catholics, but there was no strong identification of the board members as *Catholic* Catholics—you know, professional Catholics." She set about recruiting leading figures in the progressive Catholic movement. By the time she left, about half the board members were theologians. "The organization was more recognized as part of the progressive Catholic Church, not a front group for the pro-choice movement."

In 1984 CFFC was instrumental in creating a full-page ad in the *New York Times*, its headline proclaiming, "A Diversity Of Opinions Regarding Abortion Exists Among Committed Catholics." The ad included a careful, respectful statement challenging the Catholic bishops' contention that all Catholics condemn "the direct termination of prenatal life as morally wrong in all instances." The statement pointed out that "a large number" of Catholic theologians believe that under some circumstances abortion "can sometimes be a moral choice." The ad was endorsed by ninety-seven Catholic theologians, priests, and religious.[5]

The ad helped convince "the public and policy makers" that "Catholic bishops didn't represent Catholic people on abortion," Kissling says. The ad "was a very visible demonstration" of the fact that "Catholic people are all over the place on issues" and they did not march in lockstep to the pronouncements of their bishops. That was important, she says, because it made it more difficult for a bishop to threaten legislators. It would be harder for a bishop to tell a legislator, "If you don't do what we want on abortion, Catholic people aren't going to vote for you."

CFFC also set itself apart from other pro-choice groups by developing its own position on abortion. As early as 1990, Kissling stressed that the pro-choice community should understand that abortion "deals with people's deepest, most unconscious feelings about life, the power of creation, and the survival of our species," that it is both "a private and social phenomenon."[6]

In 2001, in a thoughtful commentary in the *Journal of Medical Ethics* of the British Medical Association, she wrote that she approached abortion as a Catholic, a feminist, and someone who cared about social justice for the poor. All those perspectives led her to believe that a woman's own conscience must guide her as she makes this decision, without the "intrusion" of state or faith. She explained that CFFC's position was not absolutist; the organization "never opposed laws that limit abortion after viability," so long as late-term abortions are permitted to save a woman's life and health. But all such laws, she stressed, must "respect women's moral agency."[7]

But respect for the moral dimension of abortion did not temper Kissling's battles against the institutional church. Under her leadership, CFFC took on the Vatican, criticizing its special status as a nonmember state at the United Nations. In 1996, the Vatican felt it necessary to counter CFFC's efforts by issuing a four-page response to the group's attacks. Kissling was elated. Here was proof, she told the *National*

Catholic Reporter, that her organization "is becoming a big gnat on the skin of the elephant."[8]

That gnat continued to bite. In an op-ed for *USA Today*, Kissling charged that the Vatican was using its status to align with conservative groups intent on limiting the rights of women. "Imagine the furor," she wrote, if a UN diplomat were to suggest that "condoms cause AIDS" or did not believe that women raped in war should be permitted to use emergency contraception, or argued that UNICEF did not deserve support since it "was no longer a children's agency and was involved in abortion." All those positions, Kissling pointed out, "are regularly taken by representatives of the Roman Catholic Church—a 'country' that many people are shocked to hear exists, and outraged when they learn the United Nations has accorded it the status of a state (albeit a non-member one)."[9]

The Vatican did not lose its special status at the UN. But CFFC's campaign provided a Catholic counterweight to the Catholic Right, speaking up for the UN's family-planning programs, helping the organization defend itself against the angry complaints of conservative Catholics. Likewise, CFFC's advocacy for a change in church views on contraception as the best vehicle for reducing the number of abortions helped establish the organization as a trusted voice for rational dissent.

Kissling was aware that her own power, and the public space she occupied, derived from her Catholicism. She had become, she concedes, "a professional Catholic." Indeed, one of her fears when she headed CFFC was that the church might excommunicate her.

"At a personal level," she says, excommunication "would be meaningless." She once joked that, had she been exiled from the church, she would start "going to Communion twice a day, because they can't stop you. Do you think there can be a picture of me in every church in Washington, DC?" She adds that, "since I'm not active in a parish, excommunicating me is not going to take me away from parish life."

But, she acknowledges, "at a professional level, in terms of the work I was doing, excommunication would not be helpful." She'd make some news and likely write a book about the experience. "I'd get speaking engagements. It would be the 'man-bites-dog story,' which I could ride out for a year or two." But then she'd fade away from the public sphere. "I could not speak with whatever modicum of authority being a Catholic who has not been excommunicated gives me. So my work would be damaged."

She didn't think that would happen, in part because it would draw too much attention to her, a woman church officials liked to call "a nut with a fax machine," and in part because the church would be hard pressed to justify excommunicating her when they were not excommunicating Catholic lawmakers in Congress who were "far more responsible" for keeping abortion legal than she was. But had she been excommunicated, she says she would have resigned. "I do not think it would be good for CFFC to have a president and a spokesperson who was excommunicated."

Not that fear of church retribution dampened her ardor in tweaking the hierarchy. "I have really good sound bites, and all of these sound bites are zingers," she says with relish. A barb she's fond of: "I think John Paul II really has one of the greatest minds in the church; unfortunately it's one of the greatest minds of the fifth century."

"I go for the jugular," she says. "That was part of my job." But since stepping down from CFFC, she says she's in a different place. "This is my honey period as opposed to my vinegar period."

She has sympathy for Catholic health-care providers who have a narrow window in which they can be faithful to church policy and serve women. She points to the moral gymnastics around the concept of "indirect abortion," which states that if a medical procedure's primary goal is to save a life, and the intention is not to kill a fetus, then the death of the fetus is tolerated as collateral damage. Under these circumstances, she says, Catholics may treat cancer of the uterus in a pregnant woman, or an ectopic pregnancy, when the fetus is lodged in the fallopian tube, even if the treatment results in fetal death.

Catholic health-care providers "are trying their best to figure out ways to stay within" what they consider to be a value or a tradition while also aiming to "help the woman." But the problem is that there are so many situations where fine-tuning the ethics to conform to papal directives isn't always going to work, she says. And when the fine-tuning fails, women with medical conditions who need abortions to save their lives don't receive them. She blames the Catholic hierarchy, "hell-bent on a law that bans all abortions," for this rigidity.

There was a time, she says, when theologians had more leeway in discussing these moral questions. In the sixties and early seventies, theologians were considering "the value of the fetus, the circumstances that might justify abortion," the distinctions between what the legal position should be and the moral one. All that rich discussion disappeared after 1975, she says, due to the "chilling effect of the John Paul II and Ratzinger papacies." What's happened, she says, is that bishops are doing all the talking, and "theologians are keeping their mouths shut."

She bemoans what she calls the "politicizing of theology." In Catholic churches not only in the United States but throughout the world priests and bishops are making "pronouncements for political purposes," meant to advocate for changes in secular laws, rather than giving "guidance to ordinary people who need to make decisions about these things." She's encouraged, she says, that Pope Francis seems willing to welcome more discussion on moral questions.

When she left CFFC in 2007 she was profiled by the *New York Times* and honored at a posh event at Washington's Four Seasons hotel, where feminist Gloria Steinem, novelist Anna Quindlen, and Congresswoman Rosa DeLauro paid tribute to her.[10] Her successor at CFFC, Jon O'Brien, hailed her as a "pain in the ———."[11] Her papers are stored at Smith College, and she did lengthy interviews on her life as part of Smith's Population and Reproductive Health Oral History Project.

She left an organization with a $3 million budget and international partners, primarily in Latin America. Since stepping down from CFFC, she's participated in several civil dialogues with pro-life advocates, trying to find common ground. She has written for *Salon* and other publications on abortion and other Catholic issues. And she continues to be a symbol, for those who either revile or admire her, for Catholic dissent on women's reproductive rights.

Kissling has continued to explore ethical issues and moral dilemmas, first as visiting scholar to the Center for Bioethics at the University of Pennsylvania and now as president of the Center for Health, Ethics and Social Policy, a small nonprofit that works to improve the status of women throughout the world.

Kissling enthusiastically describes her work helping health-care providers throughout the world explore their ethical qualms about contraception, abortion, and health services for gay men—in countries where health policies are often at odds with the workers' backgrounds. Her goal, she says, is not to change a pro-life worker into a pro-choice one, but to have groups of health-care managers understand the beliefs that underlie their moral values, and how those values will affect their work in the field. It is, she concedes with a smile, all about ethics and conscience and values formation. "Yeah, Catholic," she shrugs. "In the best sense of the word."

Kissling's faith is difficult to pigeonhole. She attends Mass "once in a while." And when she goes, she receives Communion. "If I'm going to Mass, it would be stupid not to take the sacraments." But she is not a fan of contemporary Catholic liturgy, calling Catholic folk masses—very popular among progressive Catholics—"just tacky." For aesthetic reasons, she prefers the Latin Mass, with "beautiful vestments, great music—and I don't need the priest to be facing me." But while she would enjoy such a Mass, it would not inspire a religious feeling. Catholicism, she says, does not have that emotional pull for her—what she calls the "smells and bells" aspect of church-going.

While she is fond of the Bible's "whole set of stories about Jesus, the apostles, his mother," she does not hold them to be literally true. To some extent, she says, the stories are "the touchstones for how I think about life." So the biblical account of the Resurrection, she says, is less about whether Jesus rose from the dead or not, and more about what the story teaches us about life—"how one can die in a certain way, but be reborn, be resurrected. . . . There is hope in despair. People make mistakes, they correct them."

Kissling insists that the question should not be *Are you a Catholic?* but *What kind of Catholic are you?* Some people choose to identify themselves as Catholics if they are very pious and attend Mass and pray. Others are Catholics because they believe in the gospel message of social justice. "The pious stuff is totally uninteresting to them. I have friends who are nuns. They wouldn't go to church if you paid them," she says. "They wouldn't put their foot inside a Catholic church other than to demonstrate." Nuns will tell her, "I get angry when I go to church because women are excluded, and I'm not going." She adds that she's "willing to let Pat Buchanan—archconservative Catholic, who doesn't seem to care about the poor or anybody else and is ready to bomb the entire world"—call himself a Catholic. "He's not a Catholic like me, but he's a Catholic."

In the end, Kissling contends that she is a Catholic because she chooses to call herself one. "I define who I am. I decide if I'm a Catholic," not the church or her critics. She also recognizes that in the eyes of the world, she always will be considered Catholic. It's part of her public identity.

But she's struggled with remaining in an institution she feels is "very, very corrupt and has been very corrupt for a long time in many, many ways." She has questioned whether staying in the church gave the institution a "safety valve," reassuring other like-minded individuals who have decided to stay in the church that it's "not really that bad."

But she believes that whatever cover she may inadvertently provide the institution is offset by the power of her role for Catholic women. "Early in my work in CFFC I discovered how important it was to many Catholics, particularly women—and young women—that they are able to see a Catholic like me," Kissling says.

She recalls speaking engagements at universities, Catholic and secular. "There would always be a priest there who would get up at the question period to berate me," she says. "I would wipe the floor with him. . . . I'm not going to cower because some guy in a collar tells me I'm wrong or I'm a bad Catholic.

"So that was another part of it, to demonstrate that you could be a Catholic woman, and you could act with dignity and authority and treat yourself as an equal to these people. Being a role model had real value for them."

4

SHARON MacISAAC McKENNA
From Convent to Commune

It was the early 1960s. Vatican II had convened. Sharon MacIsaac, a young woman religious, had been sent to Rome to assist in the preparation of the Vatican document assessing Catholicism's relationship to non-Christian faiths. Mixed with her sense of awe and excitement, she felt something quite different. At a quiet moment before the proceedings began, she visited Saint Peter's Basilica. "Everybody, every single person I saw, was male. Not a female there." She remembers thinking, "This has a bad smell. Something is off. Men should not be in such huge numbers only with men. There's something sick about this." It brought home for her the fact that, if priests are to be celibate, women must be perceived as obstacles, as seductresses. "You are a threat as a female."

A few years later, as she was undergoing psychotherapy, she would experience "a sense of Catholicism that had always been there and in my life, the hard exclusionary features of it, the maleness of it." MacIsaac was not one to walk away from these revelations. Like the pioneering generations who preceded her, she was open to new experiences, even if they were painful.

In the early 1900s, MacIsaac's grandparents braved the rugged terrain of rural Saskatchewan, Canada. They were German Catholic farmers who had moved to Minnesota and settled down in comfortable homes with enough financial stability to afford piano lessons for their daughters. But in 1906, wooed by the Canadian government and a

Canadian Pacific Railway eager for settlers, the family embarked on a second migration. They took everything—livestock, furniture, all their possessions—to "the best new West," as the railway promoters called it. They found a cold, untamed land that had never been plowed. "It was a cruel winter, and many people died," she says. But over time, her family, like so many other immigrants, reinvented themselves and built a new society.

More than half a century later, MacIsaac became her own type of pioneer, but the untamed land she explored was her own psyche. That exploration began in earnest when she was twenty-five and studying theology. She began psychotherapy, living with a group of Catholic priests and nuns in a psychotherapeutic commune. That experience helped her discover truths about herself that caused many changes in her life. She left the convent, eventually married a former priest, and became a successful psychotherapist and teacher of therapists. She challenged her church's long-held interpretation of the biblical story of original sin, using Sigmund Freud's insights to make her point. As her ancestors did, she weathered the storms, survived, and thrived, her Catholic faith changed but not forsaken.

She grew up in the 1950s in Scott, Saskatchewan, a small farming town in Western Canada with few diversions. She'd been raised a Catholic, but educated in public schools, running around with neighborhood kids whose parents were Ukrainian, British, and American, with enough faith differences to support three churches.

Left to their own devices, the town's children banded together, doing anything they could to alleviate the tedium of the small town, playing in the grain elevators, watching the trains arrive twice a day. In the summer, she says, "not very educated nuns" would come to Scott and prepare the Catholic youngsters for First Communion and Confirmation. The church was sweltering and the benches hard, but MacIsaac considered the lessons an antidote to the stifling boredom. She liked the gospel stories and the lives of the saints.

In those days, priests and nuns were on the lookout for bright young women to join the religious life. They tried to recruit her, but she had a "terrific boyfriend" and resisted. The idea frightened her a bit, she admits, because "something about it attracted me."

She had decided to follow in the footsteps of her "beautiful and smart" older sister and become a nurse. A vivid encounter with death changed all that. When she was seventeen, she spent the summer working as a nurse's aide in a hospital the next town over. The hospital matron took her under her wing and let her witness surgery and childbirth.

One summer day, an old woman, her belly bloated by cancer, was MacIsaac's charge. She remembers trying to spoon-feed her "that awful Lipton noodle soup with noodles and flakes of parsley in a watery mass." Not long after, the woman died. "I had never seen anything like that," she recalls. "This was a small rural hospital, and some alarm went off, and the matron came flying in." She summoned MacIsaac and told her, "This is what we do; we wash people who have just died."

"I was game," she says, and together she and the matron struggled to lift the patient. "She weighed a ton, dead weight." The soup started dribbling out of her mouth. They washed her and changed her into a clean gown, getting her ready for the local undertaker.

Her shift was up, and MacIsaac left. It was high noon, very hot and bright. She experienced an overpowering fear. She sat in the church to calm down, but the "horrible feeling" returned. She needed solace, someone to talk to, so she went to the nurses' residence. There she spotted a pamphlet, one of those vocational pamphlets so prevalent in the 1950s. It was titled, "Are You Called?"

She concluded it was an omen, that she was indeed being called to the religious life. She kept her decision to herself. "Frankly, I felt like a freak. In my town it was truly different." No young woman from Scott had ever entered the convent. She followed her mother's plans for her senior year, attending a "big city" high school in Saskatoon, a hundred miles away.

For MacIsaac, high school was a breeze. In Scott a single teacher taught several grades in one room, and MacIsaac had been forced to learn by herself and prepare for provincial exams graded by examiners hundreds of miles away. She aced those tests and found her senior classes "very easy." She missed the presence of boys in class and thought the girls were "spoon-fed" their lessons.

But she was impressed by her teachers, the Sisters of Our Lady of Sion. They were young, well-educated, and international, since the order had convents in Europe, the United States, and South and Central America. Even their habit was more stylish than the other orders'—a gown with a wide collar, with a black veil attached to a cap.

MacIsaac decided to join the order, a decision that wasn't easy for her family to accept. Late in her senior year, when she confided her choice to her mother, "she looked very sober," MacIsaac recalls. But she told her, "You know I'm not going to stand in the way of anything you want to do. I'll support you." While her older sister was "kind and noncommittal," two of her siblings, her older brother and a younger sister, were far more openly upset by the news. Her brother offered to pay her university tuition so she wouldn't end up "in some damn convent." Her younger sister was too grief-stricken to even say goodbye.

In that era, giving a child to a religious vocation was essentially consigning a loved one to a life devoid of family. "In those days, you went in, you didn't come home. They visited you." Nuns could attend the funerals of family members, but that was it. So MacIsaac missed the marriages of all her siblings. "If one of them had died, I could have gone to every one of their funerals," she says bitterly.

Nevertheless, she adapted well to religious life. A number of the senior girls in her class had opted for the convent. They all were appalled by a schedule that had them rising before dawn, praying before they sat down to breakfast, and in bed before dark. But the contemplative aspect of MacIsaac's training opened up a new world to her. For the first two years, she and her fellow postulants attended no academic classes. Instead, they learned how to meditate and spent hours doing manual labor, helping in the kitchen. "There was terrific respect for each of us," she says, "each of us gaining some access to ourselves." She treasured the "experience of being taken seriously and learning how serious it was to be alive and to be, specifically, me . . . the absolute importance of your own being." For the first time in her life, she was asked to be silent for long periods. "The relief of not talking when you have nothing to say was huge."

It was clear to the sisters that MacIsaac had a good mind, and they sent her to the University of Saskatchewan to prepare for a teaching career. She excelled in her studies, earning her undergraduate degree in 1962.

As her life was being planned, theologian Rev. Gregory Baum was coming into his own with the papacy of John XXIII and the convening of Vatican II. A Jewish convert to Catholicism, Baum was a rising star who had drawn the attention of the Vatican. The new pope believed in ecumenism, and Baum had written a new book, *The Jews and the Gospel*.

Baum's work meant a great deal to the Sisters of Our Lady of Sion, as their order had been founded in Paris in the nineteenth century by a Jewish convert. They cared for Jewish women and children who had fled to Europe to escape pogroms in Russia and Poland. Typical for their times, they prayed for the conversion of the Jews to Catholicism. But atypically, and as the order matured, they also taught Catholics to respect Judaism and Jewish culture.[1]

When Baum was in Saskatoon for a lecture, the Sisters invited him to meet with them at their convent. The Mother Superior told him that they had not been able to find priests who had a broad understanding of the Jewish faith. "There aren't any priests around who know anything about Judaism," Baum told them. "You girls are going to have to educate yourselves." Baum said that Saint Michael's College was opening up its graduate program in theology to the laity. "Why don't you send people down there?"

Saint Michael's was one of six affiliated colleges that were part of the sprawling University of Toronto, Canada's Harvard. In the 1960s, the university's impressive faculty included literary critic Northrop Frye and media theorist Marshall McLuhan.

MacIsaac was chosen for graduate study in theology. Because she was only twenty-three at the time, "green as grass," the nuns sent an older sister with her to also participate in the program and watch out for her. It was 1962, and Toronto was shaking off its image as the staid and stodgy capital of Ontario. "Toronto the Good" was giving way to "Toronto the Groovy."

Waves of young American men were moving to Canada to evade the draft and the war in Vietnam, settling in this big city with its low crime rate and tolerant citizens, many of whom opposed the US war. Canada, like the United States, was feeling the earthquake of youthful baby boomers pushing the envelope, experimenting with sex, drugs, and rock and roll. Bob Dylan and the Beatles were shaking up pop culture. Even something as solid as Catholic theology was feeling the shockwaves.

The sisters took intensive graduate courses along with seminarians who had already studied theology. Not only were they exposed to intellectually challenging work, they were studying theology at a time when new thinking was encouraged.

Baum and other theologians and philosophers were stirring the pot, spurred by the openness of Vatican II. Even the theology of Saint Thomas Aquinas was being reframed. MacIsaac had a professor—"a brilliant German Dominican"—who argued that the venerable medieval theologian had been misinterpreted. Rev. Ignatius Theodore Eschmann contended that Aquinas was not a strict enforcer of church law but instead believed in the primacy of the individual conscience. "The first law is the spirit," MacIsaac learned. "If a Christian is living according to the laws of the church, if that's how he lives, but not by the inner promptings of the Spirit, he's not yet a Christian."

That revelation, she says, changed her life. "I loved it," she says of her theology studies. "I felt like the horizons went away. . . . I couldn't believe that I'd been so lucky to have been in that world."

As the church developed the Vatican II document that would become the *Declaration on the Relation of the Church to Non-Christian Religions*, MacIsaac traveled to Rome to assist in the effort.[2] That's when she entered Saint Peter's and was appalled by the patriarchy of her church—and the limits it placed on Catholic women.

But it appeared that the culture of patriarchy might be on its way out. In the aftermath of Vatican II and Pope John XXIII's desire to modernize the church, women religious were exchanging habits that concealed them from the world in favor of modern dress. They suddenly found themselves being perceived as women. There were spirited discussions about the value of celibacy in the priesthood, with many in the church believing that married priests were on the horizon.

The church, post–Vatican II, was even open to nuns and priests getting psychotherapy. One sister in their graduate group was clearly having emotional problems. "She was having a lot of inner struggle, a lot of trouble. Whatever it was, she was ruthless with herself." Baum sought a referral to a good therapist, and he got a recommendation for Lea Hindley-Smith, a British therapist gaining a reputation for her ability to understand and connect with her clients.

Hindley-Smith's work led her to form Therafields, a therapeutic community that ultimately included nine hundred people, both those getting treatment and those training to be psychotherapists. About five hundred of her followers lived together in a sprawling community that included thirty-five houses in Toronto's Annex neighborhood, an area near the university, known for its Victorian and Edwardian mansions, some of which had become rooming houses. In time, the community would include four farms outside Toronto and two homes in Tampa, Florida, becoming one of the largest communes in North America.[3] The community flourished for roughly two decades, closing in the early 1980s.[4]

The sister in question began treatment and improved. But she wanted to discuss her feelings in group therapy, with people who were her peers. So a number of priests and nuns from Saint Michael's agreed to participate in what became known as the "Catholic group." By all accounts, Hindley-Smith was remarkable. Grant Goodbrand, who lived in the commune and wrote a history of it, observed that Hindley-Smith particularly impressed the scholarly priests and nuns of Saint Michael's who initially considered her "the wisest, most numinous, and charismatic person they had ever met"[5]—although that view would change over time.

And forty years ago, the notion of living in a commune was not as exotic as it is today. Indeed, in 1970 Baum theorized that the "hippie commune" might one day replace the parish as the focal point for Catholic life. "In many cases, especially in the big cities, the parish is not a community and can never become one," Baum said. "What counts is the creation of small communities, in which Christians and other people may be at home."[6]

When she was studying theology, MacIsaac hadn't even been aware that her colleagues were getting psychotherapy. It took her a couple of years to realize what was going on and to participate. "I entered therapy when I was twenty-five. I was young and still a nun and intending to continue to be a nun," she recalls.

Therapy would change her, helping her discover uncomfortable emotions and opinions she had long buried. But this focus on herself, and this deepening community with others in Therafields, also laid the foundation for a "second adolescence"; she'd largely missed out on her first one, having entered the convent right after high school. She remembers returning to campus for her third year of study at the end of summer on a "beautiful day in late August," no longer in her full habit. "I could see that others were surprised," particularly the priests. There wasn't anything inappropriate in their reaction, she says. "It was kind of shock and a recognition I was female."

She was in her late twenties when the second adolescence began in earnest, and MacIsaac explored what it meant to be a woman and to have male friends. She ultimately recognized that she wanted to be in the world—and out of the convent. But the realization was "surprising and unsettling."

MacIsaac left the convent just about a decade after she entered. "I had gone in very good faith, and it was a turnaround. I had never anticipated it, nor had they. But I had to do it." Both she, and the more senior sister sent to look out for her at university, decided to leave the order. "I remember telling the superior. She was stricken," she recalls. "She placed a lot of trust in us and our promise, and it cost a lot."

The Mother Superior asked her if she still believed in God. "Of course I do," MacIsaac answered. In those days, "nobody left the convent." But MacIsaac wasn't the anomaly; she was part of an exodus that would rock the church. Between 1965 and 1975, in the United States alone, more than forty-four thousand sisters—roughly one-quarter of all American nuns—would leave religious life.[7]

MacIsaac's family, however, greeted the news much differently. They were "profoundly relieved, overjoyed even," she recalls. She hadn't realized how "devastated" her mother had been when she'd joined the convent.

Philip McKenna, a Dominican priest and fellow student at Saint Mike's, had also left religious life. McKenna, an Australian, was a brilliant scholar and great preacher, with a beautiful voice, MacIsaac recalls. He had been attracted to her, but she initially wasn't aware of that. "I was so naive," she laughs. At one point he'd confided to her that she was the first woman he'd met whom he would ask to marry, if he ever would marry, but he would not; he was going to stay a priest.

McKenna, too, had been undergoing psychotherapy. He went home to Australia in 1968 after his studies were finished and asked his order for permission to return to Toronto so he could continue his therapy but was turned down. The order offered him sessions with a psychiatrist appointed by the diocese, but his superiors couldn't understand how much he valued the "really truthful and probing work" that was going on at Therafields and how important it had become to him, MacIsaac says.

To the order, his desire to return to Toronto "looked like a temptation," MacIsaac says. When his request was refused, he decided to go anyway. He was deprived of his authority to administer the sacraments and perform other priestly duties. When he got back to Toronto, he went through the process to formally resign from the priesthood.

MacIsaac and McKenna were among members of the commune who also pursued training in psychotherapy. The therapy they were undergoing was psychoanalytic psychotherapy, she explains. "It means you're paying attention to your dreams and you come to understand how much you do without understanding why you're doing it."

Psychotherapy so affected her thinking that she felt it important to reexamine the doctrine of original sin in light of Freudian theories about the conscious and unconscious. Our very human nature has created this duality, she says, and it is not evil. She wanted to do her dissertation on it. In pressing Baum for permission for her thesis, she argued, "We can't keep talking about sin this way." Baum was reluctant, believing the topic was far too large. But her doctorate was cross-disciplinary, and her other supervisor was a psychoanalyst. She got the permission she needed.

MacIsaac's thesis in theology and psychoanalysis became a book, *Freud and Original Sin*, which reached some groundbreaking conclusions. She argued for a different way of understanding the biblical concept of original sin. Biblical texts attempted to explain our conflicted nature, the phenomenon that Freud had written about, she says. Within the mind "there's another forum, almost invisible, that's active, and we don't have much access to it." People get glimpses of it when they free associate, paying attention to subjective ideas that cross their minds. But original sin is this state of being conflicted. It is not evil or wrong, just a part of our human nature.

Our unconscious and our conscious are often at odds. "It's not a pathology—that's what Freud was saying. It's constitutive of the mind," she says. The unconscious "is not evil, but we are afraid of it. We're afraid of it taking over," allowing hatred, violence, sexual excesses, the suicidal urge to overwhelm us.

MacIsaac believes that one way this fear can be addressed is through psychotherapy. "We need others to talk to," she reflects. "Psychotherapy is gradually being able to bear information about yourself . . . being able to bear things that frighten you in yourself. How can I turn from impulses that terrify me so much that I have to drink or deny them extremely? How can I deal with them so I can gradually bring them into consideration?"

Therapy, meanwhile, was revealing aspects of herself that she hadn't known were there. MacIsaac has written that living in a "house group" in Therafields was "like diving into the deep end; it was therapy by immersion and as such a powerful learning opportunity. Moderation was not a virtue."[8]

Her own therapeutic journey resulted in three episodes where she had temporary breakdowns. Those episodes, uncovering a memory or a feeling that has long been buried, "they're like deaths," she says. It takes a few days or weeks to get back one's equilibrium. "You're kind of weakened by it," but emerging from those experiences is a way of reclaiming a part of yourself. The "tumult" likely delayed her thesis by a couple of years, she says.

One episode occurred when the Catholic group was experiencing an intensive weekend of group therapy. MacIsaac remembers a "very scary" moment: She was in a discussion with someone and had begun to answer when she stopped short and blurted out, "I don't look for the truth of what I feel. If I feel something I don't want to feel, I dismiss it because I shouldn't be feeling that."

MacIsaac's training had taught her to aspire to holiness, she says. "So if you disagreed with someone, or didn't believe what someone had said, your instinct was to bury those feelings." The insight was so profound that "I actually broke down," she recalls. "I went into a god-awful state. It was like falling with nothing under me." The others in the group supported her, and she came to learn that, in a therapeutic community, arriving at the truth of one's feelings and communicating them to others can be "a relief and very powerful."

Another insight was equally, if not more, traumatic. She remembers one Mass, held in the living room of one of the mansions that her commune owned. As the priest presided over the liturgy, she experienced an overwhelming anger, an irrational rage, because "the sacramental life is mediated only by males." Women never read the gospel or preach a sermon. She realized the "hard exclusionary features" of Catholicism, "the maleness of it."

That one moment called up years of enduring sexism in the church, expressed by its refusal to ordain women or permit married priests, and the recurring reminder in her academic world that, even though she had a graduate degree in theology, if a priest spoke a thought relevant to her field of study, it would carry far more weight than her own view.

Often when she went to church she heard sermons that were "so bad, so uninformed, so poverty-stricken." She would find herself fantasizing about how much better some of her female colleagues might preach, "doing it with more care and more pastoral sense."

That this anger would erupt during the celebration of the Eucharist made it all the more troubling to her. "I think I couldn't bear it; it was a really awful thing, because it's the Eucharist, right?" Catholics believe that at the Mass, bread and wine are transformed into the body and blood of Christ. But she says that her "rage and rebellion" was aimed not at the Eucharist but at the "mediating" of the sacrament, the restriction of the priesthood to celibate males. Even though the Eucharist was being offered genuinely, she says, "I couldn't bear being there."

That day she also rebelled against the "Catholic triumphalism" and the contempt for Protestantism that had been part of her childhood. She raged against "having been a credulous receiver of unquestioned teaching and unquestioned ways of being."

She also was frustrated that the promise of Vatican II was not being fulfilled. "The church wasn't changing so quickly." It was already the 1970s, and still church practice "was untouched by what had been envisioned and agreed to in the council."

The last two documents the Vatican issued in 1965 heralded reform. The document on non-Christian religions was a resounding condemnation of anti-Semitism in the church and renounced church teachings that laid the blame for the Crucifixion on the entire Jewish people. It called for "fraternal dialogues" between Catholics and Jews.[9] Likewise, the *Declaration on Religious Freedom* asserted that we must come to the truth without coercion of any type, and that we must live according to our conscience.[10] Those documents met with a lot of resistance, Baum told her, because they essentially acknowledged that the church had "been mistaken" about the Jews and about "demanding obedience and not asking of yourself the responsibility for truthfulness."

"But everybody went home," she says. "Everybody went home, and . . . with everybody gone, there was a backlash." Conservative forces in the institutional church quickly reined in the promise of change.

The anger she felt at that home liturgy helped precipitate a "rocky interval" between MacIsaac and her church. She remained a Catholic, but the church was more remote to her. "I wasn't as observant for a while."

As MacIsaac was working out her feelings about the institutional church, she and McKenna became a couple. But they saw no reason to tie the knot. It was the 1970s, she says. "We were sort of hippies, and you had to give a good reason for getting married. Why would you?"

But that "good reason" surfaced after MacIsaac agreed to care for an infant girl, born into the community. The mother knew she couldn't take care of her, and it became apparent that she wanted MacIsaac to take the child. McKenna was reluctant. He said "he wouldn't be good at it, he's too much of an egghead." But MacIsaac reassured him that she'd take on most of the parenting duties. A lawyer eventually advised her that to make the relationship permanent, she should adopt the child. But adoption was possible only if the couple was married.

"So I remember that conversation. We both looked at the other and said, 'Can you think of any good reason why we shouldn't get married?' We sat there, and neither of us could. It was not very romantic, but we ended up having a wonderful, small wedding." By the time she officially became Sharon MacIsaac McKenna, their daughter was "an exquisite little two-year-old" who attended the ceremony.

They still were "hippies" at heart, MacIsaac McKenna says, so they homeschooled their daughter until she was nine years old and asked to go to a regular school. They didn't baptize their daughter until she was eight, "able to participate in what it meant."

By the 1980s, Therafields was coming apart. Many of the commune's adherents were growing disillusioned with Hindley-Smith, who had fabricated parts of her biography, whose personal life was messy, and who often was extravagant and irresponsible. The commune disbanded, tainted by a sex-abuse scandal involving Hindley-Smith's son and brought down by financial mismanagement.[11]

Goodbrand's book cites two quotes from MacIsaac McKenna that track the Catholic group's growing disillusion with Therafields's leader. Early in the book, MacIsaac McKenna described her delight in Hindley-Smith's presence. "I felt she understood me very, very deeply and cared about me. . . . I remember saying to myself that this is what love is in the Gospels."[12]

But by the end of the book, MacIsaac McKenna discussed a darker facet of Hindley-Smith, something "very disturbed" in her, a "savage envy of younger women."[13] In her interviews for this book, MacIsaac McKenna did not refer to Hindley-Smith by name, calling her "that woman up the street" from the university.

When asked about the misogyny she felt at Therafields, MacIsaac McKenna observes that "what emerged among many of us, painfully and only in its own time, was how inferior we felt ourselves to be as women." This was an era when psychoanalysis often blamed "any difficulties in a child's rearing" on the mother. The young women at Therafields agonized about whether they were good enough to be mothers. Hindley-Smith contributed to that sense of doubt.

In the commune, Hindley-Smith favored men over women, MacIsaac McKenna says. The fact that sexism was present even in a "with-it" group undergoing therapy helped her understand that the church was not the only institution where misogyny lurked. That realization helped heal her breach with Catholicism.

The MacIsaac McKenna family was becoming more settled. When she began fourth grade, their daughter transferred to a new Catholic school in town. "It just happened that the new school going up in town was going to be Catholic," MacIsaac McKenna says. They wanted her to start school where the environment would be new to all the students. But she says she's glad her daughter went to a Catholic school.

Her daughter regaled her classmates with descriptions of her parents' wedding and suggested to the principal that the school needed improvement in some areas. The faculty thought she was very funny, MacIsaac McKenna says. "They couldn't get over her."

But MacIsaac McKenna felt that she had some unfinished business. She feared that after leaving the convent she'd "forsaken God. I hadn't prayed because I was avoiding God. I started to feel actually desolate about it." So she contacted Sister Edward, a British Sister of Sion whom she had idolized.

Sister Edward lived in London and suggested MacIsaac McKenna come for a visit. When they met, she asked her why she hadn't confided her doubts about the religious life before she made her final vows. MacIsaac McKenna told her that she hadn't known what to do and at that point, just before she'd taken her final vows, she hadn't been at all clear about her future. "I genuinely didn't foresee leaving then." Sister Edward understood. "That was huge," MacIsaac McKenna says.

Today in her practice at the Centre for Training in Psychotherapy in Toronto, MacIsaac McKenna doesn't mention her faith or her past. But that doesn't mean that faith doesn't enter in. She's working with people in search of something spiritual—"trying to understand their failures in being able to love or commit or hope or not give up." They're seeking to know whether "their lives are worthwhile." To overtly mention God would be unethical, because the clients need to find their own truth. But that doesn't mean that MacIsaac McKenna can't seek divine help.

Getting to "truthfulness about your actual state, your feelings, your thoughts," is very difficult. Years after she began her own therapy, she says, "I began to think that God is truth." Saint John the Evangelist said God was truth, life, and love, she says. "When I would say, 'My father is truth,' it had such an effect. It still does to this day."

She continues, "It's very easy to do psychotherapy not well enough. You have to be open and present. . . . Nobody knows if I'm praying to God—nobody knows that." And those occasions where a client achieves a breakthrough, "how does that happen?" She feels that when a therapist "is participating in being together with another person, the Holy Spirit is with both of you."

Not that MacIsaac McKenna is the same Catholic that she was when she entered the convent. She and her spouse both grieve that the church's acceptance of married priests—something that had seemed so close to fruition after Vatican II—failed to occur. "The dawning that it wouldn't happen in our lifetime was very difficult."

Her old friend Gregory Baum, now in his nineties, is no longer a rising star at the Vatican. His outspoken views in support of artificial birth control, a married priesthood, and the ordination of women soon drew the disfavor of the Catholic hierarchy. In 1961 Baum had been the only Canadian chosen to serve on the Vatican's Secretariat for Christian Unity. In the mid-1970s, Toronto archbishop Philip Pocock rebuked him and took away his priestly faculty to hear confessions. By 1976 Baum had left the priesthood, although he continued teaching at Saint Michael's until he hit the mandatory retirement age in 1986.[14]

MacIsaac McKenna still grows angry when she perceives sexism in the church. She recalls the comments of a senior cleric who said that women couldn't be priests because they were not present at the Last Supper. "I could hardly believe my ears." It isn't clear when the ordination to the priesthood became a sacrament in the church, she says. And the notion that priests can only reflect who was present at the Last Supper? "All of them were Jews. Did Jesus intend that priests had to be Jews? . . . It's so stupid, you can hardly believe it. . . . There it is," she says. "Clarity on the clericalism and the misogyny. Absolutely gratuitous. Who knows when it's going to be altered? Who knows?"

Yet in another breath she exudes the calm tolerance of a psychotherapist. "I'd say the church is human. I never found a society, even among psychoanalysts and psychotherapists trying really hard, where we're not self-deceiving and not culturally overpowered by whatever is in the air."

The former religious has almost come full circle. She tries to attend daily Mass. "When I go to Mass every day, there's something that happens. If you're around people who do it a lot, there's some calmness in them. . . . We don't even know it. But we need it. We need something—a whole assistance that's right in your body and that comes from being with people who gather and try to find out what Jesus said."

Now in her seventies, with two granddaughters, MacIsaac McKenna remains open to new insights and experiences. "I know I'm still in process. You're changing into an era of your life that is so marked by failing, failing faculties, but there are changes going on. That growing—you keep growing. That's the thing."

5

SISTER SIMONE CAMPBELL
God's Lobbyist

Sister Simone Campbell vividly recalls the moment she first felt feminist anger. It was during her law school days, a course of study she'd undertaken when she realized that she needed a law degree to fight for the poor families she served as a Sister of Social Service.[1]

Campbell and a few other women religious happened to be doing a retreat at the same time a group of priests, members of a religious order, were meeting. At one point the entire group was together, listening to a talk. "We were all sitting around in a circle. . . . The fan was making a noise or something." One of the priests was bothered by it. Instead of asking a fellow priest near the fan to shut it off, he turned to the sister next to him and told her, "Turn off the fan." She did, walking across the room, to flip the switch.

She was angry with the priest for his "arrogance" and with the woman religious for her submission, she says. The incident helped stoke her "radical feminist phase when I was just furious at the male domination of the church, the male domination in society, the expectation that women were just there to serve."

At the time she was reading *The Church and the Second Sex* by Mary Daly, "so that stirred me up," she says. As its title suggests, Daly's book was a feminist manifesto for Catholic women, inspired by Simone de Beauvoir's *The Second Sex*.

Daly would go on to leave the church and revise her book, making it even more radical. But in its first iteration, Daly had written that her book was born out of her "ebullient sense of hope" for the future of the church, prompted by Vatican II.[2]

Nevertheless, when first published in 1968, the book was controversial. One Catholic reviewer called it a "provocative volume."[3] Boston College, where Daly taught theology, attempted to deny her tenure the following year, an action many considered retaliation for her outspoken views.[4]

For Campbell, feminist anger "was an important step for me," but it was temporary. "There was a moment that got me into the anger, but there wasn't a moment that got me out of it," she says. She got more centered in prayer, "and then I got into Zen, and when you're in Zen, you can't blame anybody. . . . I discovered that anger becomes debilitating and that anger becomes righteous. That's not helpful to me."

Campbell may not have held on to her anger, but her passion remains, and with it an acute sense of injustice and a willingness to speak truth to power, both elected officials and church leaders. In recent years, she's channeled that passion into a career as a formidable lobbyist, even if a nun in her late sixties in a modest skirt and jacket and sensible shoes may not conjure up the popular image of the people who prowl the halls of Congress.

Campbell arguably is the best-known woman religious in the country. She's appeared on *The Daily Show*, *60 Minutes*, and *The Colbert Report* and was a featured speaker at the 2012 Democratic Convention. She's written a memoir and even drawn the attention of *Rolling Stone.*

Since 2004 Campbell has been executive director of NETWORK, a Catholic social-justice lobby based in Washington, DC. No newcomer to Beltway politics, NETWORK was founded in 1971 by forty-seven women religious who worked as educators, health-care providers, and community organizers to "shape a new ministry of justice." Their aspiration—to advocate for federal policies that advance economic and social justice—was far bigger than their funds. The nuns came up with $187 at their initial organizing meeting. But the time was right—feminism and post–Vatican II optimism were still in the air, thousands were demonstrating against the Vietnam War and for civil rights, and the abortion wars had not yet begun in earnest. While they couldn't compete with K Street lobbyists and their massive political donations, NETWORK's staff had something they lacked: Saturday-evening liturgies that drew scores of activists. The group's legislative seminars featured big-name elected officials, including Democratic luminaries Adlai Stevenson, Ted Kennedy, Barbara Mikulski, Walter Mondale, and Joe Biden.

Its issues included alleviating poverty and hunger, reducing the threat of nuclear weapons, and women's rights. Its first executive director, Sister Carol Coston, even received a Presidential Citizens Medal in 2001, the first sister to have been so honored. NETWORK's goals are ambitious, to say the least: the lobby advocates for "a just society" that "values people over the accumulation of profits" and "ensures that all people—the 100 percent—have what they need to live dignified lives."[5] Within that broad goal of protecting the poor, NETWORK has also addressed climate change and trade policies.

But NETWORK remained largely an "inside-the-beltway" phenomenon until Campbell arrived. The lobby and Campbell both owe their fame to the Vatican. In 2012 the Vatican's Congregation for the Doctrine of the Faith, which traces its roots to the sixteenth century and the Inquisition,[6] issued a "doctrinal assessment" strongly criticizing the Leadership Conference of Women Religious (LCWR), an association comprised of the fifteen hundred women who head congregations of religious in the United States, representing about 80 percent of the fifty-seven thousand women religious in the country.[7] The Vatican attacked LCWR for its "radical feminism" and said it would review its ties to organizations implied to be bad companions—among them, NETWORK.

The sisters' crime? "The Church's Biblical view of family life and human sexuality are not part of the LCWR agenda in a way that promotes Church teaching. Moreover, occasional public statements by the LCWR that disagree with or challenge positions taken by the Bishops, who are the Church's authentic teachers of faith and morals, are not compatible with its purpose."[8] The nuns were going to get a lot of scrutiny from the Vatican, and three bishops would monitor them and make sure they behaved.[9]

One might have thought that the public denunciation, something Campbell told NPR felt like a "sock in the stomach," would have signaled to the sisters to lie low until the flap blew over. But Campbell did not express any sense of remorse. "When you don't work every day with people who live at the margins of our society, it's so much easier to make easy statements about who's right and who's wrong," Campbell said. "Life is way more complicated in our society, and it's probably way easier to be eight thousand miles away in Rome."[10]

Indeed, Campbell, a keen strategist, saw the Vatican's attack as an opportunity to promote NETWORK's legislative agenda and raise its visibility. It wasn't the first time that Campbell had used the media to help advance her lobby's social-justice agenda. In March 2010, when it looked like the Affordable Care Act would be defeated because of fears that it would permit federal money to pay for abortions, Campbell organized a letter from fifty-nine leaders of Catholic women religious, representing thousands of sisters. The women religious stood with Sister Carol Keehan, president of the Catholic Hospital Association, who had already cast her lot with the bill.[11]

Campbell's letter didn't mince words. The bill, she wrote, while imperfect, "will make crucial investments in community health centers that largely serve poor women and children. And despite false claims to the contrary, the Senate bill will not provide taxpayer funding for elective abortions. It will uphold longstanding conscience protections and it will make historic new investments—$250 million—in support of pregnant women. This is the *real* pro-life stance, and we as Catholics are all for it." NETWORK delivered the letter to every member of Congress.[12] The letter helped the health-care bill become law.

Two years later, when the church hierarchy went after NETWORK and LCWR, Campbell provided many of the most memorable media comments: "I wish I knew what was in their [the Vatican's] brains," Campbell told NPR. "The leadership doesn't know how to deal with strong women." She conceded that abortion, contraception, gay marriage, and the ordination of women were "big issues. But they aren't at the heart of faith."[13]

The Vatican's attention, she writes in her memoir, was exactly what NETWORK needed to raise the profile of its work advocating for the poor and marginalized. "American Catholics, and the public generally, reacted to the Vatican censure by expressing heartfelt support for the sisters at every turn," she wrote.[14] Campbell was going to channel that goodwill into an engine that would drive the public debate on poverty.

The "Nuns on the Bus," as they styled themselves, traveled 2,700 miles, drawing attention to the needs of the poor and critiquing the budget proposal of fellow Catholic and Wisconsin Representative (and eventual Republican vice-presidential nominee) Paul Ryan.[15] Ryan had proposed sharp cuts in spending on domestic programs serving the poor and the elderly, with the savings going to deficit reduction and tax cuts.[16] He contended that his budget was in keeping with his Catholic values, a remark that prompted criticism not only from women religious but from Catholic bishops.[17]

The bus traveled across nine states and stopped in more than thirty communities, most of them in the Midwest. At each stop, the sisters visited institutions that serve the homeless, hungry, and sick, meeting families who depended on the federal programs jeopardized by the Ryan budget. Nuns also stopped at congressional offices along the way.

The *New York Times* helpfully pointed out that the nuns' trip dates overlapped with the American bishops' "Fortnight for Freedom," whose call for religious liberty highlighted their objections to the birth-control mandate in the Affordable Care Act.[18] While the nuns and the bishops agreed about the budget cuts, Campbell seemed less worried about her religious freedom. She'd met Iraqi women religious and thought they had a lot more to complain about. "If you want to talk religious liberty, look at them. Their motherhouse was in Mosul until it got bombed."[19] Everywhere the nuns stopped, they attracted thousands of people and local and national media coverage.

I attended their homecoming in July 2012. It was a sweltering summer day when Campbell returned to Washington to a rally outside the United Methodist Building. It was an appropriate venue. The imposing structure, built in 1924, stands in the shadow of the Supreme Court. It was envisioned as a visible sign of Methodist commitment to social reform. Over the years, the building has served as a meeting place for groups opposing the Vietnam War and fighting for equal rights for women and for civil rights. Within its walls, disability advocates worked out details for the historic Americans with Disabilities Act.[20]

The multiracial crowd spanned all age groups. As the bus rolled in, "Eye of the Tiger," forever linked to the film *Rocky III*, blared out from speakers, amping up the already sweaty, exultant crowd of several hundred well-wishers, taking pictures with their cell phones as the sisters disembarked. TV cameras were everywhere, including a crew from Bill Moyers's public-television production company. The crew had been following the nuns the entire trip.

Campbell wore dangling earrings and black clogs. She beamed as a Methodist minister called the sisters "our rock stars." Smiling, and taking sips from her water bottle, she listened intently as an imam hailed their bus trip, stating that it was "not only a journey in space" but "a journey in time," summoning a vision for the new century of equality, justice, and interconnectedness.

She stood silently, holding her remarks in a plastic folder, shifting, smiling, clapping, and nodding as the heat and the speakers kept coming. She finally stepped up to the microphone. "I'm overwhelmed," she said. "This is so awesome. It delights my heart. . . . We left trying to explain something to the world, and the world explained something to us. . . . The Ryan budget is immoral," she said. And, ever the lobbyist, she noted that the sisters "stand with our bishops" in that judgment.

The sisters were touched by their encounters, she said, often experiencing both heartbreak and hope. They were buoyed by all the good work women religious were doing—everything from running food pantries to organizing literacy programs and staffing centers for immigrants and refugees. The hope often was accompanied by sorrow that so many needs went unfulfilled. Campbell spoke of the "oasis" sisters in Chicago had created, providing housing for the homeless that offered "light and beauty and color and security." But in the neighborhood outside the housing development, she said, "was a desert of violence and blight" where twenty minutes before their bus had arrived, a small child had been shot.

When the nuns visited Detroit, she said, she was impressed by the literacy program "where adults struggled to overcome lifelong learning disabilities." The students worked in teams of three, she said, so they would "keep an eye on each other," making sure they all showed up. "We need to make sure we each show up for the struggle ahead," she told the crowd. "Catholic sisters' commitment to justice, charity, and human dignity should be an inspiration and a model for all of us . . . and especially for our political leaders across the street," she said to loud cheers.

Buoyed by the success of their first Nuns on the Bus outing, NETWORK has continued to tour nationally to promote immigration reform, advocate for expanding access to medical care for the poor through Medicaid, encourage voter engagement, and address political polarization. The timing of the bus trip on polarization displayed Campbell's lobbying savvy. It occurred right before Pope Francis's visit to the United States in late September 2015. The trip, Campbell said, would make the case that the pope's "economics of inclusion" can't happen without "a politics of inclusion."[21]

But it was the first road trip that catapulted Campbell into the media spotlight, and even into the political campaign. During her speech before the 2012 Democratic National Convention, Campbell focused on policy, not politics. True, she attacked the budget that "Ryan wrote and [Republican Presidential Nominee Mitt] Romney endorsed," noting that US Catholic bishops have found that the budget "failed a basic moral test." But she managed to avoid using the word *Democratic*—or even to refer to President Obama by name.

She said that both Ryan and Romney "are right" in their call for personal responsibility. But she contended that "we are responsible for more than ourselves and our families; we are responsible for one another." She told stories of the people she'd met on her bus trip: ten-year-old twins in Chicago who'd been the sole caregivers for their mother, bedridden with multiple sclerosis and diabetes; a family in Milwaukee dependent on food stamps because an employer had cut back on the husband's work hours, and the sister of a woman in Cincinnati who died of cancer because she lacked access to health care.

She told the delegates that "we all have a responsibility" to ensure that the Affordable Care Act "is properly implemented" and that "all governors expand Medicaid. . . . This is part of my pro-life stance," she said.

She smiled at the crowd, seemingly surprised at the cheers and standing ovations she evoked. Campbell believes that the positive public response to her message is way beyond what she could produce on her own without divine inspiration. "I'm just willing to be an instrument," she says. "It's abundantly clear—it's more than me."

Campbell has survived in Washington by not challenging the hierarchy directly on reproductive rights, gay marriage, or other hot-button issues. NETWORK has stuck with its mission of advocating for the poor.

She's also been savvy about how things work at the Vatican. In April 2013 when it looked like Pope Francis was continuing Pope Benedict's tight oversight of the LCWR, Campbell told *USA Today* that she was not jumping to any conclusions. "The censure [of the LCWR] has always been about politics. And politics are shifting in the church right now. We know when politics shift, there are opportunities and there are risks."[22]

She was proven right two years later when the Vatican made its peace with the women religious. The new pope's actions were in keeping with a larger public narrative that essentially urged his priests and bishops to do what the nuns had been doing: preach a message of social justice and tolerance rather than focusing solely on moral and sexual issues.

Campbell wrote that the Vatican's decision to conclude its scrutiny "powerfully affirmed the ministry of Catholic sisters in this nation and ended an unneeded investigation that had fostered painful divisions within our church."[23]

It is clear that Campbell is playing the long game. She's often joked that she works to change the federal government "because I want to work someplace where I have a hope of change. Any organization that took 350 years to figure out that Galileo might have been right is not noted for rapid change."

Pope Francis, she says, "has the spiritual confidence to be vulnerable. . . . He talks about his own need for conversion. That's huge. That's a witness to all the rest of us who wrestle with the meaning of this life. Now, if he can reform the administration of the church, that would be fabulous, [and] fairly miraculous since it's been five hundred years since it was last done." She adds that people do to popes what they do to presidents—freight them with "unreasonable expectations."

Raised in Long Beach, California, Campbell entered the convent when she was nineteen. After graduating from Mount Saint Mary's College, Los Angeles, she earned her law degree from the University of California, Davis. Just a year after graduation, she founded the nonprofit Community Law Center in Oakland, serving the poor of Alameda County, where she practiced family law for more than seventeen years.

In 1995 she left the political and legal spheres to take on the role of general director of the Sisters of Social Service, overseeing communities in the United States, Mexico, Taiwan, and the Philippines. She went on to serve as executive director of JERICHO, an interfaith group lobbying California state legislators on social-justice issues. She became NETWORK's executive director in 2004.

She was born and raised a Catholic, but the brand of Catholicism she was exposed to was far sunnier than many Catholic children endured in the fifties and sixties. Her Catholic school was staffed by Sisters of the Immaculate Heart, founded in 1848 in Spain. Campbell wrote that the nuns who taught her engaged their students in the "now," in the struggles in the sixties for civil rights, and in the Second Vatican Council.[24]

The Sisters of the Immaculate Heart gained fame because it included Sister Corita Kent, whose brightly colored artwork became an icon of sixties optimism. (Kent left religious life in 1968). But the order ultimately dissolved in a bitter dispute with ultraconservative cardinal James Francis McIntyre over their decision to follow the suggestion of Pope Paul VI and modernize their rules concerning their dress and schedules. McIntyre banned the nuns from teaching in any parish schools in the Los Angeles archdiocese. Many of the former sisters created an ecumenical community to serve the poor of Los Angeles.[25]

But it was Campbell's own younger sister's struggle, and then death, from Hodgkin's lymphoma that helped her realize the fragility of life and, she wrote, spurred her to "make a difference while we can."[26] She felt a calling to service and to religious life. She was drawn to the religious order that ran a summer camp she attended that drew youngsters from all social classes and backgrounds.[27]

That order was the Sisters of Social Service, founded in 1923 in Hungary by Margaret Slachta, the first woman elected to the Hungarian parliament. Slachta had a new vision for women religious—one inspired by the social teachings of Pope Leo XIII, who had advocated for the rights of workers and the poor. These would not be women who spent their days in prayer hidden away in a cloister or who restricted their work to nursing and teaching. These would be women of faith and prayer who embraced the social gospel and worked with and for the poor and marginalized.

As the order reached beyond Hungary's borders, Sister Frederica Horvath brought it to Los Angeles in 1926. She arrived wearing a simple grey dress and hat, close to the dress of women of that era.[28] The only symbols distinguishing her and her sisters from other women were their medals inscribed with the words *Come, Holy Spirit* and their gold rings, both signs of their dedication to God and others.[29] As the order matured, sisters earned degrees in counseling and social work and then went on to train as physicians, lawyers, psychologists, and community organizers.[30]

For Campbell, this life of social action infused with spirituality is what keeps her sane and whole. "The thing that people just don't get is that the community is my family," she says. "If I wasn't a member of my community, I probably wouldn't be Catholic." But her community is based on a contemplative tradition that is fundamental to Catholicism. "We've got a lot of richness. It's the richness that made me who I am, and for me it's all about taking faith into the world." Her community nourishes her, she says. "I am nourished at times in the institutional church," she says, but "not always."

Campbell's now has a high-profile role as head of NETWORK, but much of her career was spent out of the spotlight. As a lawyer in California she advocated for children "born into chaos" who were in "really tough, tough situations." She won most of her cases, she says. "I'm very competitive."

But what made her job "heartbreaking" were the stories of the children she represented. She remembers one small boy, the football in a bitter breakup. His father's anger and fear over the divorce led him to constantly ask the boy whether his mother had "touched him wrong." The interrogation, which took place whenever he spent a night with his dad, "went on and on.

"Finally, the kid said 'Yes.' So the dad makes an allegation of abuse, and this poor little kid gets in the middle of this. He's trying to be both faithful and loyal to his dad and to his mom." He was so stressed, she says, that he "ended up having a psychotic episode. . . . Isn't that horrible? Doesn't that just break your heart?"

What also broke her heart was the Loma Prieta earthquake in 1989. "It was really traumatizing," she says. The earthquake killed sixty-three, injured nearly four thousand, and devastated neighborhoods in Oakland and San Francisco and other parts of the Bay area, leaving thousands homeless.[31] When she did a retreat later that year, she was angry with God about what had happened. In her prayers, she asked him, "'Where the hell were you?' In my head, that's what I said," she recalls with a laugh. And God's response to her was, "I was in the earthquake."

She did not let that go. "Well, what the hell were you doing there?" she asked God. In the course of that exchange, she says, she understood that God is present and feels our pain. "God suffers in the heartbreak as much as I do," she says. "My faith teaches me that God hums us at every moment. God is creating us at every moment. We are not orphans. The reason we don't see God is that God's so close."

Campbell believes that to live in faith is to be willing to "walk towards trouble," to encounter people whose stories may break your heart, and to listen to people who may surprise you and cause you to rethink your assumptions. Speaking in 2014, she recalled some of the people she met in the United States through her advocacy, people living on the margins. She described a 2008 trip to visit Iraqi refugees in Syria and Lebanon and meeting with a mother so desperate she'd sold her eldest daughter to spare her other children from hunger. "She wept when she told me that story," Campbell said. "And I wept with her, because I had been so judgmental about anyone who would sell a member of their family."

Such encounters, she says, are antidotes to certitude, which leads to righteousness. They help to open us to the "holy doubt" that permits us to hear "a different story" than we expected and to learn from people with perspectives that may differ from our own. [32]

Campbell does not get tied up in knots over the question of ordination of women to the priesthood. She admires the "courage" of women who have gone through a formal ordination, something the institutional church condemns. But, she says, "we have to open our eyes to the broader story. We're thinking of ordination too narrowly." To be priestly, to be called to nourish one another in community, is not confined to men who are formally ordained, she says. It's a mistake, she says, to fight the bishops "on their definition of ordination." Doing so puts everybody "in a push-me/pull-you situation where you both get stuck."

Campbell is a published poet, and she often speaks in metaphor. She describes the church, often called the Ship of Peter, as sailing on the sea. The "ordinary folks" hear the gospel, share stories about the best places to go under water, and, with their air tanks on, they jump into the sea, looking to spread the gospel. "Now the problem is the hierarchy," Campbell says. "They swagger on the ship. They don't know the beauty of the sea." When there is a disconnect between ordinary people trying to live out the gospel and the institutional church, whose leaders are not connected to their struggles, the faithful don't get what they need when they return to the ship looking to "get bolstered up." If the concept of ordination were more expansive, if all Catholics could find more ways to express themselves as a "priestly people," there would be more avenues for nourishment.

Campbell went on to discuss some abstruse areas of Catholic doctrine that I didn't fully understand until I read her memoir. Catholics are taught that ordination is an extension of baptism, she says. "So we're baptized into being a priestly people." The concept of ordination, she says, could be as expansive as the Catholic view of baptism. Typically, a priest baptizes, but that's not always the case. "There's ordinary baptism, where you get your godparents and you have a celebration . . . and you get a baptismal certificate," she says. But then there are things like baptism of desire, baptism of blood, baptism of necessity. I mean, there's other ways to be baptized."

Baptism of necessity permits a member of the laity to baptize someone if there are "urgent circumstances," she explained in her memoir. Baptism of blood occurs if someone is martyred for his or her belief, even if they have not been formally baptized. If a person truly wants to be baptized but can't join the church, or is prevented from joining, then the church recognizes baptism of desire.

"If ordination is an extension of baptism," she says, "then why aren't there other forms of ordination?" Even the sacrament of the Holy Eucharist, she wrote, is present not only in the bread and wine transformed into the body and blood of Christ. "As the Second Vatican Council stressed, Jesus is also present in the people assembled there, and in the Word proclaimed, as well as in the celebrants of the sacrament."[33]

"When I was president of my community, I was a priestly person for my community during those five years," she says. "I heard confession, I anointed the sick. I presided at amazing celebrations that were Eucharistic."

She explains that while a priest came to say Sunday Mass for their community, a few times he didn't make it, and on those occasions she'd preside. "We had readings, we had bread and wine, we shared faith, we had a homily. We did all that."

She wasn't celebrating Mass, she says, but adds, "Was it Eucharistic? It was Eucharistic. Was it 'The Eucharist?' I don't know. Did it matter?"

She asks, "Wouldn't it be enriching just to live our faith freely? . . . Our prayer should be not that the bishops have a brain transplant," she says with a laugh, "but rather that we have eyes to see the priestly roles that are being done, acknowledge them, lift them up, and celebrate them."

Campbell believes that people are hungry for spirituality and that women religious are uniquely equipped to offer that nourishment. "We lament that there are not enough sisters like in the good old days, and that frustrates the hell out of me," she says.

Nuns don't have to be the church's "labor force" as they did in the 1940s and 1950s, she insists. In the old days, she says, "we were forever moving tables and chairs." That's something communities of mostly elderly sisters can't do.

"We're getting old . . . we're having to wrestle with death and dying because our friends are dying, we're dying." But sisters are in the position to respond to what society needs, she says. "There's a deep hunger for the sacred, for spirituality. There's a deep hunger to belong and to be in community and to know we're not in this alone. There is a hunger to be listened to—I mean actually listened to, in the physical presence, not just tweeted or Facebooked. . . . And there's a huge, huge need in our society to wrestle with death and dying."

Sisters, she says, have the gifts to respond to those needs. "We've got to find a way to put them out in the universe" for others to share. "Folks in the parishes, they have horrible struggles," she says. "As women religious we have to find a better way to share the wealth, richness, and nourishment that we have."

Some of the struggles Catholic women deal with concern moral issues, such as contraception. NETWORK doesn't take a position on artificial birth control. "Women know what to do," she says. "Let's be real about this." She explains that she teaches a course on the differences between church law, known as *canon law*, and Anglo-Saxon jurisprudence. Canon law, she says, is about "the desired result, not the minimum." Canon law "is moon and stars for the most part" and "aspirational. . . . Anglo-Saxon jurisprudence is all about the dirt. It's just the floor [of what's expected]."

The problem, she says, comes when we apply Anglo-Saxon interpretations to canon law. "We bring our Anglo-Saxon version of law" to judging our moral conduct and "think the Vatican police will come find us if we don't follow every jot and tittle." But that's not the case, she says. "The fact is, people make the best choices they can, and we just have to encourage them in the best choices." That's reflected in the views of Pope Francis when he asks that church leaders not be "righteous" and judgmental, she says.

In her memoir, Campbell takes a similar tack on the Catholic bête noire, abortion. When she was practicing family law, she was "appointed to represent a thirteen-year-old girl who had been raped and impregnated by her uncle." In this case, the girl had a miscarriage, but Campbell got some understanding of the "horrible, agonizing choice" faced by "this terrified girl and others like her. . . . I'm pro-life, but I'm not pro–criminalization of abortion," she writes. Noting that "poverty is the great driver of the abortion rate," she believes that the way to curb abortions is to "nourish women and take care of them and support them and do what's necessary so they can make that choice for life."[34]

What does make her angry, she says, is when moral issues become politicized and when "our church leadership gets hijacked by right-wing politicians who want to use [these moral issues] for their own gain. . . . I don't know whether it's naïveté on the part of the leadership or it's their own political desires for affirmation. . . . But that's wrong—just plain wrong."

She contends that faith should not be about the rules. "It's about the vivid life. Jesus was never about the rules, Jesus was about life." Sometimes church leaders, she says, have "hidden behind the rules because they don't know what else to do. And that is crippling us.

"Faith is so much more than the church. . . . For me that's a huge comfort—that Jesus is bigger than the institution."

Nevertheless, Campbell remains firmly within Catholicism. "For me, I was born and raised and lived all my life in this church." She adds that in Western cultures "nobody else" has either the Christian "contemplative tradition" the church has or the Catholic social-justice tradition. "We've got a lot of richness. It's the richness that has made me who I am, and for me it's all about taking faith into the world. . . . The richness of faith is worth it to me," despite having to deal with "some pesky unenlightened leadership," she says. "Besides, we're probably a means of conversion for them, and they're a means of conversion for me."

Campbell's days are hectic. But she always finds an hour each morning to meditate. "That's the anchor," she says. "I grew up in Long Beach, California, so the only experience with snow I had was my snow globe," she recalls. "But ordinary life is just a snow globe, all shaken up. Meditation is like sitting still and letting it all settle down." Doing so, she says, "provides clarity. I do the best I can."

6

MARIANNE DUDDY-BURKE
Beyond Catholic Incorporated

Like any happily married spouse, Marianne Duddy-Burke warmly remembers her Catholic wedding—a nuptial Mass with a "sublime" choir and more than two hundred guests, including four generations of the couple's families. Writing in 2013, Duddy-Burke described that day and fifteen years of marriage—with the job changes, health challenges, and children—that followed. It is a marriage and a family rooted in faith. As many Catholic parents, she wrote, she and her spouse "have lit advent wreaths, placed the infant Jesus in the manger, prayed for peace on New Year's, and celebrated Holy Week liturgies and Easter vigils."[1]

But unlike most Catholics, Duddy-Burke has to worry if she'll be denied Communion if she attends the funeral or baptism of a friend or relative, or if her daughters will be thrown out of a Catholic school because someone complained to the pastor. For Duddy-Burke remains both committed to Catholicism and committed to living a full life as a lesbian.

Catholicism is just too important to Duddy-Burke to abandon. So she's found a different space to practice her faith, a space outside the norms of the institutional church. The Catholicism she practices, she contends, more authentically follows the gospel.

Duddy-Burke is executive director of DignityUSA, which represents thousands of lesbian, gay, bisexual and transgender Catholics throughout the country. Dignity offers these Catholics the recognition and acceptance that the institutional church—what Duddy-Burke terms Catholic Incorporated—has withheld. Founded by a priest in 1969, at a time when LGBT persons were often shunned and discriminated against, Dignity sought the official approval of the church and conferred with bishops and theologians. Initially many diocesan and order priests officiated at Dignity services, and many dioceses even had special programs for gay Catholics. Dignity chapters often met in Catholic churches. But since the late 1970s the church has increasingly marginalized gay Catholics and attempted to restrict any pastoral outreach to the gay community. In 1986, after the Vatican issued its *Letter to the Bishops of the Catholic Church on the Pastoral Care of Homosexual Persons*, the institutional church severed "any official collaboration between Dignity and diocesan structures," Duddy-Burke says.

Whatever steps Pope Francis may take to soften the church's position on same-sex marriage and LGBT issues, she believes that real change has to come from the people in the pews, not the church hierarchy. And she continues to immerse herself in a Catholicism that embraces the sacraments and service to the poor and marginalized.

Duddy-Burke is a round woman with short, reddish hair, a warm, expressive voice, and a throaty laugh. She's someone you'd expect to run into at a parish PTA meeting or Sunday Mass. Nothing about her bearing suggests the hidden trauma of her childhood, the advocacy that has shaped most of her adult life, or the knowledge that, in some Catholic circles, even today she would be scorned.

Duddy was born in 1960. That was the year John F. Kennedy was elected president, Pope John XXIII was about to renew the church, and American Catholics found that they were suddenly considered cool.

She grew up in an Irish-Catholic family where the famous porcelain sculpture of praying hands was on the coffee table in the family living room, a sculpture that was the focal point of family prayers together. (Her father was entirely Irish Catholic—her mother a mix of Irish, Polish, and German ethnicities, but the Irish culture prevailed.) They said grace before meals and never missed Sunday Mass. They and their extended families would get together for baptisms, First Communions, Confirmations, weddings, and funerals. "It was part of the everyday fabric of our lives, totally inseparable from who we were."

They lived in Central New Jersey in what she calls the "new suburbs" in East Brunswick, in a predominantly Catholic neighborhood.

These were good years for the white American middle class and for the descendants of Catholic immigrants, who now were fully accepted into American culture. Jobs were plentiful, families were nuclear, and the economy was strong. One man could support a stay-at-home wife and four or five kids, living in a suburban home close to a new Catholic parish.

Saint Bartholomew's parish was founded in 1959, spurred by rapid population growth in the state's Middlesex County. It began with nearly nine hundred families and, like so many Catholic churches of that era, soon built a proper church and parish school. Its patron, Saint Bartholomew, was one of the twelve apostles. He preached the gospel to the people of Egypt, Ethiopia, Persia, India, and Armenia, where his efforts drew the wrath of the king and won him martyrdom. The church has a stained-glass window that depicts the saint with the knives thought to be his instruments of torture. He was flayed alive.[2]

A young Marianne Duddy looked to martyrs like Saint Bartholomew for inspiration in dealing with the challenges of her childhood, much more turbulent than it appeared. She looked to the church for stability. "The church that I grew up with was seen as a very powerful and positive institution," she recalls. "It was a force that was changing the world for good. There was a sense of the church triumphant." That church wasn't challenged by the faithful. In her family, the last word always was *What did Sister say?* or *What did Father say?* The admonitions and judgments of the parish priests and nuns trumped even her parents' authority.

Duddy was so steeped in that Catholic world that before she turned eight she felt a calling—to the priesthood. "I used to say Mass in our backyard and play Confession with all the neighborhood kids," she says. With Necco Wafers substituting for Communion hosts, she would take the sacraments to the sick in hospitals—bandaged pets serving as patients. "I buried every one of our pets that died with a funeral service that I led." Since her family believed in the American dream—that anything was attainable through hard work and perseverance—Duddy felt that her dream, too, could become a reality. "I figured that by the time I got to be an adult there would be women priests. Or maybe I'd be the first."

She got some inkling of what she was up against in third grade. The boys of the parish were invited to be altar servers. Since the pastor spoke to the entire class, she assumed that she, too, was welcome to fill out the requisite forms and come to the meeting at the church and bring a parent. Her parents were skeptical, but Duddy insisted that both boys and girls had been included. This was long before the church permitted female altar servers, so when they arrived at the school, they soon learned she was mistaken.

But in the optimism of the day, the parish offered some creative problem-solving. The priests told her that, while she could not serve at the altar, she could be a lector, someone who goes to the pulpit and does the Scripture readings for Mass. "I don't remember being mad that I couldn't be an altar boy," she recalls. "I remember my parents turned it into, 'Look, you are going to be the youngest reader that our parish ever had. We're going to be so proud of you when you stand up there.'"

But Duddy was drawn to the church for more complex reasons. Contrary to appearances, she did not live in an ideal Catholic family. Her childhood is "a very mixed story," she says. Her father "really tried to be a good father, a good husband, a good person in the community." But he was an alcoholic whose drinking problems likely were exacerbated by the chronic pain he experienced after being struck by a motorcycle when Duddy was six or seven years old. "The leg was shattered, and it was reset a couple of times," but he walked with a limp and "was plainly in pain."

By the time she was nine or ten, she had learned to help him with his office work. After her younger sisters went to bed, she and her mother would go through his bulging briefcase, sorting the documents into files. Her father was a credit manager for a major oil company, and his job was to analyze oil and gas deals and determine which should be approved, which raised questions, and which should be rejected. She learned how to read a credit report. Looking back, she says, it's "scary when you think about a ten-year-old making these business decisions," possibly having on impact on "the overall American economy."

By middle school, her father's drinking bouts, which had been episodic early in her childhood, had grown much worse. He would become angry and violent, sometimes striking her mother. When she would try to intervene and get him to stop, she would get hurt, too. "The level of violence and intimidation and fear in our house was pretty high."

Sometimes he would force her into the car when he went out drinking. She remembers harrowing drives with a drunk father at the wheel and her fear that they wouldn't make it across the bridge on the way home. "My father eventually killed himself, and I think I knew from a young age that was going to happen. I was really scared that he wanted to take me with him. It was terrifying."

But the worst times were after his alcoholism had cost him jobs and he didn't have the money to drink. Then he'd take her with him for another reason: She'd be passed from bar buddy to bar buddy as they held her on their laps. They'd pay for his drinks. "It was a very sexual thing," she says, her voice growing husky and hushed.

Her mother went to their pastor, hoping for support and some guidance about what to do. But what she met was not so much indifference as incredulity. The family was friendly with all three priests who staffed the parish. The pastor, Duddy-Burke says, was a good man, but he just couldn't believe what her mother was telling him. "Oh, that just couldn't happen," was his message to her mother. "There was such a lack of understanding of what happens in family life," she says. Priests accepted "the subservience" of women and were "totally unprepared" to address the real-life problems of nuclear families or understand "the role of women in the family."

Catholic culture made it harder for women to change unacceptable situations. At that time, she recalls, a maxim often repeated at school was "God, others, you." It was only years later that Duddy-Burke realized how "problematic" that message is, "particularly for women, because there's always tons of 'others.' You never get around to paying attention to you or understanding what's right for you." Her mother, she surmises, "was caught in that trap." And in those days Catholic families did not divorce. "It was out of the question. I remember wishing for it, but it was clear—Catholic family: marriage is forever."

As a child, Duddy understood there were "cracks" in her family and that what appeared fine to the outside world was "fairly turbulent" inside. But any critique of the pastor's inadequate response to her mother would come much later. With the topsy-turvy life she was living at home, the church became even more of a rock for her, "a safe place. I was a very good student, always top of my class; school was very easy for me. I liked doing the extra things. I loved hanging out with the nuns." She threw herself into school and parish activities, singing in the choir, joining the youth group. Within the sheltering confines of this Catholic world, she found affirmation and a respite from what was happening in her family. She also found a way to process what she was experiencing. The lives of the saints gave her vivid portrayals of people who had undergone great trials and triumphed in the end.

Duddy got a reprieve from her turbulent family life when she earned a full scholarship to Mount Saint Mary Academy in Wachtung, New Jersey. The venerable school, founded in 1907, sits on a hill, graced by an impressive portico with four columns and its own bell tower.[3] It was "several towns away" from her home, and by her junior year, she was boarding there as well.

An experience there fed into her persistent dream of the priesthood. She would attend Mass in the chapel daily, along with the nuns. The school chaplain was blind and needed assistance at the altar. "Since I was there anyway," the nuns asked Duddy to help the old priest. "It was amazing to be right up there in that inner sanctum with the priest and know all the words and know all the gestures. It felt like another step that was naturally leading me to become a priest." She remembers that chapel with great fondness—as a place of peace and light, with stained-glass windows, and "smelling of incense and old nun."

Duddy felt that the church was changing and that the ordination of women priests would happen. After Vatican II, she saw the nuns discard their old habits and diversify their work. No longer just teachers, they were running hospitals, becoming lawyers, working with the homeless. "They were involved in politics and antipoverty work and housing rights. So the whole definition of what it meant to be active in the church and who could do what was just exploding right around me. So of course women could be priests."

However, Duddy's ambitions for her immediate future were more modest: After high school graduation, she planned to become a Sister of Mercy. But the nuns advised her not to follow that plan. They wanted her to leave the safe Catholic bubble and experience the world before entering the convent. "It was really the nuns who said to me, 'You need to experience life in a different way, and then come back to us if it's right for you.' So they really led me to try something new."

With the support of her "advocates" at her high school, Duddy applied to Yale, Princeton, the University of Michigan, and Wellesley. She was accepted wherever she applied. Her one act of rebellion, she laughs, was to resist her parents' dreams that she would attend either Harvard or Notre Dame.

In 1978 she began her freshman year at Wellesley, a women's college and one of the "seven sisters"—all-female schools with reputations for high intellectual standards and an upper-class patina, the women's version of the Ivy League. Wellesley had cross-registration with MIT, nearby in Boston. In its 1978 bulletin Wellesley described itself as the college that "takes women seriously as individuals, as scholars, and as leaders. . . . Throughout the years, Wellesley has encouraged women to make unconventional choices. . . . This conscious effort to prepare women for a full range of career and life choices is an integral part of Wellesley's rigorous and demanding academic experience."[4]

To say that Duddy was out of her comfort zone was an understatement. She had grown up in a world nearly entirely comprised of Catholics. Her largest experience of a world beyond Catholicism was babysitting for a Jewish family. Now she was on a campus brimming with people of other faiths or no faith, opening herself up to new ways of looking at the world.

Her best friend in college was a Jewish pro-choice advocate, and "people were talking about things that you would never bring up in my house. . . . I was like at sea, just feeling like an innocent abroad. It was an entirely different world. It was shocking, and it was really hard for me not to judge everything through the lens of this restricted, sheltered Catholicism which had been my life. Letting go of that sense that this is the only way to be in the world" was the great work of her freshman year, she says.

And then there was the fateful night when she was working in the school's science library, one of her student jobs. "While it was quiet, I was flipping through books in the reference section and found *Our Bodies, Ourselves*, the great bible for women in the seventies. And there was a chapter called 'In Amerika They Call Us Dykes.' I had no clue what it was talking about, so I started the chapter, and I was like, 'Oh, there's a word for me. There must be other people like me.'"

That chapter, famous for its "unabashedly positive portrayal of lesbianism," explained to her the platonic good times she'd had with the boys she had dated and the fact that all her "deep relationships" had been with women.[5]

But she had been sheltered as a Catholic schoolgirl, so she wasn't frightened by the realization. Catholic boys might get a health class where homosexuality came up, but Catholic girls were not warned about their sexuality. It was just assumed that a good Catholic girl would not be sexually active until after marriage, Duddy-Burke says. And the notion that a woman was a sexual being beyond procreation was simply not part of the church's thinking. "The big evil for us was birth control or abortion, so it was totally outside my frame of reference.

"Coming out for me was putting a name to an experience that I didn't even understand was atypical," she says. Discovering lesbianism "was very normalizing in some ways for me. And I never, ever had a sense that there was anything wrong with this spiritually."

There were "so many taboos" against premarital heterosexual sex, she says. "But I'd never been told that sleeping with a woman was wrong," she laughs. "I mean, I didn't know how to do it. Some trial and error, but it's amazing what the body knows when given a chance."

Once she identified herself as a lesbian, she went looking for others on campus. The pictures of lesbians seemed to indicate that they all wore flannel shirts and work boots, so that was a clue. She posted a note in a school elevator asking if anyone had Cris Williamson's tape, since she had lost her copy. (Williamson's 1975 album, *The Changer and the Changed*, is considered the first in a "women's music" genre sung by a lesbian artist.[6])

As Duddy was getting her bearings at Wellesley and making new discoveries about herself, her one anchor continued to be Catholicism. She was president of the campus Newman Center, which offers Catholic students a place to worship and socialize. It was a job she enjoyed that gave her a sense of community in a radically new environment.

She had a lot of fun with the two seminarians she worked with. *Star Wars* was very popular then, so at Christmas, they put some *Star Wars* action figures in the nativity crèche. She took one of the seminarians home one weekend to meet her mother. "We'd do off-campus trips together, and they had a great sense of humor." It was all very steadying and reassuring for a coed thrown into a radically different world.

But she lost that anchor during her sophomore year. She was summoned to a meeting with the Newman chaplain. That wasn't unusual; she often met with the chaplain to discuss Newman business. He was a middle-aged priest of Indian extraction whom Duddy considered an odd match for Wellesley, because he spoke to the girls as if their futures were as mothers and wives and nothing else. "I mean, these were Wellesley women!" But she respected his office, and never thought to challenge the church's decision to place him on campus.

But this meeting was to be her last. The priest had a blunt question. "He stammered and stuttered, and finally he said, 'I have heard from someone that you are a lesbian. Is that true?'" Duddy-Burke recalls thinking that this was the first time her coming out was not voluntary. She asked herself, "Do I tell the truth, or do I hide?"

"Yes, it's true," she told him.

He responded, "Well, we cannot have someone like you representing Catholics on this campus. I am accepting your resignation."

Duddy's first reaction was anger. "This is a stupid, stupid man who is enforcing a man-made law, not something that came from God. Eventually it would change." But she didn't challenge the chaplain's decision. She did as she was told, briefly calling the Newman Center's vice president to tell her she now was in charge.

The sadness came when she realized that the community that had been her anchor was lost to her. No one stood up for her—something Duddy failed to do for herself. She continued to remain friendly with the two seminarians who had been active in Newman. But things were different. "We didn't have the structural commitment of Newman to connect us."

She felt out of place attending Mass on campus, and Masses at suburban churches near Wellesley, focused on family life, didn't fit the bill. She got involved with other Christian groups on campus, but that didn't serve as an adequate replacement either. "I think Catholics feel most at home in a Catholic environment."

Duddy-Burke never knew who the "someone" was who told the Newman chaplain about her lesbianism. In fact, she never thought about finding out. "It's so funny that question has never crossed my mind. Isn't that silly, that it's never crossed my mind?"

The experience failed to sour her on Catholicism. "I never lost my faith," she says. "I continued to have an individual spiritual life." But she lacked a home for putting "those values into action." No place for social service, no place for her music, no place to exercise leadership.

And in the late seventies and early eighties, being gay even at a college as progressive as Wellesley was not easy. Lesbians formed an "underground community," forced to communicate with one another through messages written in the reference-card room of the library, she says.

There were threats of violence when they tried to hold their first dance, and their posters were torn down. Nevertheless, Duddy became a leader in the student lesbian movement and was interviewed for a *Time* story on homosexuals and lesbians on campus.

Just before the story came out, she realized her parents didn't know she was gay. She made a trip home at Thanksgiving, and just before she left to return to school, she sat them down. She told them, "I realized while I've been at school that I'm a lesbian." She let them know about the upcoming *Time* story. "I'm sorry you don't have a lot of time to process this before it comes out in print."

Their reaction, she says, was unexpected. "They were amazing." Both parents told her, "You're our daughter. You are always welcome in our home. You're welcome to bring anyone home, and we'll figure out the sleeping arrangements later."

But when it came to her relationship with the church, Duddy didn't really get her bearings again until she went to graduate school, at the Weston Jesuit School of Theology, which later became the Boston College School of Theology and Ministry. Once again, she was among Catholics. She had promised herself that she would not disclose her lesbianism. Nor would she express her still-active desire to be a priest. She thought there were "spaces" where she could slip through, serving the church and fulfilling some of her pastoral longings. She could be a chaplain at a hospital or university.

At this point, she was living with a woman and figured she would keep the relationship secret. She couldn't do it. "Within the first few days it became very clear to me that I could not live with integrity without being clear as to who I was. I just couldn't play games. . . . I was out within the first week."

At Weston, she says, being a laywoman studying theology was more of a struggle than being a lesbian. Only a few laywomen were taking classes there. But there was still some reason to hope that eventually the church would become more tolerant. Her teachers at Weston expanded her view of the church, teaching her to look far beyond what she had been exposed to in her Irish-Catholic childhood.

She was learning that the church was expansive and complex, more than a structure solely revolving around a hierarchy of priests, bishops, and pope. Theologian Cardinal Avery Dulles had written an influential book that explored the various ways the church manifests itself in the world. The concept of "the church" included the community of the faithful, serving the needs of the world, receiving the sacraments together, and following the gospel.[7]

In the 1970s, Duddy-Burke adds, the institutional church was among the first organizations to oppose the legalization of discrimination against gay people in the workplace, and several dioceses had offices of lesbian and gay ministry. In 1976 the US Conference of Catholic Bishops released a pastoral letter, *To Live in Christ Jesus*, which Duddy-Burke appears to have almost memorized. Quoting a passage, she closes her eyes and recites, "Gay and lesbian people, no less than anyone else, deserve to live with dignity, respect, and friendship." It's good that Duddy-Burke has committed those words to heart, for a search of the document on the website of the US Conference fails to turn up the actual text of the letter.

In 1982, while she was at Weston, Duddy discovered Dignity/Boston. Her roommate noticed a story in the *Boston Globe* about the group. "Marianne, there's something you really have to see," she told her. "This sounds perfect for you." The *Globe* story had quoted a chaplain for the group who said the group provided gay people who had been shunned by the institutional church "a way back to Catholicism."[8]

Duddy attended a Dignity/Boston service that night. "I went in the door, and I was hooked," she says. The service gave her "a sense of being home." She recognized the songs so popular in the folk Masses of the day—the piano and guitar accompaniment. The members of the congregation were warm and welcoming. "I just felt at home."

She was so taken by Dignity that she arranged to do her fieldwork there, working with LGBT Catholic young people. Prior to Duddy's graduation, a senior professor objected to her getting credit for her work there because it was a gay organization. "He made an issue of it and was really unpleasant with me," she says. With the credit in question, Duddy received a master's degree in theology rather than a master's in divinity.

"During the four years I was at Weston, it became clear to me that there was no way I could work for the institution with integrity," she says. "I realized, as a woman, I could get a job as a chaplain someplace, but I would need to hide my lesbianism and my relationships if I wanted to work for the institutional church."

As Duddy completed her theology studies, her male peers, the seminarians in all her classes, were looking forward to ordination. She desperately wanted what they were going to have. That desire was more painful because she knew what her classmates were like. "You spend every weekday and some weekends with all these people. You know their capabilities and their pettiness and their blind spots."

She recalled that during the first week of classes at seminary she'd had to teach a few of the seminarians how to write a check. She was twenty-one, and the seminarians were six years older, but they'd been insulated from everyday matters like money management. "They'd never had to do it." Many of her classmates were not able to "cope with basic world things," and yet "these are the folks that are going to be unleashed to run parishes."

Watching priests say Mass at Dignity services was heartbreaking. "I remember sitting there and sobbing, week after week after week. I had this deeply felt call and no way of seeing it through. Seeing a priest up there on the altar doing what I knew I was totally capable of doing but knowing I would never have that status was excruciating."

She concedes, however, that ordination would have required the church to change its policy on two issues: the fitness of women for the priesthood and the requirement that priests be celibate. "I knew that the love relationships I had were sacred, and I saw no reason that they would prohibit me from being effective in a priestly role," she says.

It was at a Dignity event that Duddy developed her own lasting love relationship. She met her partner on Easter night in 1994. At that point, she says, she was still "shell-shocked" from the end of a twelve-year relationship. She met Becky, then a member of the Sisters of Mercy, who had realized she was a lesbian and not yet decided what that meant for her future.

"The fact that she was still a nun was in some ways safety," Duddy-Burke speculates. She was wary of forming a relationship on the rebound, and Becky needed time. But that first meeting made an impression. "I remember calling my best friend the night after Becky and I had this amazing conversation and saying, 'Oh, my gosh.' I hadn't had that sense of excitement in a very long time."

Becky's background was complicated. She was a Catholic convert, still suffering from the guilt of her upbringing in the very conservative Free Methodist Church. It was her exposure to Catholic theology that led her to believe that sexuality could be a force for good in one's life.

The two were married in a religious ceremony at Dignity in September 1998. They were legally married in Massachusetts in 2004. They are the parents of two adopted daughters. "When we were first looking to adopt, the first place we called was Catholic Charities," Duddy-Burke says. But the adoption specialist told them that while the organization could train the couple to be foster and adoptive parents, placement wasn't going to happen. The specialist said, "Our supervisors will not allow us to place kids in the homes of same-sex couples."

Duddy-Burke, by then a full-throated advocate for gay Catholics, was tempted to challenge Catholic Charities, since much of their work was supported with state and federal funds and Massachusetts bans discrimination against individuals on the basis of sexual orientation. But she and her partner were both pushing forty and worried that stirring up a fuss would hurt their chance to become parents.

Instead they contacted the Massachusetts Department of Children and Families and were accepted. "DCF in Massachusetts has a long history of placing kids with same-sex couples," she says. The training for gay adoptive parents was "beyond tolerant," she says. "It was affirming."

One of their daughters attended an urban Catholic school for kindergarten. The family was welcomed and had a good experience there. But they worried about the future. Duddy-Burke was working as Dignity's executive director. "I knew it would be just a matter of time before some right-wing crazy person complained to the school that this critic of the church has her kid in Catholic school." They'd also heard that a homosexual couple whose children were enrolled in a Catholic school had been forced to leave after a parishioner complained. Neither she nor Becky wanted their daughters to be in the middle of that kind of trouble.

And since both their daughters had been adopted from foster care, they had "learning issues," and access to the special services they needed was easier through the public-school system. Their daughters are being raised Catholic, although not as members of what Duddy-Burke terms "Catholic Incorporated—or Catholic Inc."

Catholic Inc. "has done such a good job of taking the word *Catholic* and making it a brand," she says. "It has this particular connotation of a parish, headed by a male priest, where people come on Sunday mornings and get Communion and then go back into their lives, and the parish feeds into a diocese and the diocese feeds into the US Conference of Catholic Bishops, and then there's the Vatican—this whole linear chain of command."

Indeed, Duddy-Burke's growing unease with a hierarchical church made her rethink her desire for ordination. She has come to believe, she says, that "the whole structure of ordination is as much an issue as the exclusion of women." In baptism, she says, all Catholics are anointed as priests and prophets. Her call, she says, is "really showing that you don't need a collar" to do ministry. By focusing so intently on the role of priests and the Mass, she says, the institutional church neglects "following the gospel in everyday life."

She insists that Catholicism is much broader and richer than Catholic Inc. She points to Catholics who've left the traditional parish to join "intentional communities," who come together for liturgy in diverse meeting places ranging from churches of other faiths to homes, community centers, and libraries. There are women religious who live among the poor. The church, she contends, also includes people who "don't affiliate with a structural Catholicism but who hold the values very dear."

Progressive groups like Dignity work to "shatter that sense that Catholicism only looks one way." She points to the challenges that Catholic Inc. has faced lately—a sharp decline in vocations to the priesthood, the scandal of priest pedophilia compounded by efforts by the hierarchy to cover it up. Will the scandals "eventually humble the institution? I hope so."

Dignity, she contends, is authentically Catholic in that it welcomes diverse communities all with the shared goal of following the gospel. "There's nothing that says to me that the gospel of Jesus has to be carried out in the way the Catholic Church is currently structured. Nothing."

Some Dignity groups conduct liturgies with validly ordained Catholic priests recognized by the institutional church. Other groups "haven't seen a priest in twenty-five years. We have a national structure that is accountable to our local people but that doesn't dictate liturgical practice." For example, in 2011 the Vatican revised the missal, dictating the responses the faithful make during Mass.[9] The nation's sixty-eight million Catholic parishioners simply accepted what had been decreed, but Dignity did not, Duddy-Burke says. "Dignity chapters all across the country sat down with the wording and the information about the history of how this was developed, and the chapters made decisions about whether they were going to use this text or not. What parish could do that?"

That diversity is reflected in her family's own practices. Emily, their oldest daughter, was baptized by an ordained priest who had been placed on "permanent leave" from his order and by a woman priest whose ordination is not accepted by the official church. Infinity, their younger daughter, was baptized by lay members of the Dignity community. Likewise, their daughters received Communion when they could understand the significance of the sacrament. It was not a matter of a special ceremony or "a big white dress." They took Communion "when they were ready."

Duddy-Burke doesn't know how many people consider themselves members of Dignity, although she estimates that the group "touches" about ten thousand individuals a month. "Dignity's original purpose was to provide a sense of shelter and sanctuary and a safe place for people who needed it," she says. When it began forty-five years ago, LGBT Catholics were very vulnerable, often the targets of physical violence, even murder, often suicidal, "living in a culture and a church that called them sick, sinful, and criminal."

But as LGBT rights have become more universally accepted, Dignity's mission is changing, she says. The minority of Dignity members attend a liturgy at a Dignity chapter. Many more members belong to Catholic parishes or meet in small groups at churches of other denominations or are not affiliated with any institution.

Dignity now sees itself as a force reaching out to all Catholic communities marginalized by the institutional church—everyone from married priests and women priests to Catholic homeless people. She believes that Catholic Inc. won't change its positions until and unless Catholics in the pews demand change.

There are so many areas where Catholic Inc. is wrong, Duddy-Burke says. While polls consistently show that Catholics support equality for the LGBT community, "why," she asks, "is it okay for schools and parishes and Catholic Charities to fire folks who marry their partners? Why is it okay that the pope has not said one word yet about the violence against LGBT people in Uganda and Nigeria?" She criticizes the Vatican for appearing to tolerate the "corrective rape" of lesbians in Iran and India. And she asks, "why are Catholic healthcare providers still not giving out condoms" to prevent the spread of HIV/AIDs?

Duddy-Burke is heartened that Pope Francis appears to want to change the church. But she doesn't think change will come easily or quickly. She applauds the pope's effort to move the church to "a more collaborative governance style." But she predicts that he will be "fought tooth and nail by the existing power structure." Even if the pope succeeds, she adds, "it will take decades for that to trickle down" to the people in the pews.

"Most Catholics seem to feel that their options are either to remain quiet when they have a concern or disagreement or to leave. . . . Very few of us are either lucky enough, blessed enough, or stubborn enough," she says, to not back off and to choose "this sort of third way." It's not easy, she concedes. "Catholic Inc. branding . . . so dominates people's minds, hearts, and souls" that it is very hard for Catholics to conceive of finding "ways to be Catholic outside of the norms" laid down by the institutional church.

But if change is to come, she says, the laity will be its drivers. "We own our church. That's where the hope comes from."

7

DIANA L. HAYES

The Thorn in the Church's Side

When Diana L. Hayes was teaching at Georgetown University, one of her students asked about the role of the Jesuits during the slavery era. "To my shock," she says, she found that in the nineteenth century before the Civil War, Jesuits were among the "largest slaveholders" in the Delmarva Peninsula, a region bordering the Chesapeake Bay that includes portions of Delaware, Maryland, and Virginia. "They had huge plantations in southern Maryland." The Vatican demanded that the Jesuits free their slaves, she says, but they sold them instead, ostensibly to white Catholics in New Orleans who promised to keep the slave families together.

When the Jesuits checked back a few years later, they learned that the slave families had been "broken up and sold all over the country." The profits from the slave sale helped build and endow Georgetown University, then Georgetown College, Hayes says.

She would remind Georgetown administrators, "to their distinct lack of humor," that in light of its history Georgetown owed each black student free tuition. "They had already paid for it." School officials "didn't take too kindly" to that idea, she says with a laugh. "What the heck. You've got to keep them stirred up." (It was not until 2015 that Georgetown students sought justice for the victims of Georgetown's slaveholding, bringing public attention to the school's shameful legacy.)[1]

An African American laywoman who converted to Catholicism in 1979, and then ultimately became an eminent theologian, writer, and lecturer, Hayes always has managed to "stir up" the institutional church. Her deep faith and spirituality have not blinded her to its flaws, ones she is willing to call out. She thinks of herself as a "thorn in the church's side," someone who reminds church leaders of the racism and sexism that still exist in the institutional church. "I'm a thorn so deeply embedded that it irritates the hell out of the church. But . . . so deeply embedded that they can't pluck me out."

She has done groundbreaking scholarship on the role of African American Catholics in the United States. Through her many books and lectures, she's also expressed her faith, and her reading of the Scriptures, in a voice that honors her identity as an African American woman. In her book *Hagar's Daughters*, for example, Hayes dramatically reframes our image of Sarah's slave and Abraham's concubine. Hagar is no longer a bit player in the drama of salvation but emblematic of the power and spirituality of all black women.

Hayes's conversion wasn't as dramatic as Saint Paul's: she wasn't knocked to the ground by a bright light and directly addressed by the voice of Christ.[2] But the circumstances that transformed a shy, introverted African American lawyer in her thirties into a Catholic theologian and an influential scholar and public speaker are almost as dramatic.

In responding to God's call, Hayes writes, she found her own voice and her own unique identity. No longer seeing herself through others' eyes, as the "odd one," she embraced all her qualities—a lay African American celibate Catholic woman and theologian. "I did not fit the stereotypes which our society has set forth for black women," she writes, noting that she was neither "brazenly promiscuous nor a mother, nor was I ignorant and dependent." Her existence challenged both the perceptions of a "dominant white structure" and of a sexist culture that defined women "as a reflection of our men—fathers, brothers, uncles, husbands, and even sons."[3]

In her books and lectures she embraces womanist theology, which opposes the oppression of all people. She is committed to "the survival of an entire people—male and female, rich and poor, gay, lesbian, and straight, physically and/or mentally challenged, and of every race and ethnicity. . . . I believe that no one can be free until all are free."[4]

Even as she embraced Catholicism and began intensive studies in theology, Hayes struggled with prejudice and sexism herself. She encountered "professors who could not and would not accept the validity of my vocation and did not want me, or were uncomfortable with me, in their classes."[5]

One incident stands out. She had to take a course on the sacrament of Reconciliation. Her classmates were seminarians who were learning the nuts and bolts of hearing confessions, something Hayes would never have to do. The priest who taught the course questioned why Hayes was enrolled in it. He even went to the dean of theology to complain. But the course was required for all students in her theology program, so he had to accept her.

In the class's confessional role-play, the professor "was always the confessee. He was always a woman. And it was always, as far as I can remember, a sexual issue," Hayes says. "And the woman always was at fault." The penitent would confess to prostitution or to refusing to have sex with her husband because she already had eight children. Worse, he'd identify each of them as either "this slut" or "this tramp" or "this bimbo."

Hayes told him that she found his language and his attitude "disgusting" and threatened to go to the dean if he didn't clean up his act. He did clean up his language but not the misogyny. And some of her fellow students displayed their own resentment. They were upset because they'd been looking forward to the "terribly raunchy, misogynistic" jokes the professor was known for. He didn't tell them in her presence.

"I spent the whole class basically angry," she says, not only because of his overt sexism but also because he ignored her and denied her any participation in the class. "He was such a sort of hateful person. Not what you would imagine a priest to be."

It was another education about her new faith. "I was learning that Catholics—priests, seminarians, and religious—I had experiences with sisters as well—are human and just as sinful and finite as anyone else, that you can't put them on a pedestal."

The church is bigger than the people who are its ministers, she adds. It is an imperfect institution. "Your faith has to be bigger than this institutional structure. . . . It has to go beyond to the Spirit, to the being of God, and that's what sustained me."

Growing up with three sisters in Buffalo, New York, Hayes always was pegged the "different" one. As a teen, when her sisters were listening to rock and roll and rhythm and blues, she often would be listening to classical music. She liked their music but loved classical music just as much, if not more.

Her mother taught her to read when she was three, and she "devoured" books. She loved languages, particularly French. Her sister Cindy was two years ahead of her in school, and Hayes would read all her textbooks. She even liked reading chemistry books. She was a tomboy, fearless and athletic, befriending the boys in the neighborhood. But in other settings she was "very introverted," she says. "I was terrified of public speaking." Even standing up in church to recite a Bible verse "would tie me in knots."

All her life, she's marched to her own drummer. "I lived in my head and in books, and God was there with me. When things would be particularly rough for whatever reason, I knew I could go to God and talk about what was bothering me and He would listen."

One of the things that bothered her was her father. One summer evening, ten-year-old Hayes lay awake and miserable in her bedroom. She could hear her parents. Her mother was crying. When her father drank, he would get angry and abusive, and her mother would bear the brunt. Hayes, a sensitive, bright and religious child, found herself making a solemn vow to God that night. "I promised God that if He would let me take care of her and my sisters, I would never marry. I would belong to Him for the rest of my life."

Her father, she is quick to say, was a good man. As she got older and learned about alcoholism, and the pressures on African American men, she realized that her father's problems grew worse after they bought a home in what was then a leafy Buffalo neighborhood close to a park. The "pressures of paying the mortgage" dogged him. "It was a Jekyll and Hyde thing," she says. "When he was drinking, you just stayed out of his way."

But Hayes did not find her God at the African Methodist Episcopal Zion church her family attended every Sunday. When she was sixteen, she told her parents that she wasn't going to go to church with them anymore. "I thought I could do better things on a Sunday, like read a book."

"With the wisdom of a teenager," she says, she looked around at the congregation and found hypocrisy. Within the confines of Saint Luke's, her family church, everyone would be devout. But as soon as they left the building, they would gossip about each other.

Her father did not take Hayes's declaration well. But her mother, she says, "understood me." Her mother told her father, "Di hasn't said she doesn't believe in God. She hasn't said she's leaving God. She simply says she doesn't want to go to Saint Luke's. I think we should give her the chance to find out where she wants to go."

Hayes found God in nature. She loved all outdoor sports—hiking, skiing, kayaking, canoeing, and mountain climbing. She was at peace with her nonaffiliation. "I felt revived every time I went out into the woods," she says. "I talked daily literally with God."

If God was close to Hayes, that didn't mean He spared her. To reach her ultimate destination, she faced many obstacles as a black woman from a family of limited means with aspirations far beyond those of most black women of the sixties and seventies.

She'd been an excellent student throughout elementary and high school and earned a full scholarship to attend the University of Rochester, about eighty miles from her home in Buffalo. But on the first day of class, she discovered that her public high school had not prepared her for her major in organic chemistry. She was far behind the other students. For the first time in her academic life she got poor grades, which drove her to tears.

She also had expected that the university would be racially diverse. But her freshman class included only four black students—two girls and two boys. "That was traumatic," she says. "We all assumed they did that so that we'd date each other," she says. "We hated each other on sight."

Before she went off to school, her mother persuaded her to get a permanent to straighten her hair. The day she dove into the university's chlorinated pool for her required swimming class, most of her processed hair fell out. "Shortly after that, I went to afro," she says with a laugh.

There also were financial problems, exacerbated by the fact that Hayes was the first in her family to attend college. In addition to her full-tuition scholarship, Hayes earned a New York State Regents scholarship, which was supposed to cover all her other expenses. But her father, trying to impress the authorities, had inflated his income, making her ineligible for the financial aid that she was entitled to.

Her poor grades led her to transfer to the University at Buffalo in her sophomore year. But deprived of Regents aid, she had to earn her tuition. Her first year at UB, she worked full time at the Millard Fillmore Hospital night nursery, where her mother worked, and went to school during the day. It took her three years to get her Regents money.

In 1968 she met New York Senator Robert Kennedy, who was running for president. Inspired, she worked as a campaign volunteer, "knocking on doors and handing out leaflets," shocking her family, who had never expected their "shy introvert" to do this. An uncle influential in Democratic politics had lined up a job for her working for Kennedy in Washington.

The day she arrived in the nation's capital was the day Kennedy was assassinated. She ended up working for the US Postal Service that summer. But Kennedy's life made an impact. As she began her senior year, she changed her major from foreign languages to prelaw and political science. School officials told her she would need an extra year to meet the requirements, but she doubled her course load and graduated on time.

When she entered New York University School of Law, once again there was a misunderstanding about scholarship aid. Her grant covered tuition and room but not board, something she did not realize until after she arrived. NYU gave her $500 to pay for food, but "even in 1969 that didn't go very far," she says. She lived on yogurt and hot dogs. "Great for my weight," she jokes, "but you were hungry a lot."

In law school, she still hadn't found her voice. "I hated speaking in public. There were times when I wouldn't even answer to my name in class because I didn't feel like being grilled like they would grill you," she says. She believes that her teachers knew she could master the materials but would never be a trial lawyer. She liked the scholarly side of the law, doing research and writing briefs.

But her dream of working in urban and poverty law met the reality of the Nixon administration, which was shutting down Lyndon Johnson's antipoverty programs. Instead she began her legal career at the US Department of Labor in Washington.

While she was facing, and overcoming, these obstacles, she continued to commune with God on her own terms. But that relationship, which had given her much joy and sustained her, was about to change radically.

Dissatisfied with her career, Hayes had returned to Buffalo in 1975 to earn a graduate degree in environmental science, with the goal of working for the Environmental Protection Agency or the Department of the Interior.

But the historic blizzard of '77, which inundated Buffalo with below-zero temperatures, gale-force winds, and eight-foot snowdrifts, helped bring on a long and nasty bout of pneumonia.[6] Hayes was ill for "a very long time," and when she recovered she dropped her plans for another degree, and moved to Albany to first take a position with the New York State Consumer Protection Board and then later a post with the New York State Office of Children and Family Services.

1978, the "Year of the Three Popes," may have initially piqued her interest in Catholicism, she recalls. During that year, Pope Paul VI died and was succeeded by Pope John Paul I, who died thirty-three days after his election. He was succeeded by the church's first Polish pope, John Paul II.[7]

Hayes found herself drawn to him. "I liked his charisma." She admired his fluency in several languages and what appeared to be his "openness at the time. That changed," she says with a laugh.

But it wasn't just the new pope. "Something just kept saying to me, 'I want you to become a Catholic.' I remember thinking to myself, 'Why in the world would I become a Catholic? I'm not even a practicing Methodist.'"

When Hayes decided to "check out the church," she called the Albany diocese, where she was routed from department to department until she ended up with the vocations office. She explained that she didn't want to become a nun but wanted to discuss Catholicism with someone. She was advised that she needed to find a priest. Then she asked, "Okay, where do I find one?"[8]

Fortunately, her search ended with Rev. Nellis Tremblay, pastor at Saint Patrick's Church. Tremblay was active in Albany's civil-rights community. He was more than a "liberal" Catholic, she says. "He was a radical."

The same year she was considering Catholicism, she had applied for a position in the US Foreign Service. She was accepted, scheduled to begin her orientation in January 1980. Once again, her plans were disrupted by illness. Her knees and legs became more and more painful. She was forced to use crutches as the doctors tried to discover the cause. She postponed her Foreign Service orientation. She found herself unable to walk, unable to even stand up, having to take sick leave from her Albany job.

The one thing she could do was continue to meet with Tremblay. The fact that her disease came on as she was preparing for conversion was troubling, she wrote. She had become "a pain-filled grieving, angry woman, bed-ridden and questioning both her own sanity and that of God." Why should she become a Catholic, she asked herself, when she couldn't even kneel in church, making her even more conspicuous in an almost exclusively white parish?[9]

But Tremblay saw God's hand in her pain. Later he told her, "God has to knock you down to make you listen because you're always running away," she laughs. "To a certain extent, I think that's true. When I was asked to become a Catholic, I didn't say immediately, 'Sure, no problem.' I fought hard."

The doctors ultimately diagnosed her with chondromalacia, a degenerative disease that "simply means that the cartilage in your knees has disintegrated. Your knees become like a mortar and pestle, and it's excruciatingly painful." The illness likely was caused by the damage her knees had suffered a few years earlier during a long hike in Vermont. Hayes had been injured in a landslide. "The doctors feel that was what came back to haunt me."

She did convert to Catholicism in December 1979. "God grabbed me up and threw me into the Catholic Church, to my shock and occasional horror," she says drily.

At the same time that illness was sidetracking her career plans, Tremblay was praying that Hayes would become not only a Catholic but also a Catholic theologian. "I kept talking about coincidences, and Father Tremblay kept talking about God acting in my life."

The time was right. There was a period, post–Vatican II, when there was "a window . . . of opportunity that opened," Hayes recalls. "The church was in a spirit of renewal and the acceptance of things new; even the conservative bishops were open to change."

"God knew not to ask me into this church prior to Vatican II," Hayes wrote. "I wouldn't have been able to participate in a church where women, especially women of color, were relegated to menial, domestic, or restricted religious roles."[10]

But if Hayes thought that becoming a Catholic would be enough to satisfy God, she was wrong. Still battered by pain, and unable to work, she'd spend her mornings in prayer and meditation, engaged in a do-it-yourself religious retreat. Each afternoon, she would take a break and read a mystery novel.

As she was reading her novel, she found a discordant and alarming message. She read a sentence that made no sense: "You will go to Catholic University and study theology."

Hayes looked again, and the sentence was still there. "I called Father Tremblay and told him he'd better come get me and take me to the state hospital because I was becoming crazy." She explained to him what had happened, and he asked her to pick up the book one more time. The mysterious sentence had disappeared. Father Tremblay advised her that the sentence had not been in the book, but in her own heart.

She didn't even know what or where Catholic University was, or what it meant to study theology. But Tremblay answered some of those initial questions and put her in touch with Sister Primrose, a woman religious who was a Catholic University of America alumna. Going back to school was "the last thing I wanted to do," she says.

Hayes's letter to Sister Primrose led one of Tremblay's seminary classmates, a CUA former acting president, to contact her. "You know, I don't go small," she jokes, "I start at the top." When he asked her what she wanted to do, she remembers "all of a sudden, this peace came over me." She told him, "I want to be a theologian." He was welcoming and encouraging. The next spring, still on crutches, she visited the campus in Washington, DC.

CUA officials were equally receptive. She took two philosophy courses that summer and passed the Latin test. "The next thing I knew I had been accepted in the pontifical doctorate program, the first lay-woman and the first African American ever to be accepted at Catholic University in that program." The course of study took seven years, which she thought was a good thing. "I had been a Catholic for just six months, and I needed something that would give me the most background into the Catholic Church that I could get," she says.

Her family didn't understand why she had converted to Catholicism. Indeed, her younger sister told her, "You've finally become white!"[11] And they had trouble with the career switch. "You know my poor father was so proud of his daughter the lawyer." He told her, "I know what I'm talking about when I tell people you're an attorney. What's a theologian?"

Hayes told him, "To be honest, I don't know. But I'm sure I'll figure it out along the way." Hayes still wanted to be true to the compact she had made with God twenty-two years earlier, when she'd promised to remain celibate if He would let her take care of her mother and her sisters. Even though her three sisters were married, "I was always there to help them as best I could."

But resuming school for seven years meant "being poor." She let her loved ones know that she "would not be able to help them financially as I'd been doing literally all my life" but that she would always do what she could in times of crisis. It was difficult for her to tell them and difficult for them to accept. But they did, she says.

Becoming a Catholic-convert theology student offered many surprises, pleasant and unpleasant. Hayes had been told that she had entered the program too late to apply for a scholarship, so she planned to take courses part time. She could not afford full-time tuition.

She was asked if she wanted to be a graduate assistant. If she took the job, which gave her free tuition, she'd be doing research for one of the professors. She quickly agreed to that.

Still hobbling on her crutches, she went to the library, and discovered that her disability meant she would not have to roam the stacks to get the materials she needed but that a student would help her. Later she learned that an anonymous donor had funded that assistantship. After that first year Hayes received scholarships to continue her studies until she completed her degree.

Hayes only gradually came to realize how exceptional this opportunity was. Post–Vatican II some progress had been made. "Women were no longer required to sit in the hallway to listen to lectures," she wrote in 2002.[12] But she found it "shocking" that she was among so few women.

Hayes had entered the church and theology studies assuming that the church was essentially all white. "That was a big problem," she says, because she couldn't understand "why in the world" she felt a calling to a white church. When she was in Washington, she met black Catholics for the first time and attended Saint Augustine Church, considered "the mother church" of black Catholicism in Washington, experiencing their "fantastic gospel choir and wonderful integrated community." As she progressed in her studies, she met black priests and religious, and she discovered black theologians.

She recalls a course taught by the late Carl Peter, her mentor and then-dean of CUA's School of Theology and Religious Studies. Peter was discussing the notion of "subversive memory," a memory that "turns all reality upside down." The memory of Christ's life, death, and Resurrection "basically doesn't make any sense," Hayes recalls the lesson. "Why would God allow himself to be crucified? Hung on a tree, lynched?"

When Hayes asked Peter for a modern-day example of a subversive memory, Peter responded, "Martin Luther King Jr." At the time, Hayes explains, there was a push to commemorate the birthday of the slain civil-rights leader with a federal holiday. The King holiday, Peter told his students, "would be a subversive memory," challenging the notion of an all-perfect United States and reminding people "how sinful we were in terms of slavery."

It was the first time Hayes had heard a black person mentioned in any of her classes. When she approached Peter after class, he told her about black liberation theologian James Cone. "I went out and got all his books," she says. "I was just literally blown away."

Cone described the Crucifixion of Jesus as a "lynching," tying the black experience of oppression to Christ's experience of oppression and his struggle and victory against it. "I knew from then on what I was going to be—a black liberation theologian; and then further down the road, as womanist theology emerged," she realized that she was a womanist theologian, someone who believes that faith should be inclusive, respectful of diversity, and opposed to oppression based on race, gender, sexual orientation, or class.

The fact that her theology program did not cover the black Catholic experience that fully did not surprise her. Students in US schools did not learn about the role of blacks in American history until the civil-rights movement, she says. And at that time, very few African American Catholics were studying or teaching theology. What "saved my sanity," she says, was the fact that she could take some courses outside campus.

She met black Protestant theologians at Howard University, one of the premier black colleges in the country.

Of course, she notes, the Howard theologians could discuss the history of the black church but not the history of the black Catholic Church. Hayes found that she had to do her own research, along with a few of her black Catholic contemporaries, to bring to light the history of black Catholics in the United States. Ultimately she would discover that the roots of black Catholicism were deep and went back to Africa. When she studied theology, she says, she studied history, archeology, anthropology, and evolution so she could put black Catholicism in the "context of the world in which it emerged."

There was another person in her life who also saved her sanity during these challenging years of study. When she was still living in Albany, awaiting her entry into Catholic University, Hayes had visited a Catholic bookstore where she ran into Bishop Howard Hubbard, then the youngest bishop in the United States and head of the Albany diocese.

Hayes walked up to Hubbard and told him she'd just been accepted into CUA to study theology. He was pretty floored, she says. It was rare for a woman, particularly a black woman, to earn a graduate degree in theology.

But he also was intrigued. He gave her his card, asking her to call him so they could meet at his office. She called soon after. His secretary brushed her off, telling her the bishop didn't make appointments during Holy Week, the seven-day period before Easter. But Hubbard did return her call, that day. "We met on Holy Thursday and just hit it off," she says.

She told him the story of her conversion and her call to study theology. But they also discussed music and books, and he asked her to send him her contact information when she arrived at university. He promised to look her up when he attended the yearly meeting of US Catholic bishops in Washington, DC.

Hayes thought he was just being polite. But he wasn't. For the next five years, the bishop would call, and they would meet for lunch or dinner. He'd help her financially with her books and extras. "He just really kept me sane." She would often wonder what she was doing, studying Catholic theology, and he would calm her down and "talk me out of my panic."

When she was between semesters, he even arranged for her to have housing in Albany at the Sisters of Saint Joseph Cathedral Convent. She also grew to know Albany seminarians and would attend their annual banquet. She became known as the "closet Albany seminarian."

Hubbard was also instrumental in helping Hayes broaden and deepen her theological studies. By then she had been studying five years at CUA, supported by a series of scholarships. Her chondromalacia had been in remission for a few years. Her plan was to continue at CUA until she earned her doctorate. Hubbard suggested she complete her degree somewhere else.

He told her, "I have to be honest: You're a woman and you're black. It's going to be very difficult for you coming out with your doctoral degree. A lot of people aren't going to want to accept it or to acknowledge it. You have to have the best grounding that you can as a Catholic theologian."

He initially suggested Rome, but by then Pope John Paul II was "starting to push back on things," she says, requiring seminarians to wear priestly garb. She had been used to studying with seminarians who wore jeans. The thought of being the only woman in a room full of priests in collars did not appeal to her.

Hubbard then asked her to consider Catholic University of Louvain in Belgium. She recalled how much she'd liked Belgium when she visited in 1984. She remembered that Leuven (Dutch for Louvain) was "a beautiful medieval village" with a racially diverse population. She began the application process only to learn that she would need to either put all her money in a Belgian bank, which wasn't possible for her, or have someone take financial responsibility for her. Members of religious orders had their superiors, and priests had their bishops take on that obligation, but she was a layperson.

Once again Hubbard was willing to help. He agreed to sign the papers that made him financially responsible for her. It amounted to "letting the world know that I was his seminarian, for all intents and purposes," she says.

Hayes still was not quite sure what she'd do after receiving her degree. Teaching seemed the most likely option, even though "that was the last thing I had ever wanted" to do, she says. But at this point in her studies, and in her deepening faith, she'd decided to let Providence take over. In the black community, she says, it's called "letting go and letting God."

There was a lot of letting go when she was in Belgium. For her last two years at CUA, she had been able to walk without crutches or a brace. But now pain again stalked her, this time from rheumatoid arthritis, exacerbated by the cold Northern European climate. "That was a devastating blow," and one she contends with to this day. She tussled with God. "Come on. I've done everything you want, and then you're going to do this to me? What the heck is going on?" But Hayes says that she always felt that "God talks to me through my illnesses."

Her "many years of struggle and pain . . . have forged me in the fiery furnace of God's love," Hayes wrote. Experience of that pain helped her "feel the struggles of others. . . . I know what it is like . . . to be discriminated against because of my poverty, my race, my gender, and my disabilities." She believes that her mission is to serve those, who, "unlike myself," have not found their voice and do not yet realize that "as children of a loving God, they are sent, not to suffer, but to live a life free from oppression."[13]

Despite the pain, she views her years in Belgium as "some of the best years I've ever had in my life." Even with the help of scholarships, paying for her education had always been a struggle. But at Louvain, she says, the tuition costs were much lower and the scholarship help went much farther. "I didn't have to work and finally had the freedom to read and write and think, participate in classes the way I'd always thought college should be."

And she persevered, writing her doctoral thesis on the prospects for an American liberation theology that would be based on the perspective of the developing world rather than the developed world. When she started looking for jobs in the fall of 1987, she struck pay dirt. She landed five job interviews. Georgetown University in particular was eager to hire her. When she hesitated, they upped their offer. In light of her law degree, they decided to add $5,000 to the salary they had initially discussed.

Hayes had trepidations about teaching. "I was an anomaly for my students when I walked into that first class," she says. All freshmen were required to take the course, The Problem of God. When she walked to the front of the classroom, her students, all white, gasped.

"They were in total shock," she says. She turned to them and said, "Yes, I'm your professor. Good morning."

In that moment, Hayes became a teacher and found that her aversion to public speaking was gone; she could hold the classroom. That didn't mean that Hayes did not meet challenges from people on campus who thought she must be a janitor or a secretary, not dreaming she was an academic. Her credentials would be scrutinized.

"Especially priests—white priests, sadly—would come up to me and say, 'I understand you teach theology.'" When she would affirm that, they would always want to know where she had received her degree. Many priests would assume she was a Protestant theologian who'd studied at Howard. They would be stunned when she told them she'd studied at Louvain. "I would watch as the blood drained from their faces," she says with a laugh, "because Louvain was and is considered one of the best Catholic universities in the world."

Hayes became a pioneer at Georgetown, her writing and research expanding what was known about black Catholics in the United States. "So much of my work has been in recovering, exploring, and finding the voices of black Catholics," she says. Her research often answers her own questions. She was curious about black Catholics and slavery. And she discovered that one of the first slave revolts—the Stono Rebellion in South Carolina—was led by black Catholics. "We just didn't sit around happy that we were Catholic and accept slavery." She says that "few scholars, except Father Cyprian Davis, had explored that history before."

Hayes is more apt to use humor and quick wit to make her points than to wage frontal assaults on the flaws she finds in the church. She remembers being asked to address a conference of Catholic women in Johannesburg. She was asked to talk on the theme "Women's Rights Are Human Rights" but specifically asked not to speak "from a feminist perspective."

She thought "that was a lot of gall on their part," telling her how to address the topic. But then she brightened. She said to herself, "No problem. I'm not a feminist. I'm a womanist." And that was how she prepared her speech. The bishop attending, she says, did not realize how "much more dangerous the womanist movement is than the feminist movement."

Hayes was being true to herself. Feminism, she believes, is not expansive enough to include the experience of African American women. It's not that black women don't experience sexism; they do. Rather, prejudice is often combined with discrimination on the basis of race and class. "It's a multiplicative impact . . . race times class times gender." And initially, she says, the feminist movement was both secular and "anti-men." Black women, she says, "can't afford" that, because "we have to stay together as a community—black women, black men, black children all supporting each other."

In contrast, womanism started in the theological realm and then moved into the "secular world," she says. Hayes says that womanist theology is a critique of both the feminist movement and the black-theology movement. Black theologians, she says, tended to focus solely on the experience of black men. "Black women began critiquing that," and affirming that their experience counted too. Womanist theology, she adds, calls attention to the ways that the institutional church has not lived up to its principles. Womanism "challenges everything that the church supposedly is about," she says. "We say we're for justice, we say we're for equality, we say we affirm the roles of women, and yet everything we do denies that."

When she taught womanist theology, Hayes says she would lay a foundation by explaining that the Bible has been interpreted through a "Euro-American white male perspective." People of color and women now are reading Scripture "from their own context."

Hayes has interpreted the Old Testament story of Hagar from that new perspective. Hagar appears in the story of Abraham, the patriarch who became the father of the Jewish people. Abraham's wife, Sarah, was unable to conceive a child. She asked Abraham to sleep with her Egyptian slave, Hagar, and to conceive a child with her. Hagar became merely an instrument for the couple, a way to ensure they'd have an heir. When Hagar became pregnant, Sarah began to abuse her, and she ran away. An angel spoke to Hagar and asked her to return, prophesying that her son, Ishmael, would be a leader. So Hagar returned.[14]

But after Sarah, through divine intervention, bore a child in her old age, she was dismayed when she saw her son Isaac playing with his half brother. Sarah demanded that Abraham force Hagar and Ishmael to leave the household and cut Ishmael off from any inheritance.

Abraham reluctantly did so, and Hagar and her son fled into the desert, with only the bread and water Abraham had given them. When the bread and water ran out, Hagar wept, believing her son would die. But an angel spoke to Hagar, assuring her that Ishmael would not perish and would found a great nation. When Hagar opened her eyes, she saw a well. She was able to save herself and her son.[15]

Hayes has written that black women are the daughters of the Old Testament's Hagar, "the rejected and cast-out slave, mother of Ishmael, concubine of Abraham, and threat to Sarah, his barren wife."[16] They are victims of both sexism and racism, often oppressed not only by men but also by white women. Sarah did not understand that she was as much a victim of a patriarchal society as Hagar, Hayes wrote. Instead, the only way she could feel she had any power was to dominate the only person who had less power than she had—her slave. But like Hagar, the deep spirituality of black women has helped them overcome oppression and pass on hope, and a spirit of creativity, to the next generation. Their faith has saved them from despair and loss.

Hayes also looked at Mary in a new light, "not as this docile, submissive young woman, but a woman who questioned the archangel Gabriel." Mary "demanded explanations," Hayes says. She wanted to know how this miraculous birth was going to happen. For many women, her insights were "very refreshing. Men are less likely to be open to it; but, again, many of them do eventually," she says.

But not always. Hayes recalls a talk she gave at a religious-education conference in Los Angeles. She discussed the history of black Catholics in the church and their role as a "subversive memory" reminding the institution of the way it had failed them. As she finished her presentation, a priest challenged her. Slavery, he said, "brought blacks to this country" and thus exposed them to Christianity and a better life. So slavery, he contended, "was beneficial in some ways."

The crowd reacted with a stunned silence for a few moments, she recalls. Then a few people rose to challenge him, and "the whole place sort of erupted." After things calmed down, she told him, "Seeing as how Christianity started in the Middle East and Africa . . . it was already on their continent before it even reached Europe. . . . Many were already Christians."

"Of course he had nothing to say to that," she says.

Hayes now is retired, but she continues to write books and give lectures. She has never regretted her vow of celibacy. "It fit me," she says. Without a spouse or children to consider, she was able to take a career path that demanded years of study both in the United States and abroad. She came to realize, she says, that she could love someone without needing a sexual connection. She's fallen in love with two men in her life, she says, and each time she found that the love she experienced did not require sexual fulfillment to be real and meaningful.

Hayes knows that her church continues to be racist and sexist. She has been dismayed that Catholic parishes are not welcoming enough to black Catholics in their midst, something she's experienced firsthand. When she's been asked to speak at a white parish, she's gone in and sat in a pew and had no one sit near her. She has felt what she calls "the limp-fish handshake" from white parishioners whom she's met. She's grown impatient with white Catholics striving for diversity who think reaching out to black Catholics means establishing ties with poor black parishes in the inner city, unable to "conceive" of a black parish whose members would have the same economic and educational status as they had.

Nevertheless, she remains optimistic. "I am actually very hopeful about Pope Francis," she says, although she concedes she'd like him to talk more about "the issues surrounding women." But Francis is "willing to listen to people instead of just giving ultimatums, like [Pope] Benedict."

But that doesn't mean she doesn't yearn for larger reforms that go way beyond one pope. If she could change the church, she says, "it wouldn't be a hierarchy," with all the power in the hands of celibate men. Laity would have a much stronger role in the governance of the institution. "Women would be involved at every stage; women would be ordained. . . . We certainly would be working much harder to eliminate racism, sexism, and homophobia and heterosexism in the church."

8

TERESA DELGADO

Trauma and Faith

When she was in her teens, Teresa Delgado discovered that the Italian and Irish boys she knew weren't that attracted to her. Instead, her dark Latin looks and figure drew the attentions of older men. When she was seventeen, one of those older men raped her. It was a setup. She'd been invited to what she thought was a party and found that she and her date were alone. There was no party. She didn't call it *rape* at the time. After all, this was someone she knew and previously had consensual sex with. She called it a punishment from God. Only much, much later would she call it rape. And only much later would she understand that, while it was an experience she would never wish on anyone, including herself, it helped shape the person she became.

Delgado is director of the Peace and Justice Studies Program and associate professor of religious studies at Iona College in New Rochelle, New York, a private Catholic institution run by the Christian Brothers. Petite, slim, and attractive, she lacks the laugh lines you'd expect of a woman in her late forties, married for more than twenty-five years and the mother of four children. Her voice is strong and authoritative. It has the cadence of a seasoned teacher, but one whose lectures are popular. It is dramatic, falling and rising as she tells a story or states an opinion. Within the space of a long interview, she is often moved to laughter, and once to tears.

It was her sexual assault, she says, that "helped fuel my passion for healing this bifurcated sense of self between sex and faith" that dogs so many Catholics. That purpose infuses her teaching at Iona. "I think my journey to seminary, my journey to God, is, in some sense, a journey that was initiated by that trauma." The experience, and the insight it gave her, she says, "has allowed me to speak in a way that is authoritative around issues of sexuality and faith."

Delgado has remained a Catholic, despite her deep reservations about the church's approach to sexual issues, and its misogyny. She regrets that an institution that developed a nuanced ethical position on the concept of a "just war" has failed to explore the nuances of sexual ethics. Within her classroom, where she teaches Christian sexual ethics, she faces students deeply confused about how to apply Catholic principles to their sex lives. Her goal, she says, is to offer them a safe place to discuss their feelings, and to share her own insights about navigating these moral dilemmas. Her Catholic students, she says, aren't "even comfortable writing about God and sex in the same paper."

But many other experiences inform her voice. Every aspect of Delgado's life and background seems to have shaped her deeply personal critique of Catholicism and the institutional church. Delgado is one among a new wave of Latina theologians probing the impact of Catholic culture and the culture of "machismo" on Latin American women and Latinas. Her Puerto Rican heritage informed her doctoral dissertation, which proposed a framework for a distinctly Puerto Rican theology embracing Puerto Ricans' unique status as US citizens, living on the mainland and the island, still dogged by prejudice and suffering the injustices of colonization.

Her theological views have been influenced by both liberation and womanist theologies. Liberation theology is based on the belief that Christians must actively work to eliminate the structures of oppression that contribute to poverty and powerlessness. Preaching to the dispossessed and marginalized that their hope lies in heaven is not enough. Christians must do all they can to build a more just society.

Delgado describes womanism as "a discourse and an ethic of living that lifts up the entire community" and perceives one's value in relation to others in community. "I am because we are." But she also emphasizes its particular importance to women of color. Womanism cherishes "that which has been so despised in our world—namely, blackness," loving and affirming it "for its beauty and its fruitfulness." Her role as a womanist theologian, she adds, in no way rejects her Puerto Rican roots. "I don't see blackness as separate from Puerto Ricanness, because blackness is part of Puerto Ricanness, historically, culturally, spiritually."

Delgado knows what it's like to be a teenager without the tools to resolve the opposing "gravitational pulls" of wanting to be a good Catholic and yet wanting to "push boundaries" and explore one's sexuality. In 1976, when Delgado was ten years old, her parents moved the family from a diverse neighborhood in the Bronx to the far less diverse and more upscale New York suburb of Pelham, in Westchester County. She became a teen in the 1980s, a time when disco was still popular and sexual freedom was taken for granted. Popular culture celebrated comedies like *Risky Business*, whose hero, teen Tom Cruise, runs a brothel out of his parents' suburban home.

She attended the Academy of the Resurrection, an all-girls Catholic high school in Rye, New York. She excelled academically, performed in all the school plays, ran track, was vice president of the student council, and was, from all outward appearances, a happy, well-adjusted high achiever. At the same time, she had a teenage social life that her parents did not know about.

She thinks that many other girls in her school did the same, compartmentalizing what they did at home and at school and their separate existence as teenagers. They felt that they could make that work as long as each aspect of their lives did not intrude on the other and the attempt to push the boundaries "didn't get out of hand."

For a couple of years, Delgado had an Irish boyfriend. "He broke up with me to date, I guess, a white girl from Pelham Manor. I was devastated," she says." The breakup sent her the message that "I'm too ethnic, my body's too ethnic." This was the era when top models tended to be white and willowy. Tall, blonde, lithe Christie Brinkley graced magazine covers of the day. "I was so self-conscious about my rear end," she says. Now, she laughs, "they've got songs about big asses." She became "very obsessed with food and running and exercise." She'd restrict her daily food intake to an apple and a salad and would run five miles. Five feet, three inches tall, she was down to one hundred pounds. "I was definitely anorexic."

Her rape left her with a sense of shame. She thought it was "a punishment" from God "for all the things that I had done." She didn't tell anyone about what had happened to her. She did not process the event as an assault because she had previously slept with her attacker, someone she'd worked with. But her body told her something else. Her response, she says, was "very, very different" from the way she had felt when the sex had been consensual.

Indeed, right after the assault, Delgado's first concern was secrecy. She insisted on taking a shower and drying her hair before going home. When she returned, her parents were still up. She worried, "Are they going to notice my hair is a little wet? . . . I can't let my parents see that something is wrong." Reflecting on her behavior, she says, "How messed up is that?"

Delgado kept her secret, throwing herself even "more intensely" into her academic and extracurricular activities. But the guilt didn't go away. She remembers attending Mass with her family and being bothered by an odd purple light glowing from one side of the crucifix in a niche behind the altar. The purple light likely was the result of a renovation that partially blocked a stained-glass window. Growing up, she and her friends had often wondered where the light was coming from. But now, she says, the light seemed like an "eye" watching her. It felt "ominous."

Emotionally, she says, "I shut down." She remembers her senior year, following the rape the summer before. But she can't recall the details of events or how she felt about them. Her senior prom and her boyfriend the last year of high school are memories, but they are not vivid. "I've blocked it out."

Nevertheless, the accomplished, high-achieving young woman moved forward with her plans for college. She wanted to study away from home, and her parents wanted her to go to a school within New York State to benefit from the state's Tuition Assistance Program. She settled on Colgate University in Hamilton, a small private liberal arts college in Upstate New York, known for its quaint village, founded in 1795, and lots of snow. Colgate offered her an "excellent financial-aid package," she says.

She majored in religion and women's studies. Colgate turned out to have a long-lasting impact on her life. She met her husband there.

Pascal Kabemba was a senior, born and raised in the Congo. They met when she was a freshman. Her first impression was not positive.

"He was very arrogant in my view," she says. He used to try to provoke her in the school cafeteria, where she worked, checking meal cards. The school didn't permit students to take food out of the dining hall, but Kabemba would do so routinely and would ignore her commands that he stop. At one point, she got so angry, she threw a fork at him. It was only when she learned that he was trying to deliberately provoke her ire that she realized that he was interested in her. "He thought it was kind of cute," she says with a smile.

The relationship began when they found themselves on an empty campus in January. Delgado had stayed to take a course and because she was applying to be a campus resident adviser. As an international student, Kabemba couldn't go home for the break. "So we spent more time together. Quality time. Really beginning to have conversations. And that's kind of how the friendship began."

That Valentine's Day, Kabemba handed her a red rose, she wrote in her alumni newsletter. "Our time together at Colgate overlapped only one year, but Colgate was the foundation upon which our love and life together were built."[1] The couple married in 1989.

Having kept her secret for so long, she tried to explain what had happened to her to Kabemba. But he didn't understand, Delgado says. His reaction now would be completely different, she adds. "But at the time, given his own experience as an African man, and as a man, to him someone who is sexually assaulted comes out looking bloodied," and the perpetrator can't be someone the victim knows or had sex with. "I didn't have the language or the wisdom at the time to reject that interpretation or to communicate it differently. To shift it." It reinforced her sense that this was something she shouldn't share with anybody.

Delgado really wasn't able to process what happened to her until her junior year, when she took a women's studies class with noted Catholic theologian and feminist Mary Hunt. It was in that class, she says, "that I had the profound revelation that this was, in fact, rape." That knowledge, she says, "opened up a whole other path for me that was both heartbreaking and freeing at the same time."

As she was still trying to recover from her own rape experience, Delgado was hearing from other Colgate coeds, complaining about being "groped" and "harassed" by the same boys she'd see at Sunday Mass on campus. When she was a resident adviser, one of the students told her that she'd been raped by two boys, Delgado recalls. Those two young men also were Catholic. "Why isn't our Catholic chaplain challenging our students to think about their faith beyond Catholic Mass" and linking the faith to "how they live day-to-day?" she asked herself. "So I was very self-righteous and holier than thou," she says. "If this priest can't address some of these concerns, this Mass is not worth my going to."

She switched to the Protestant service. "That proved to be a tremendous blessing," she says, because she met university chaplain and religion professor, the late Coleman Brown. She called his sermons both "humble" and "incisive. He spoke right to the core. And he challenged us. Every single Sunday. And made us think about what our faith meant. What it means, what it can mean. How it can inform our lives and inspire us to be our best selves."

When she was a child, Catholicism had given her serenity. She remembers her Catholic kindergarten and the "beautiful" statue of the Blessed Virgin in the foyer of her school. "The kindergarten classroom was right by the statue of Mary," she recalls. "It almost felt like she was the sentinel," keeping watch. It gave her the sense that "my schooling in a Catholic environment was always under the watchful, protective eye" of the Blessed Virgin. Delgado grew up thinking that "faith and intellect, faith and education, were not separate entities. They were one and the same."

Before she could even read, she had memorized the Mass prayers. She'd sometimes watch the Mass on TV with her grandmother, who lived with the family, her diabetes preventing her from going to church in person. Her grandmother would pray along with the priest, and so would she. Adding to the reality of the ritual was the fact that her father would bring a consecrated host from church to his mother so she could receive Holy Communion at home.

When she was six, awed by the Mass, Delgado desperately wanted to be a priest. After going to church on Sunday she would "bully" her sisters into playing Mass with her so that she could pretend to be the celebrant. The design of their parish church in the Bronx, Nativity of Our Blessed Lady, placed the altar in the middle of the structure, surrounded by the faithful. To Delgado, it looked like the priest was "enveloped in light," she says. She wanted that light, that "majestic spiritual connection" that imparted a sense of peace. She once got into trouble for trying to light all the candles in the church. "I ended up getting dragged out of the church by my ear by my father," she says.

When her father discovered that she was saying Mass in the family basement, he told her "very gently" that she couldn't be a priest when she grew up. She did not take it well. "I had a tantrum," she says, and then she took off, running away from home for a few hours. "Thankfully, we lived in a neighborhood where everybody knew each other," she recalls. "They knew I was sitting in front of the bodega down the street."

When she was older, she got into spirited discussions about women's ordination with the pastor of Saint Catharine's parish in Pelham. "We would go back and forth on this question, and I never felt his responses were satisfactory for me," she says. But, she adds, "he was very gracious, because he let me argue."

But that was one of the few high points in her experience at her Pelham parish. Her Bronx parish school conveyed no sense of the punitive, she says. But she found that at Saint Catharine's the priests and nuns were much older and seemed much more rigid. "They yelled a lot. It was more about getting in line, being in line, staying in line."

She also faced culture shock, she says. Nativity was very diverse, but Saint Catharine's had few Latino or African American students. The Italian and Irish kids would call Delgado and her sisters "spic" and "greasy." They'd joke about seeing their mother "turning tricks" on the corner. Their hostility grew because the Delgado sisters excelled at school, she says.

Their teachers did not intervene, as far as Delgado could tell. So she did, throwing blows, pulling hair. She took on one of her tormentors in a dramatic way. The "most vocal" of the bullies "said something about my mother," she recalls. "I went over to his desk. It was one of those old-fashioned desks, the chair and desk are one unit. I just picked up the desk and dumped him out of it. I got sent home for that," she says with a laugh. But the bullying stopped after she stood up for herself.

That sense of justice, of taking action when a wrong is committed, didn't leave her. After college, she joined a management-development program at Chase Manhattan Bank. She ultimately became a manager in a department launching software to streamline the way Chase handled electronic requests. She was in her early twenties, but two supervisors, both older than she, reported directly to her, and they, in turn, oversaw a department of between thirty and forty workers.

Delgado found a way to develop positive relationships, telling the supervisors that she knew she had much to learn, seeking their guidance. When the software project proved successful, Delgado was given another assignment: She was asked to fire half the workers in her department. The new technology had made them redundant.

Delgado couldn't do that. "Most of these employees were people of color. Most of them were single-income households making less than $20,000 a year. I felt that it was criminal to do anything other than trying to get them another job within the company."

But the head of her division refused. "He was interested in head-count reduction and what was going to be positive for the bottom line of our department, not shifting it from one to another. So he didn't want me to get human resources to help.

"Everything that I got from a Catholic education kicked in," she says. She paraphrases the message of Christ in the gospels: "'When I was hungry, you fed me; when I was thirsty, you gave me something to drink. You didn't abandon me.' All those messages were crystallized for me in that very moment. . . . I decided to leave."

In this moment of ethical crisis, she contacted Brown, the Colgate chaplain she revered. She told him, "I can't do this anymore. It's unjust to me. Why does there have to be a divide between my sense of what's ethical as a Christian and what happens in our financial world?" Their discussion touched on the social-gospel movement at the turn of the century and the work of Dorothy Day, the Catholic convert who founded the Catholic Worker movement to serve the poor and dispossessed. Brown told her, "I think you're having a seminary moment."

Delgado quit her job at Chase and entered Union Theological Seminary in New York City, the same seminary Brown had attended. The seminary and graduate school of theology has a distinguished past and a distinct mission. It was founded in 1836 by people of faith "deeply impressed by the claims of the world upon the church."[2] During its early history, the seminary tried to apply faith to the many problems that still dog New York City and the nation as a whole: the influx of immigrants, poverty, and racial unrest.[3]

Delgado chose Union for two reasons: she could continue to live in the New York area, and would avoid a commuter marriage, and Union included both Protestant and Catholic scholars and "celebrated diversity" in all its forms—ethnic, racial, and sexual. At Union, she says, she also received the unexpected "gift" of being able to study under groundbreaking womanist theologian Delores Williams.

Delgado began a fourteen-year course of study culminating in a doctorate in 2005. As she was pursuing seminary studies, Delgado was embarking on what she terms her "most serious and creative enterprise"—her marriage and four children, two girls and two boys.

At seminary she could have fulfilled her childhood dream. Many of her fellow women students were training to be Episcopal priests. Indeed, Delgado had been approached by her Episcopal friends to enroll in the ministry track. She remembered her "sense of a call to the priesthood," she says. This opportunity, she says, "seemed to me to be the next best thing. I mean, I would still be considered a priest—an Episcopal priest, but still a priest."

But she felt that leaving the church would make it very difficult for her to be an agent of change. In her head, she kept hearing the phrase "a negligible factor in the equation," she says. In other words, her critique "would be meaningless and have no credibility" if she stood outside the institution. While criticism from the outside can be "valuable and show solidarity," she says, there have to be people committed to change who remain in the church—people who say, "We envision a church very differently than the way that it exists now. And we want to boldly live into that vision."

Delgado's doctoral thesis details some of that vision. It reflects her growing immersion in Puerto Rican culture and traditions and its relationship to her own life and religious belief. She grew up in a home where English was spoken and not much family history was discussed.

The silence was even more pronounced because of a decades-long rift between her mother and her father's mother, who lived with the family. It was only when her mother got together with her sisters that she learned more about her roots. The sisters would play Scrabble, Delgado recalls. That was the time, she says, "when you wanted to eavesdrop." But she still thought that the stories of her mother and aunts were just that—their stories. It wasn't until she started reading Puerto Rican literature and nonfiction that she realized that her family's stories were connected to a much wider community and experience.

That revelation helped her understand her discomfort. "I felt like a fish out of water, but I didn't know I was a fish out of water." She now realized that her "sense of restlessness," of things not "feeling right," were "not because of me," she says. She was living in an "environment somewhat alien to me."

Delgado's theological approach views the Puerto Rican experience as distinct from the experience of other Latin American countries. There is more ambiguity in the Puerto Rican experience, Delgado explained in her dissertation. Puerto Ricans are a mixed-race people, so the distinctions between black and white are blurred.

Puerto Rico also has a complex relationship with the United States. Its residents are US citizens, subject to federal laws, having the right to participate in presidential primary elections, but with limited representation in Congress, and denied the right to vote in the general election for president and vice president.[4] As a colonized people, Puerto Ricans often have been oppressed, Delgado says, contending that a Puerto Rican theology has to acknowledge that ambiguity and discomfort. Christ lives with them in that ambiguity, loves them as they are, and will support them as they seek to declare themselves free and independent, whatever the political outcome may be.

More broadly, her critique also addresses the Latin culture of "submission" that the church has reinforced. She contends that Latinas have been betrayed by both their culture and a church that for so long has "devalued" women.

Church doctrine and biblical accounts long have been interpreted through the lens of patriarchy, she says. As a consequence, the church tends to extol the woman who sacrifices herself, even her identity, for the good of the family and the community. Self-giving can be a very positive thing, she says, but only when the giving of self does not harm the person's identity as a child of God.

Church teaching, she adds, often reinforces a Latin culture that extols a women's subordination to a man. The Virgin Mary, for example, is usually depicted as a model of submission and obedience to God. Women learn that "obedience to a male image is the fundamental starting point for female humanity," Delgado wrote in 2009.[5]

Also detrimental is the church's emphasis on Christ's suffering and death on the Cross as redemptive in and of itself, she says. Delgado contends that it is not Christ's suffering and death that carries redemptive power. It is the life and resistance that led to his execution that is redemptive. She makes the same point when speaking about Archbishop Oscar Romero, assassinated in 1980 in El Salvador, reportedly by a member of a right-wing death squad.[6] Romero is not Christ-like because he was shot to death, she says, but because of "the way he led his life," publicly confronting El Salvador's military leaders, defending the poor and the oppressed.

"This emphasis on submission, obedience, and dependence as the fertile ground within which God's grace is sown has violent implications for Latin American women and Latinas," she wrote.[7] When a woman believes that submission and obedience are central to her faith, she may sleep with a husband who is unfaithful and insists on unprotected sex, abetted by a church that frowns on condoms, making her vulnerable to AIDs. She may give her body to a sex trafficker to help her family financially.

Part of the problem, she says, is that the hierarchical structure of the church seeks to keep power concentrated, excluding women from the priesthood. Too often church leaders are more concerned about their power within the church than they are about the people they are meant to serve. Consider the ritual of the Mass, she says. In most churches, the altar is at the front of the church, and the priest, dressed in robes, processes down the aisle, like a king. The priest stands apart from the people.

That's what makes Romero's life so exemplary, she says. He understood that he did not "own" his power. He would tell the faithful, "What you see as my power and authority is simply your power being reflected back to you."

"Where liberation theology—and, for me, womanism—comes in so strongly as a critique is that those who are at the bottom are clamoring" to tell the institutional church that they "experience God differently," Delgado says. She insists that "those who are voiceless, those who are abused, those who are oppressed" have the clearest insight into Christ's message. Almost every parable Christ told, she says, "was a critique of those who think they know who God is, and He's suggesting, 'No, you don't have that right.' Who are we going to listen to?"

The church is able to think through serious ethical problems that affect society, she says. Citing church just-war doctrine, she notes that the church "has been very creative about finding ways to work out real ethical dilemmas like war and killing." The church recognizes "situational nuances that may allow it," she says.

But when it comes to sexual behavior or reproductive issues, the church has not shown the same creativity, whether it concerns condom use, contraception, or even abortion. "I want to at least ask the question: Are there occasions when abortion is ethical? Are there occasions when condom use is ethical? Are there occasions when multiple partners in a marriage is ethical? I want to ask those kinds of questions. Is it ethical for a spouse to have sexual relations outside of a marriage if their spouse is in a persistent vegetative state?"

But the church looks at all these hypotheticals and declares them to be wrong and sinful, she says. She contends that the reason these theological lines of inquiry have been "foreclosed" is because the questions themselves present "a threat to institutional power."

In 2005 Delgado began her teaching career at Iona College. She could have found herself teaching theology at Yale Divinity School, a position most academics would salivate over. But as she was being considered, she took herself out of the running. She wasn't thinking about her career, she says. She was making her choice based on love, assessing what would be best for her husband and four children.

"Iona was here," she says of the college based in New Rochelle, minutes away from her home. But a decision made for practical reasons also became the best institution for her for other reasons. She "would not have become as passionate about sexual ethics" if Iona had not required her to teach the subject, she says. "And in a way it led back to my own healing." It allowed her to have the "conversation" about her rape that she had avoided having with herself for years, because the incident "was too close, too raw, too painful. I was able to have it with my students."

But her initial experience at Iona was rocky. She was acutely aware of her presence as the only Latina professor on campus, and felt she had to prove herself. Her "need to assert credibility as a Puerto Rican Catholic female scholar in an environment with no other visible Latino/a presence" changed her teaching methods into something she didn't even recognize, she wrote in a letter to the editor published in 2014 in Iona's campus newspaper. The letter was based on a presentation on diversity she had given at Princeton University in 2010.

"As a Puerto Rican scholar, I wanted these students to know I wasn't a 'charity case' hired to fill a quota," she wrote. "As a woman of color," she didn't want students to relate to her as a "mother, midwife, or friend" but as a teacher worthy of as "much respect as any white male faculty member." As a feminist theologian, she wanted to prove that "men with clerical collars do not hold a monopoly on the language of moral theology."[8]

She drowned her students in too much work and too much material and an exam that was far too daunting. A few weeks into the class, she changed course. But the experience taught her the harmful impact of a lack of diversity among faculty. Since she felt her presence as a teacher of color might be the only experience her students received, she needed to "uphold something even if it went against everything I believed in as an educator."[9]

Diversity hasn't improved much at Iona over the past decade. But Delgado changed her teaching methods to be true to her own nature and to her belief in an inclusive faith. For example, in her sexual-ethics classes she strives to create a welcoming environment for students that enables them to think about sexuality in a Catholic ethical context. That isn't easy for them to do, she says. Her students, she says, are "grateful to be in a space where they can actually ask some questions and not be judged."

But they have a lot of baggage to unpack. Early on, she gives her students an "anonymous essay" assignment. They are asked to discuss a situation when either their sexuality and sexual expression "collided" with their faith, or they found a way for their faith and their sexuality to "work together." She takes great pains to ensure that she does not know the identities of the writers. What her students disclose, she says, is both "heartbreaking and familiar." Most are Catholic, and most write that they had to give up either sexual activity or their faith. Catholic students who opt for any sexual exploration, she says, lack any "resources" within their faith to guide them "through the labyrinth of sexual growth."

Their struggles, she says, reflect the continued impact of the church's "hierarchical-submission model" where Catholics are required to either obey or "live in sin." Those struggles are particularly hard on women, because women are the most affected by church teachings on abortion and contraception.

Nevertheless, she does not believe that ordaining women to the priesthood alone would greatly alter the church's unbending orthodoxy. "It really doesn't matter if women are in positions of power within the church if the structure is still the same," she says. If the structure continues to concentrate all the power at the top, with church leaders, then the model of "dominance and submission" stays in place.

Despite her critique, Delgado continues to love the church. But that love, she says, comes with some wariness and a desire to keep some distance. She calls herself an "in-and-out" Catholic. For example, she no longer goes to Confession. It's not because she thinks she's perfect, she says. "It's very difficult for me to make myself vulnerable in that space to a church that refuses to see its own sinfulness."

Not that long ago, and for a time, she stopped going to Sunday Mass, consistently and every week. She was angry with a church policy that required her children to attend Catholic Catechesis and Doctrine (CCD) classes before they could receive Holy Communion, Penance, and Confirmation. She and her husband sent their children to a Lutheran school with an excellent religious-education program, she says. The school is a "real Christian community—loving, compassionate, biblically informed in the best possible sense—and yet the Catholic Church doesn't recognize that as a valid religious education."

She resented having to bargain with her children to attend the classes, and they resented going. Her boycott of weekly Sunday Mass was her retort to the institutional church for not accepting her children's religious education, she says. "Okay, you don't want to accept that? Well, fine. I'm not going to church."

In the aftermath of the great recession of 2008, Kabemba, an investment banker, lost his job. The family worried they'd lose their house, a modest two-story home on a leafy street in Mount Vernon, very close to Iona College. Pictures of Delgado's four children are on the mantle, and African art and statuary dominate the living and dining rooms. They call it the "love shack," Delgado jokes. They moved in when she was expecting their second child.

Delgado wrote about the impact of unemployment on her family in the context of black history that always has made it more difficult for people of color to survive economically. She mourned this "new slavery of unemployment, underemployment, and financial ruin" and worried how it would affect her children and the larger community.[10] "Christian theologians have a responsibility to lift up the voices of those who hunger and thirst for justice in these devastating economic times," she wrote.[11]

She rewrote the Beatitudes to address these concerns. Among the blessed, she included both the unemployed "for they shall know their lives are precious," and "those who fight to keep a roof over a family, who work against foreclosure and homelessness, for they shall give the children new life."[12]

One of Delgado's immediate concerns was her son's education. She had planned to send him to Iona Preparatory School, a Christian Brothers boys' school affiliated with Iona College. "We knew that that was the best school for him." But in 2012 money was tight, and she didn't know how she could cover his tuition. "I just prayed about it, essentially saying, 'God, show me the way, because I have no idea how this is going to happen.'"

Delgado thought she might be able to find work at Iona Prep to offset the tuition bill. As it turned out, the school's director of campus ministries was overwhelmed. When she met him and offered her services, he said her coming was a "godsend. I need someone so badly. There's so much that I'm expected to do, and I'm one person."

For the next two years, she was a jack-of-all-trades. She arranged for community-service opportunities for the boys and drove the school's minibus to get them there. She used her academic contacts to bring in outside speakers. She planned the school's retreats. She met the couple who helped direct the school's music ministry, and they became friends, she says. "They are 'Protestant Catholics' like I am," she says, critical of the institution but with a strong commitment to the church's "social-justice tradition."

Delgado was invited to sing at the liturgy, along with the boys' choir. She called the invitation a "wonderful opportunity to go to Mass, to be nurtured by it, to do what I love to do, which is sing—to be part of that wider community but also that smaller community of music ministry. It was such a blessing."

Delgado says this type of "self-giving" is totally different from Latinas forgoing their identity and risking their safety in a self-sacrifice that is not life-affirming. She chose to do this, and while she lost some sleep, her work enriched her life. Likewise, as a womanist she had no qualms about doing all she could to keep up her spouse's spirits for the four years he was jobless. She was willing to have a "meal ready for him when he's home and do all those things that would be considered a traditional woman's role" as a way to "affirm his personhood" when "society is breaking him down."

Delgado was prepared to work part time at Iona Prep for eight years, covering the tuition for both her sons. But in 2014 Iona College and Iona Prep agreed to offer a new benefit to all Iona College faculty, free Prep tuition for their sons. The news, she says, "felt like a miracle," not only because of its direct impact on her family, but also because it "validated" her contribution to the preparatory school. The schools' decision to offer this benefit also was an acknowledgment that the college's faculty members might not otherwise be able to afford the prep school's tuition, she says.

Delgado still has her frustrations with the institutional church, even with a more progressive pope. "I'm not drinkin' the Pope Francis Kool-Aid just yet." She finds the pope's comments on the environment and on poverty "really refreshing" and says she's "grateful" about the way the pope has "moved the conversation." But the sticking point for her "is the status of women. And there's really no change there. I'm not disappointed in him, because I never really had expectations," she adds. "I don't really expect much from any of them, to tell you the truth."

But Delgado is far from cynical about the church and its future. While she does not expect the institutional church to fundamentally change any time soon, she believes that faith can find outlets in other ways. "What is necessary is other models of doing church, other models of being in community, other models of faith that are not dependent on the hierarchy for their sustenance," she says. "And that's where women's leadership is really at the center."

In a way, Delgado's classes have created a community and given her the opportunity to do pastoral work, she says. Many of her students reach out to her long after they've taken her classes. They will e-mail or call or ask to meet, seeking "advice, counsel, guidance about lots of different things. . . . I'm thinking, 'Is this what priests do?'" She says she doesn't know, because she's "never walked in their shoes." But she assumes that it must be similar, "this responding to a call and a need and saying 'Yes' to that." In the past, she might have had a less-positive reaction, she says. "Can they just leave me alone?" Now she welcomes this outreach as "a wonderful gift."

She serves on the board of trustees of the Westchester Peace Action Coalition—WESPAC—which addresses a variety of social-justice issues. She's also been active in the Hispanic Theological Initiative and the Forum for Theological Exploration, both encouraging more diversity in the theology community. She perceives all these organizations as "communities of faith," if the cornerstone of faith is "having a vision" of "what might be" and an investment in establishing a just world "on earth as it is in heaven.

"I'm tired of being discouraged," she says." I want to have my courage empowered by a vision of what else is possible." What's possible, she adds, is finding church in local communities, both within and outside the Catholic tradition, where people work for change and nourish one another. "As long as we invest our energy and our time and our hope in those communities," she says, "our faith can continue to sustain us."

9

BARBARA BLAINE
Still Seeking Justice

When she was eighteen, working as a Catholic missionary in Jamaica, Barbara Blaine was horrified to see what multinational corporations had done to the countryside. "The aluminum companies were in Jamaica, and they ravaged the land by taking the bauxite out of these mines," she recalls. What had once been a green and verdant mountainside was left barren. "In its wake were these huge red lakes. . . . Nothing could grow there. . . . It was so disrespectful."

Blaine worked in Jamaica as a volunteer for three years and spent more than a decade running a Catholic Worker homeless shelter in Chicago. She lived the social-justice gospel vividly and directly.

But she, too, had something buried within her. And that secret scarred her as deeply and as permanently as the Jamaican countryside had been scarred by mining. But it would take years for her to fully acknowledge what had happened to her, and even longer for her to feel fully whole.

If there is a modern-day Job—a person of faith who endures a series of trials—Blaine could qualify. In her fifty-plus years, she probably has done more to actually live the faith than most Catholics. And yet over and over again God seems to have tested her. In the face of all these tests Blaine has never wavered in her service to others. Although it has become increasingly difficult for her to trust the institutional church, she believes her advocacy has improved it.

She isn't comfortable talking about her experience of God or her Catholic identity. But if faith can be expressed through a determined commitment to social justice, Blaine has never faltered.

Someone who did so much for so many people should have the comfort of knowing her fundamental goodness. But Blaine spent nearly two decades feeling the opposite. Always present within her was a sense of guilt and inadequacy.

What she experienced, and why, took a lot of unpacking. That process began in earnest one otherwise uneventful day in 1985 at the Catholic Worker homeless shelter for women and children that she ran in Chicago. She was twenty-nine.

Blaine remembers that moment. She was reading an explosive story by investigative reporter Jason Berry in the *National Catholic Reporter* about sex abuse by priests. "I didn't know what was happening," she says of the cascade of physical reactions she experienced. Her heart was racing, she was breathing heavily, and she felt like she had to race to the bathroom, about ready either to vomit or experience a bout of diarrhea. "I tried to wash my face and catch my breath," she says.

She sensed she was experiencing the symptoms of post-traumatic stress disorder and had some insight that it was related to what she had experienced during her early teen years.

The symptoms led her to a therapist. She was asked the typical questions about her childhood: Did she get enough food, sleep in her own bed? Was there alcohol in the house? Did she have clean clothes? Had she been beaten? Everything was fine, she says, until she was asked to recall her first boyfriend and her first kiss. It happened the summer between seventh and eighth grade, Blaine told the therapist. "It was the priest in my church."

Hearing herself say those words made her realize, "Maybe this *was* some kind of abuse." Up until then, she had never thought those four years when the assistant pastor of her church had molested her had been abusive. Indeed, Rev. Chet Warren, the perpetrator, made her feel as if she were to blame. He told her conflicting stories about their relationship—claiming that they were "holier" than the others and that no one would understand the sacred bond they shared, while at the same time insisting after each incident that she go to Confession. He also told her that it was the seductiveness of her own body that aroused him.

She had internalized that message. "Guilt and shame formed the essence of the image that I had of myself," Blaine says. "It was an image of someone who was bad, dirty, evil. I didn't understand why he did this to me. And my only explanation was there must be something wrong with me."

Blaine was able to break free of this abusive relationship when she was seventeen and about to graduate from high school. But the impact of the abuse stayed with her. She spent nearly two decades believing that she needed to atone for her conduct. Blaine was driven to root the evil out of her soul and to "cleanse myself."

It was only much, much later, after she had gone public with her accusations, that Blaine realized that the priest who had ruined her childhood had harmed other children. Her growing understanding of her own experience, and her growing awareness that her story had been repeated thousands of times in churches throughout the United States, drove her to channel her activism in a different direction. The members of the community she now served were not the poor and homeless. They were the victims of sexual abuse by priests.

Today the Survivors Network of those Abused by Priests (SNAP) reports that it has more than twenty-two thousand members in the United States and abroad. It has done groundbreaking work holding the institutional church accountable for abusive clergy and changing state laws to extend the statute of limitations on sexual-abuse complaints. Blaine has done scores of media interviews, held press conferences throughout the country and abroad, and even taken the SNAP grievances against the institutional church to United Nations tribunals.

But the core of her work is revealed in the dozens of portraits of seven- and eight-year-old boys and girls that hang in the conference room of her modest Chicago office. Their school pictures show trusting eyes and smiling faces, often with a few front teeth missing. They are the "before" pictures of abuse victims. They do not yet reveal the guilt and sorrow that will be etched there. Blaine's mission is to offer comfort to those victims and prevent any more children from going through what they did.

Blaine was one of eight children growing up in a conservative Catholic family in Toledo, Ohio. The family was not wealthy, but they made do. Whole milk was stretched by adding powdered. Blaine's mom made many of their clothes.

The focus of family life was Saint Pius X parish. Blaine and her twin sister and siblings attended the parish school. She and her sisters learned the guitar to participate in the folk choir that accompanied the post–Vatican II liturgy. Growing up in parochial school she thought of God as "a benevolent fatherly figure" who required His children to "behave and be disciplined," but if you had a misstep, "He loved you anyway."

She was among a group of about a dozen seventh- and eighth-grade girls—nicknamed the deaconettes by their pastor—who did a lot of the grunt work at the parish, everything from selling raffle tickets after Mass to running the parish bulletin off on the precomputer mimeograph machine and stapling the pages together.

Armed with irons, they'd take to the sacristy and literally clean up after the altar boys, who let candle wax drip onto the carpets. They'd have to melt the wax with an iron, and then carefully scrape it away. Indeed, when it came to doing chores, it was "never the boys; it was just the girls."

All this parish work placed her in the sights of the assistant pastor there, Father Warren. Warren was a favorite of the children of the parish. "He learned everybody's name. That was a big deal," Blaine says. When a child went up to the altar to receive Communion, Warren would say his or her name as he distributed the host. "That made everybody feel special."

By the time Blaine met him, Warren was a middle-aged priest with a receding hairline, a round face, and even features. He did not look dangerous; indeed, his formal priestly portrait, where he looks directly into the camera, conveys quite the opposite—the appearance of quiet, stolid wholesomeness. He learned the Top 40 hits of the day and would incorporate allusions to some of those hits into his homilies, which were briefer than the other priests'. He was a favorite with parishioners. "He was put on a pedestal in my world," she says.

It wasn't unusual for parish kids to hang around the rectory. Indeed, one of Warren's colleagues complained that the house was bursting with kids all the time. So no alarm bells went off when Warren invited Blaine to dinner. It was the summer after her seventh grade, and she was a pretty girl with brown hair and green eyes and a nice smile, who aspired to holiness and dreamed of being a nun and missionary. "I was extremely devout," she says. Unlike her twin sister, who "questioned everything," Blaine was more accepting.

Blaine's feelings for the priest were conflicted, she says. "I felt like he was holy and everybody revered him. . . . But the kid inside of me could tell something was wrong with this man. At the same time, since I was only a child, . . . I was very attracted to him. I loved how he made me feel special." He would tell Blaine that "he could tell I was closer to Jesus than the other kids."

After dinner, as the other priests drifted out, Warren and Blaine were left alone. Warren began what would become a four-year ordeal for Blaine. She was thirteen years old. It was a sexual assault so intrusive and traumatic, falling just short of intercourse, that Blaine calls it rape. After this first instance of abuse, Warren promised her, "This will never happen again." But he didn't mean it, she says. "He said it all the time."

He played mind games. He'd tell her that what they did together "is a sacrament. No one will understand, because they're not as close to Jesus as we are. And so they won't understand, so you can't tell them."

A little voice inside her head would challenge what the priest said. "I mean, I would never question him. Remember, I didn't question anything. But in my mind, I was saying to myself, 'This is not a sacrament. We learned the seven sacraments, and this is not one of them.'"

But he also accused her of seducing him. "He made it as if I somehow caused him to have an erection. . . . He would say, 'This is what you do to me.'" And he would demand she go to Confession, but not at her parish, where he feared discovery. Instead, she'd have to lie to her parents and go to a parish farther away. He didn't tell her what to confess. "I always assumed that I was making him sin."

The mental abuse took many forms. Even though money was tight, Barbara and two siblings had their hearts set on high school jackets. She took "little kid" delight in her navy blue windbreaker with the gold emblem of their school and the words *Notre Dame Academy* written across the chest, she recalls.

When she appeared at the rectory, the pastor noticed and complimented her. She was very pleased—until Warren accused her of trying to "show off" her breasts. "That hurt me, really hurt my feelings. . . . Gee, I didn't even think of my breasts." Warren had managed to make her feel that there was something wrong in her joy about the jacket. He reduced it to something that was evil, she says. "There were lots of moments like that."

Even something as harmless as the Catholic Youth Organization offered Warren another avenue to exploit Blaine. He insisted she head up the group, declaring that she was more mature than the other young teens of the parish. She had the responsibility of planning all their events—bowling outings, trips to amusement parks—only so Warren could grope her as they parked the bus or abuse her when she met with him to discuss arrangements.

Warren would demand access at the same time her sister wanted her to attend practice for the swim team or when she had homework. She was still so young that her parents had a set a bed time for her. She would sneak her algebra book into the bathroom, able to work in peace, until a family member needed to use the facilities. She felt, she says, "like a puppet on a string being pulled here and pulled there and in the middle of it, trying hard to be a good girl."

The years of abuse took their physical toll. She started getting terrible headaches, so bad she vomited from the pain. Her parents, alarmed, sought medical care, and she was hospitalized. Warren sought her out in the hospital and abused her, even there.

She lost interest in school, and her grades flagged. She felt guilty and dirty. She was incapable of forming friendships with her fellow students. She dreaded lunch because she couldn't bear finding a place in the cafeteria. "Who wants me? Nobody would want me."

Increasingly cut off from any other supports, locked into a secret that alienated her from others, Blaine was in a vise. When she'd go to Mass and see him at the altar, she'd grow disgusted watching his hands. A priest's hands are supposed to be consecrated, because they change the bread and wine into the body and blood of Christ, she says. "I remember thinking lots of times at Mass, looking at those same hands that were supposedly so holy and were the same hands that were doing these sexual things to me."

The turning point came when she was a high school senior. It was during a three-day retreat, based on the Cursillo movement, which emphasizes the power of God's love to change lives. Participants meet in small groups and hear a series of lectures in an attempt to deepen their spirituality. "It's very high emotion, little sleep," she says. Much of it involves listening to other people's personal stories. Priests are available to hear confessions, but confessor and penitent meet face to face. The retreat convinced her that "it's possible to live this better life—that you could be free and you could be happy."

In that setting, Blaine told a priest about her relations with Warren The priest told her, "Barbara, Jesus loves you. Jesus can forgive anything." It was a very inadequate response, but enough to give Blaine the courage to break off the relationship.

She returned and told Warren: "We're never going to get to heaven if we keep doing this. So let's just agree. I'm not going to come over anymore, and that way it won't happen anymore, and then we'll both get to heaven." She thought Warren would be happy, because it would align with their plan. He had told her that they couldn't marry now, because he was a priest. But if she didn't marry anybody and became a nun, they "could spend all eternity in heaven together. He was going to marry me in heaven," she says. They would be "engaged on earth."

But he was furious. It was then she realized that Warren did not really believe all the stories he had been telling her. But she continued to feel completely responsible for what had happened between them. "I had this sense that I was forgiven, but I was an evil, bad person," she says. "But I was going to try to become a good person."

Not thinking she was a good enough student for college, Blaine was drawn to an order of religious sisters serving the poor in Jamaica. She volunteered to work with them at their complex in the heart of Kingston.

Barely out of high school herself, she was teaching high school and working at a children's home during the day, and sometimes singing and playing the guitar at night, entertaining the street boys from age seven to eighteen at the boys' school. She helped reunite boys with their families in the Jamaica countryside. A boy might be sent to Kingston to visit a relative and discover the relative had moved. Or kids might jump on a bus to Kingston only to be picked up by police for stealing food, and they'd end up with the nuns. She'd interview the boys and then contact clergy in the areas they had come from. "We had several happy family reunions," she says.

She also worked with poor expectant mothers, trying to convince them to breastfeed rather than use baby formula. Not even twenty, Blaine felt that she could never tell anyone how young she was. She didn't feel up to the task. "But I did the best I could," she says.

During her first year in Jamaica, Blaine felt called to be a nun, something the sisters happily endorsed. She became a postulant—a nun in training. But it was "not a good experience," she says. She was living with women far older than she. She was always being scolded for being too noisy or running when she should walk. She was working "a million hours a week" but felt "it wasn't enough. . . . I couldn't keep everyone happy."

After serving two years as a volunteer, she concluded that the problem lay within her. "I was too young and too immature and needed to grow up and get educated."

Blaine spent the next five years in college, ultimately earning a master's degree in social work. She had chosen Saint Louis University in Saint Louis, Missouri, for its social-work program. But once she arrived at the Jesuit school, whose motto is "Higher purpose, greater good," she developed a strong desire to study theology and so completed a double major. [1]

She also started living in community with laypeople and Jesuits. "I wanted to live the gospels," she says. She no longer felt called to the religious life, but she wanted to "live out the social teachings of the church."

Her Jamaica experience in the early 1970s, and her shock at how corporations had ravaged the land there, dovetailed with the liberation theology movement and its concerns about the exploitation of the poor. "It just seemed so unjust, the dichotomy of wealth—that the poor could live in these shacks 150 yards from their [the corporation's] fancy compound. They do all the labor, and their land is raped, and the minerals are taken, and they're left with nothing."

Blaine wanted to be part of a movement that would create "the world as God meant it to be"—a world where all life was respected and all people "were treated with justice."

After completing her graduate degree, Blaine returned to Jamaica for one more year. It was her way, she says, to give back to the community that had given her so much as an inexperienced high school graduate.

Satisfied that she had fulfilled her commitment, she returned to the States and became deeply involved in the Catholic Worker movement. Founded by Dorothy Day during the Great Depression, the movement embraces the notion of direct service to the poor and marginalized, its followers living a life of poverty.

Blaine took on a plethora of social-justice causes, fighting against apartheid in South Africa, striving to end the proliferation of nuclear weapons, and growing more aware of the unequal status of women, particularly women of color.

Her experience running a Catholic Worker house in Chicago sensitized her to that inequality. She was the person who handled many of the "domestic chores" there, she says. And she began to conclude that many of the homeless men were abusers of one type or another. They would abuse alcohol or drugs or women and children, she says. She persuaded her Catholic Worker community to designate the house specifically for housing women with children.

After many efforts and false starts, Blaine was ultimately able to find a former convent on Chicago's South Side to house the families. The Saint Elizabeth's Catholic Worker House could accommodate up to a dozen families at any one time.

Blaine lived in a simple room and shared a bathroom with the other residents. "I ate what everybody else ate" and relied on donated clothing. She earned ten dollars a week in pocket money. Sometimes her family might pay for her to fly home for the holidays, or a donor would take her out to dinner. That was always "really nice and special," she says. "We didn't have a lot of material things, but there was a lot of wealth in terms of the wealth of compassion and maybe respect," she says, her voice hushed.

At the Worker house, the volunteers formed bonds with one another. Blaine says she was "madly in love" with one volunteer, Gary Olivero, who co-ran the house with her. Their relationship had its ups and downs, she says. But it abruptly came to an end when Gary was killed while out on an errand for the house. "He was on his way to pick up food from Catholic Charities when a semi-truck jumped the median" and pushed another car into his path. "He died almost immediately," she says.

She wasn't certain the Worker house could keep going, but other volunteers came to help. "We picked up the pieces and kept on." Gary's legacy to her was a very old man Gary brought to Chicago from the Catholic Worker house in Michigan. The man had been a volunteer, but as he grew old, he became ill and needed care himself. He lived to be one hundred years old. Blaine called it a "great privilege" to tend to him.

Blaine continued at Saint Elizabeth's as she began to work out some of the long-term impacts of Warren's abuse. "I was happy and did good work there," she says. But over time, she realized that her service at the Worker shelter "was almost blocking me from dealing with my own issues. It was almost as though my pain and woundedness was never as important or as serious as the crises people came to us with." She decided to move on and go to law school. "Many people thought I was selling out, joining the establishment," she says. "It seemed right for me."

And then began Blaine's second life of service, focused on people who had experienced abuse by priests as she had. The first potential victims she tried to protect were children that Warren might encounter.

She had told her family about the abuse. They were shocked and supportive. She went to the church authorities in Toledo and told her story. It was the late 1980s by now, and she was asking only four things of the institutional church: She asked that Father Warren be kept away from children. She asked that he get treatment to stop his ever being a predator again. She asked to be reimbursed for her therapy. And she asked for an apology.

The requests were "so minimal," she says. She didn't even ask that he be kicked out of the priesthood. But the Toledo diocese and Warren's religious order took years to even admit that Warren had been an abuser. He was transferred to the pastoral ministry at Saint Vincent's hospital.

A few years later, Blaine's father was hospitalized at Saint Vincent's after suffering a stroke. She called the ministry office to ask that Warren not visit him. When the nun asked her why, Blaine responded that Warren had molested her when she was a child.

The ministry office had no idea about Warren's history and had done nothing to protect hospitalized children from him. The bishop had promised Blaine and her family that Warren would be closely monitored at Saint Vincent's. "It was a like a knife going through my stomach," Blaine said in a 2014 radio interview. "I felt so betrayed. I immediately started wondering, 'If they lied about this, what else did they lie about?'" She later learned that Warren had continued to abuse many more girls. "It's heartbreaking because I feel somewhat responsible," she said.[2]

Blaine also struggled with the realization that the adults in whom she had confided during her high school retreat had done nothing to help her. Blaine tracked down her retreat confessor and asked him why he hadn't reported the abuse to the police or at least called her parents. Why hadn't he told her that the abuse was not her fault? By then, he had left the priesthood. He told her that he didn't remember her confession. "Look, I trained myself," he told her. "I forgot what people said the minute they left the confessional. That's the only way I could survive as a priest."

Blaine also confronted one of the adult leaders of the retreat. The woman told her, "Barbara, you were not clear on what was really happening. You said you were guilty, and you acted like you were guilty." She added that in those days people were "just taught to believe that if anything sexual happened it was the girl's fault."

Warren's religious order put him on leave in the early 1990s, but only in the face of Blaine's threats to publicly name him during her upcoming appearance on "The Oprah Winfrey Show." The Oblates of Saint Francis de Sales eventually kicked him out of the order but did not remove him from the priesthood.[3]

It wasn't until 2005 that Blaine and Warren's other victims received a formal apology from then–Toledo bishop Leonard Blair, who declared that Warren's conduct had been "grievously sinful and criminal."[4]

By that time, Blaine had been running the Survivors Network of those Abused by Priests for eighteen years. During the organization's infancy, she had felt it necessary to gain media attention to the problem. It was something she did not like to do. She recalls, for example, her first TV appearance on a talk show hosted by Geraldo Rivera. She felt that his questions "were insinuating," implying that she could have done something about the abuse, that she had "contributed to the sexual violence" she had endured.

She also was insulted because he called her only by her first name, which made her feel like she was just a "token victim," not "allowed to be my real self. I felt that he was sensationalizing my being a victim."

Appearing with Oprah was not a great experience, either. She got the sense that the host "did not care about any of us," she says. "The minute there would be a commercial break, she would . . . be laughing and joking with members of the audience," ignoring the victims on stage or in the front row who were asked to "share these horrific experiences."

But the TV appearances, she says, were "the price that I had to pay in order to build our movement. Because that was how we were finding other victims." SNAP told TV bookers, "If we come and tell our story, you have to agree to put our contact information out there so other victims can find us."

Blaine had moved from the Catholic Worker to law school in 1993. It was a different kind of life, she says, but her goal remained social justice—in this case "the justice of sexual violence, domestic violence, mostly of women and kids." After law school at DePaul University, she would go on to work for the Cook County Public Guardian, charged with representing abused and neglected children.

Law school meant long hours of study, and much pressure, particularly when newly trained lawyers worked in the school's legal clinic. But recalling those years seems to bring a lightness to Blaine. She smiles, particularly when she recalls her efforts to organize an outing for her class to see the Chicago Cubs play. The outing was a big success, and it brought her into contact with Howard, the legal clinic's director. He was so pleased that he told her he had a friend who had box seats for a Cubs game and that he would take her to one. He never followed through. When Blaine returned to the clinic for an annual Christmas party, he remembered and offered to make it up to her. They eventually started dating.

But the first date could have been the last. When they returned to her apartment, Blaine had to explain why there was a man in her bathroom, taking a bath. Of course, that prompted a lot of questions, she says with a laugh. It turns out that Blaine had not let go of her Catholic Worker approach to life.

"Ray lives in a halfway house for mentally ill and handicapped people. This guy is obsessive compulsive and, anyway, he just has a hard time. He takes a long time to use the bathroom and take a bath. He usually comes to my house to take a bath." The presence of Ray "was a little strange, I think, for Howard. But now Howard has befriended Ray, accepting that Ray comes with me and so Ray is part of our life. Ray still comes to our house."

As Blaine was trying to understand what had happened to her and to heal, she began to seek out and find others who also had been harmed and to help them heal. She also was beginning to crusade for changes within the church and for legal reforms that would help abuse victims make their case and achieve justice.

Over and over, she says, bishops broke the promises they made to police abusive priests and ensure they did not harm more victims. Blaine does not like to discuss her personal faith in God, but it's clear that church efforts to block reforms and to cover up incidents of abuse have tested that faith.

When asked to name any bishop who did the right thing, Blaine can name only one: Auxiliary Bishop Thomas Gumbleton of Detroit. Gumbleton was on the board of Pax Christi when she was working for that organization. At that point, she was upset that Toledo, Ohio, bishop James Hoffman was not following through on her accusations against Father Warren. Gumbleton happened to hear her complaints and tried to intercede for her.

In 2006 Blaine asked Gumbleton for help in the SNAP effort to push for changes in state laws to extend the statute of limitations concerning sexual-abuse allegations against members of the clergy. A legislative hearing was coming up in Ohio, and Gumbleton agreed to testify in favor of a stronger law.

Ohio's bishops, Blaine charges, got the hearing cancelled two days before it was scheduled. But by then SNAP had released Gumbleton's testimony. It was powerful not only because he was advocating for law changes that other bishops opposed, but also because he revealed that he, too, had been abused by a priest when he was a young seminarian.

When she read his testimony, Blaine was shocked. She told him, "I'm so sorry this happened to you, but all these years you've never told me that."

She remembers that he replied: "Well, there was never any reason to tell you. I never wanted to tell anybody. I didn't think there was any reason. But this time I thought my telling might help the lawmakers to understand."

The Vatican and church officials, so slow to punish sex offenders, moved with lightning speed to sanction Gumbleton. In a speech to the Catholic reform group Call to Action, Gumbleton discussed the Vatican's reprisals for his frank testimony. Within ten days of his statement, the Vatican had written to him, detailing the canon law he had broken. Essentially, he'd broken the rule that states that bishops ought to speak with one voice in public. By publicly disagreeing with a bishop in another diocese, he had broken that rule. He was asked to resign immediately as bishop and as pastor of Saint Leo's parish in Detroit.

Since he was older than the mandatory retirement age for bishops, he was not surprised by the Vatican's request for his resignation. But he couldn't understand why the Vatican had felt it necessary for him to give up his parish work—work he loved, even with the lesser title of parish administrator.

He'd been a bishop for thirty years, and knew and worked with many of his colleagues. Yet not one bishop called him, he said. Not even to express anger.[5]

The fact that the only bishop sympathetic to SNAP goals was swiftly punished dramatizes the obstacles the organization has faced. Over the years, Blaine put her trust in church leaders who promised reforms only to be disappointed when those promises were not kept. The incident that appears to have been the last straw for Blaine occurred in 2014, when Minnesota Public Radio broadcast a scathing exposé of three Minnesota archbishops, including Archbishop Harry Flynn. Each archbishop had conspired to deceive abuse victims and cover up priestly misconduct.[6]

When she learned that Flynn, like so many other church officials, "had been lying to us," Blaine says, the realization was "heartbreaking. He was the head of the US Conference of Catholic Bishops committee that drafted a policy on sexual abuse in 2002. "He met with us more than once and led us to believe that he really understood, and at least he was doing the right thing." The "zero-tolerance policy" for abusers that Flynn had claimed to be promoting simply wasn't the policy he was following, Blaine says.

Even in small ways Blaine has encountered a church that rebuffs her at every turn. When she wanted a church wedding, she was told, erroneously, that it couldn't be done because her partner had been married before. But Howard was Jewish and that earlier marriage would not have been recognized by the church, something Blaine knew from her graduate theology studies. She initially challenged the priest but then conceded. "I thought, 'Oh, I must have misunderstood, even though I studied canon law,'" she recalls. "I had just assumed that, 'Oh, he's the priest. He knows better.'"

But Blaine had been right all along. The priest she had consulted "actually apologized later" for his error. "But that was just so unfortunate because it caused so much pain and suffering for me and for my family—to say, 'Oh, Barbara can't get married in the church.'"

They found another priest who agreed to marry them. But things soured when he encountered Blaine at a public meeting about the priest abuse scandals. He was leading the meeting, and it got contentious. She had come with no intention of speaking, but he directed a question to her, asking her about priests who are wrongly accused.

She bridled at the notion that priests were being victimized by false accusations. To counter that charge, she mentioned a priest by name who had actually told her he had abused some boys in his parish. The moderator excoriated her for that response, saying she had no right to expose someone who was not there to defend himself.

Again, she felt a wave of guilt and recrimination. "Being scolded in front of those people, it tapped into those feelings that I had of 'There's something wrong with me.' You know, like, 'I shouldn't have said that. And you're not supposed to say publicly what happens privately.'"

"I really didn't want sex abuse to be part of my wedding day." So the couple searched for a third priest to marry them. They found Rev. Bob Bossie, someone Blaine knew from her Catholic Worker days. "He had a very big heart for homeless people and for the outcast, and he was just somebody that I thought would kind of be good for us."

Bossie had recently discovered his own Jewish roots. His grandmother had converted to Catholicism to escape the Holocaust. So they were married by a priest who also wore a yarmulke for the occasion, Blaine says with a smile.

Blaine was married in 2002. That was also when *Ms. Magazine* named her one of their "Women of the Year." Other honorees included House Minority Leader Nancy Pelosi, who later would become the first woman House Speaker; actress and body-image activist Jamie Lee Curtis; and Ruth Simmons, president of Brown University and the first African American to head an Ivy League school.[7]

They were recognized as "women who demand justice in everything they do." Blaine was praised for being a pioneer in exposing priestly sexual abuse, founding SNAP fourteen years before the issue became a front-page story. She spoke to the gathering of four hundred well-wishers at the National Press Club in Washington where she made the point that priestly sexual abuse is not about homosexuality in the church. Abusive priests, she said, "are equal-opportunity molesters . . . damaging girls as well as boys."[8]

"I didn't feel like I fit in that caliber of award recipients," Blaine says. "I was very humbled by it. But I was also inspired by it, and I found it touching." Not only did her family attend, but her boss in the Public Guardian's office showed up to support her, along with the judge she had clerked for after law school.

Despite all the accolades, the organization Blaine founded was still small and financially vulnerable. Blaine took no salary as SNAP president until 2003, when the group had adequate financial resources. And it very much operated on the Catholic Worker model. "It's like I moved away from the idea of living with homeless people, but then my little studio apartment became kind of a drop-in center for survivors, and I'd have support group meetings in my home," she says.

Even after she married, the SNAP "office" was a bedroom closet. She recalls a group of volunteers gathered in the bedroom "sitting around a computer and a fax machine" one late night when her spouse walked in. "We were faxing out things and preparing for an event the following day, and it was very hectic," she says. Howard didn't say anything, she says, but it was clear that "this was the moment I realized that we can't do this." Her husband, she says, helped her learn to set boundaries.

For all its influence and its growing visibility as the priest sex-abuse scandal exploded in 2002 in Boston, then spreading throughout the United States and abroad, SNAP still is a very small operation, housed in an old office building in Chicago, replete both with character and unreliable elevators. In 2014 the organization marked its twenty-fifth anniversary. Slim and attractive, Blaine, now in her fifties, looks remarkably youthful and unbruised. But she remains frustrated with the progress of the institutional church and skeptical that Pope Francis will embrace fundamental reforms that would ensure speedy action to address complaints of sexual abuse, public disclosure of offenders who are the targets of credible complaints, and support for laws that would make it easier for sex abusers and their clerical supervisors to be held accountable in civil and criminal courts.

Still, she retains pride in what SNAP has been able to do. "I think we've made our church safer, because many perpetrators have been removed. Certainly not all, but many." She says that the group's "continual" exposure of incidents of sexual abuse by clergy has changed the attitudes of church leaders. They can no longer claim that abuse is an aberration.

Nor can church leaders claim that abuse is a problem limited to one country or one region of the world. "We were able to go to the United Nations and have the committees [one on torture and another on the rights of children] confirm that priest abusers remain in ministry" and that there is "a systemic and widespread problem," she says. The international scrutiny is important, she says. "If we don't acknowledge the evil, we cannot begin to rid the church of evil."

But for Blaine it is the "little things" that matter the most. "It's the survivors who think that they're the only one and who are so frightened and filled with shame and guilt—for them to know that they're not alone." She says these small moments—when a victim comes in and perhaps for the first time tells his or her story and receives validation—happen all the time. She recalled a recent visit when a wife persuaded a very reluctant husband to come to the office. "Once he was here, we talked a little bit, and it was great to see this transformation." The victim moved beyond the "little boy that felt so helpless to the grown adult, to the professional that he is."

Blaine knows all about transformations. She lives her own every day. Having been a victim of abuse, she says, is like having a chronic illness like diabetes. "Someone who's a diabetic can live a normal life" but has to be aware of nutrition and sugar levels and take medication. "It's something that requires attention every day."

Every day, Blaine also has to pay attention. When she wakes up feeling that she is a "bad, inferior, and dirty person," she can use the skills she learned in therapy to "transform" that image. She can tell herself, "No, that isn't true. That is not exactly who I am." And then, she says, she can go out into the world. "I can function."

10

GRETCHEN REYDAMS-SCHILS

Breaking Through the Silence

In early 1994, as Gretchen Reydams-Schils was considering an offer to join the faculty at the University of Notre Dame, she happened to hear a rebroadcast of Pope John Paul II's 1983 visit to Nicaragua. Left-wing Sandinistas were in power, and many Catholic priests and lay people supported them. Two priests even held government positions.

As the pope addressed a huge congregation in Managua, the crowd interrupted his homily on church unity with shouts of "We want a Church that stands with the poor," and "Power to the people!" and "Between Christianity and the revolution, there is no contradiction." Three times the pope shouted back, "Silencio!"[1]

That *silencio* was emblematic of a pontiff who would crack down on liberation theology and the priests and theologians who espoused it, promoting instead a Catholicism rooted in obedience and fidelity to the institutional church.[2]

Hearing that stern *silencio*, Reydams-Schils says, "I just felt this chill running down my spine." His approach, she explains, was "so authoritarian." The pope was addressing people "who had lived this issue" and "who had suffered," believing that Christians should do all they can to lift up the oppressed. "This is not the way I want to see the leader of my church behave. It wasn't pastoral."

She asked herself, "Do I really want to go back to this?"

Born and raised in Belgium, she'd already had one unsettling encounter with the more conservative side of Catholicism during her senior year of college, an experience that drove her to the United States to complete her studies at the University of Cincinnati. She ultimately earned her doctorate in classics and ancient philosophy at the University of California, Berkeley.

But her wariness was balanced by a sense of obligation. "All right, I'm Catholic. I have to assume my responsibility." So she accepted Notre Dame's offer, filled with both dread and excitement—dread because she knew that she would face challenges, excitement at the prospect both of possibly changing things from the inside, and of simply being "part of the conversation" about Catholicism and its future. More than twenty years later, she says, "the challenges have been even bigger than I would have anticipated."

And being part of the conversation? That, she says, "is exactly what didn't happen. I have been encapsulated in silence. There is that word again."

Reydams-Schils chairs the Program of Liberal Studies at Notre Dame and holds a concurrent faculty appointment in the university's philosophy and theology departments. Aside from visiting professorships in Europe and Africa, she's spent her entire teaching career at Notre Dame, a university where she's seen her brand of Catholicism increasingly marginalized by a conservative Catholicism focused on sexual morality. She doesn't like living "on the barricade," being forced to prove her genuineness as a Catholic.

Reydams-Schils is not someone you'd think of as embattled. She speaks in Flemish-accented English that manages to blend jokes, personal asides, and scholarly allusions at a breakneck speed. She began Latin lessons at age twelve, started Greek at thirteen, and, when she was sixteen, fell into a love-hate relationship with Plato—not your usual teenage heartthrob.

Reading the *Symposium*, Plato's account of Socrates' discussions of the nature of love with his male followers, "was so beautiful," she recalls. But Plato's work also infuriated her. "I felt like throwing the book against the wall." The *Symposium* excludes women from all the relationships of a higher love, and left her with "a deep sense of betrayal—to be lured into this powerful thought and then to be left out at the same time."

A more earthly relationship commenced after she met Luc Reydams, a friend of her brother's. They started dating the summer before she began her studies in Berkeley. They were apart for two years, keeping in touch only through letters and phone calls, and then he joined her in California. "Like me, he's Belgian. I imported him," she jokes.

They did not put off children while she was pursuing her studies. She had three—twin girls and a boy—while earning her doctorate. She credits her spouse, who was between careers when they started a family, for being a stay-at-home parent. He was her "secret weapon," she quips. When she came home from school, she didn't face "a second shift. . . . He was just always there." Having trained as a lawyer in Belgium, he restarted his career at Notre Dame where he switched from the legal to the academic track.

I met her in the hotel lounge of a Chicago hotel on a very chilly day in early April 2015. Reydams-Schils had driven to the city from Notre Dame's campus near South Bend, Indiana. I had flown in from Washington, DC. Brown-haired and smiling, she moved quickly through the busy hotel lobby to a quiet area of the hotel. She was happy and eager to do the interview, to finally have the conversation she hadn't experienced at Notre Dame. My request, she told her husband, would open up "a floodgate. I'm so grateful that somebody finally is asking me."

Likely most famous for its prowess on the football field, the University of Notre Dame is also known for its Catholic roots. The institution calls itself "the place where the Catholic Church could do its thinking." Founded in 1842 by the Congregation of the Holy Cross, a French missionary order, it now has a student body of more than twelve thousand undergraduate and graduate students and more than a thousand faculty members. Its endowment is valued at nearly $10 billion. In the academic year of 2014 and 2015 its alumni donated more than $246 million to the school, a level of participation that, the school brags, puts it among the "best in American education." Eight out of ten students in its 2015 freshmen class were Catholic.[3]

When Reydams-Schils arrived in 1994, the challenges she faced were still manageable. "The first impressions were quite positive, "she says, noting that on campus, "the Hesburgh atmosphere was still very much alive." Rev. Theodore Hesburgh had been Notre Dame's president from 1952 until 1987. He built the school into an academic powerhouse. A priest revered for his tolerance of diversity in the church, Hesburgh believed in academic freedom, and in civility.

In 1974 he urged Catholics to "be effectively concerned and thoughtfully articulate about abortion, not backing unworkable solutions, not engaging in calling the opposition murderers." He said that "mindless and crude zealots" would not help the pro-life cause.[4]

He also was disturbed by the church's laser-like focus on this one ill. "We cannot be loud in condemning abortion," he said, "after being silent about napalmed Vietnamese or seemingly unconscious of the horrible present fact" that 60 percent of children in the world's poorest countries "die before the age of five."[5]

In 1973, shortly after his criticism of the Nixon Administration's record on civil rights cost him his job as chair of the US Commission on Civil Rights, Hesburgh established the Center for Civil Rights at Notre Dame, now the Center for Civil and Human Rights.[6] The center was where Reydams-Schil's spouse earned a doctorate and found a career at the "intersection of international law and politics," she says. The center imparted an "international, very dynamic feel" to the place.

Mass at the university's housing complex for married graduate students was also welcoming, a place where the couple could bring their children, sure to meet other families. "That's the space where we leave the politics at the door," she says, and "just focus" on "what the core of the faith is supposed to be."

But even in those early years, she felt some sense of alienation. She was not yet thirty, had a doctorate, and was a parent. "All of a sudden I felt I had aged ten years," she recalls. "I was sort of surrounded by mostly men and mostly people quite a bit older than me, and that was socially very difficult at first." American women her age, unlike their European counterparts, put off raising their children until they were more established in their careers. "I couldn't invest every waking hour in work," she says, because she had small children. She didn't want to be "one of those academics" who work a sixteen-hour day, she says. She wanted a balanced life.

She discovered that her background put her at a disadvantage. "Being a European Catholic, a non-American, gets used against me all the time." The impression, she says, is that "we're not true Catholics. Call it whatever you want, cafeteria Catholics, wishy-washy Catholics." She regrets that the Notre Dame community doesn't consider the possibility that European Catholics may have something valuable to share: "a Catholicism that is a little more confident, that doesn't have to assert itself, that doesn't have to play the game of identity politics all the time."

The irony is that Reydams-Schils, a serious, committed Catholic, has kept the faith largely because of her European background. Catholic schools are publicly funded in Belgium, and they have rigorous academic standards. In Belgium, she says, religious education was very values-based. In discussing sexuality, for example, the focus was not abstinence but responsibility.

"Social justice was a big component of the religion I grew up with," she adds. "Liberation theology was very big." At the core of liberation theology is the notion that Christians must work to free all people from privation and oppression. "And liberation is both for the oppressor and the oppressed," she says, because both are caught up in a structure of sin. The goal is societal change, addressing the structures of exploitation and oppression.

Her Catholic schools in Belgium largely had been insulated from the conservative pushback that shaped the church following Vatican II. Her all-girls high school was considered one of the best in the country. The nuns "encouraged us to be strong, independent women and not to settle for less than that," and to take pride in their achievements. Her high school, she says, flew beneath the radar, out of view of the church establishment. "You sort of had a niche where you had some freedom."

There was a period as a teen when she fell away from the church a bit and stopped going to weekly Mass. But when she was sixteen, her mother's cousin, a Jesuit, brought her to a retreat that changed all that. The retreat was sponsored by the Focolare Movement, an international spiritual movement emphasizing universal brotherhood. It was founded in Italy in 1943 by the mystic Chiara Lubich.[7]

The retreat "came at the exact right time for me," she says. For the first time, she met people her age who were equally serious about their faith but in a way that emphasized joy and camaraderie. Together, with the guidance of an exceptional priest, they explored how to be Catholic in the world, with an emphasis on social justice. "What difference does that make in your day-to-day choices?" The retreat was charismatic but not just "flowers and guitars and garlands." It also was "liturgically serious," she says.

The retreat, she says, marked a moment of "awakening" for her faith. That faith deepened after she read *Christ Recrucified* by Nikos Kazant-zakis, the author of *Zorba the Greek*. The novel, written in lyrically earthy prose, tells the story of a Greek shepherd asked to play the role of Christ in the village's passion play, who over time takes on the sanc-tity of Christ. He advocates for the destitute refugees who have fled to the town. The villagers end up crucifying the Christ figure again, she says, which brought home the "social dynamic" of Christianity, that as Christians we all are complicit if we see injustice, need, and suffering and do nothing.

Not that her faith wasn't tested, even then. During her senior year of college, she encountered sexist attitudes "partly informed by a very misguided Catholicism," she says. She was at the top of her class in classics at the Catholic University of Leuven, Belgium's oldest and most prestigious university.[8] She wanted to earn a PhD in ancient philosophy but was turned down. The scholar who would supervise her studies deemed her "too vivacious" to pursue a doctorate.

She was "flabbergasted" by that remark, she says. She assumes her scholarship was contested because of "the way I dressed, my laugh." She was a "girly girl" who wore makeup and jewelry and "would actually go to parties and dance." And, she recalls, there was "one exam where I talked back. It was a philosophy exam, so I thought we were supposed to have a discussion, so I did." The academic who assessed her con-cluded that "I didn't have the right temperament to be a scholar. In other words, I didn't look, talk, and behave like a monk."

There was another reason for the rejection, equally sexist. European cost-cutting was shrinking employment opportunities in the humanities, and her teachers wanted to make sure that male candidates had suffi-cient job options. "Miss Schils," she was told, "we don't even have enough jobs for our boys."

"You could argue that they forced feminism down my throat because I ran into a wall," she says. The discrimination left a scar. She felt so wounded that she bolted for the States just two days after graduation.

She flourished at the University of Cincinnati, which had offered her a scholarship for a graduate degree in classics, and where one teacher helped repair her wounded confidence. He encouraged her to earn her doctorate in classics and ancient philosophy.

The woman whose Catholicism would be considered suspect at Notre Dame found that her religion puzzled her Berkeley colleagues. Her faith was viewed as quirky and inexplicable. "My adviser, Anthony Long, who was really one of the great names in the field, didn't know what to do with me; he didn't know what to do with my Catholicism. And he used to quote [George] Bernard Shaw at me. 'A Catholic university is a contradiction in terms.'"

That didn't affect her productive relationship with Long, she says. But those who study ancient philosophy tend to believe that Catholics really aren't equipped to be scholars. "We're being brainwashed. We can't be true intellectuals."

Nevertheless, her Berkeley experience was "very, very happy," she says. While her Catholicism was considered eccentric, it didn't affect her academic progress. But that wasn't true later on, when she was trying to establish herself as a professor by getting her first book published.

Reydams-Schils was exploring "the notion of the divine, of God, in ancient philosophy." US publishers rejected the manuscript. They told her, "That's so outdated; nobody has any interest in that anymore." She eventually realized that they were bothered by her looking at ancient texts in a way that was not averse to the notion of God. What saved her career, she says, was finding a European publisher. She adds that since then the topic has made "a bit of a comeback." But at the time, she says, "the edict of atheism" prevailed.

The barricades have grown higher since she began her career at Notre Dame. The fight over abortion had not yet totally dominated the church's focus and moved the politics of its hierarchy to the Right. The battle had been even more muted in 1984, when New York governor Mario Cuomo accepted an invitation from the head of Notre Dame's theology department to discuss his views, as a Catholic governor, on religious belief and public morality.[9]

The 1984 speech followed a public controversy over abortion that involved Cuomo and then–New York archbishop John O'Connor. O'Connor had stated that he didn't know how a Catholic could vote for any politician "who explicitly supports abortion." Cuomo took umbrage at what he felt was an unprecedented aggressive intrusion of the church into national politics, since the Democratic candidate for vice president that year was both a pro-choice woman and a Catholic.[10]

Cuomo's appearance at Notre Dame drew only a few protesters. While some bishops objected to the speech itself, the criticism was civil by today's standards. Even so, Baltimore's archbishop at the time thought the controversy "had been blown out of proportion by both sides."[11]

In 2009 President Barack Obama gave the commencement address at Notre Dame, an honor that had been bestowed on five previous presidents, including both George H. W. and George W. Bush.[12] Protests by the alumni and Catholic clergy made the headlines for days. Notre Dame's current president, Rev. John I. Jenkins, drew the ire of more than seventy bishops.[13] The Cardinal Newman Society, a Catholic nonprofit that monitors the orthodoxy of Catholic education, circulated a petition asking Notre Dame to rescind the invitation. It garnered 367,000 signatures.[14] Scores of alumni cut off their ties, and their donations, to the school.[15]

The Catholic identity that Reydams-Schils believes permeates American Catholicism has been shaped by "white, male Americans" who are "conservative or ultraconservative" politically. It hasn't been priests who have driven this but laypeople, she says. "Catholic identity began to be defined more and more narrowly" by what she calls "litmus-test issues" such as abortion, contraception, and gay marriage.

One example that infuriates her is Notre Dame's litigation against the Obama administration over the "birth-control mandate" in the Affordable Care Act. When Catholic and other religious groups raised concerns that they would have to offer their employees coverage for something that violated their conscience, the Obama administration offered a compromise: The institution would sign a statement declaring its opposition, and a third party would pay for the contraceptive coverage and undertake all the administrative work. Notre Dame found that unacceptable.[16]

The controversy pained her for several reasons. "You are a faculty member, and all of a sudden you're presented with this approach to the mandate in which you had no say whatsoever," she says. And then there is the primacy of sexual ethics over social justice. "The extension of health care to a large number of Americans is probably the most important social-justice development of our generation in terms of what access to health care means for quality of life," she says. But Notre Dame rejected the compromise. "We say no? We go down in history for what Dante calls 'the Grand Refusal, the Great No.'"

Notre Dame also did not acknowledge that the college employs many non-Catholics and failed to respect the rights of Catholic women to make their own decisions about birth control, she says. "Catholic women are the ones who need to make the choice here, not their institution."

Reydams-Schils was among more than 180 Notre Dame students and faculty who signed a petition respectfully declaring their opposition to the lawsuit, and stating that the university would better serve its Catholic mission by ensuring that its own graduate students and their families had access to affordable health care.[17]

This wasn't the only time Reydams-Schils has publicly opposed the Notre Dame administration or its leaders. In 2012, just months before a presidential election, Bishop Daniel Jenky, Notre Dame alumnus and member of Notre Dame's board, compared President Obama's "radical proabortion and extreme secularist agenda" to the policies of Hitler and Stalin. Reydams-Schils joined more than 130 faculty members to ask that Jenky either resign from the board or retract his incendiary remarks "loudly and publicly." Their letter also asked the college administration to distance Notre Dame from Jenky's remarks.

"We try to teach our students that even if you disagree with someone, you have to make your case in a thoughtful and respectful argument, rather than with incendiary language," Reydams-Schils told the *South Bend Tribune*.[18]

Reydams-Schils does have sympathy for Jenkins, Notre Dame's president. "I wouldn't want to be in our president's shoes. I think he has a very tough job," she says. Not only is the Newman Society constantly monitoring Notre Dame and other Catholic colleges in the United States, Jenkins has to deal with alumni, bishops, and a range of faculty positions, she says. "The pressure is very real."

For her, Catholicism's power and strength is much more expansive and positive. In Europe, particularly in countries where Catholicism is the majority religion, Catholics don't feel as if they're an embattled minority.

There's a downside to European Catholicism, she concedes, in that Europeans can become blasé about their faith. But in the United States she finds that, while Catholics may be more committed to their faith, the Catholic culture often is very combative and narrow-minded. Identity politics, she says, "leads to a horrible form of self-righteousness," where sexual ethics can be used as "a weapon to judge others."

As a Catholic, she says, "I am pro-life," but she doesn't support making abortion illegal. Making the battleground "women's bodies," she says, is "reinforcing the image that women are not moral agents," that "we're not capable of making the right moral choice."

She also believes that abortion is "at the end of the chain of a lot of things that have gone wrong." By isolating it, she contends, "you are lowering the chances of being able to address it effectively. . . . Disrespect for human life? It starts with whether you provide health care or not, whether people have a normal work week." Addressing abortion requires creating a more just and equitable society.

Guided by that ethic, the church also should support extending benefits to legally married same-sex spouses of employees, something Notre Dame has done, she says. (In 2014, two days after the Supreme Court declined to hear appeals from Indiana and other states of lower-court decisions that struck down their bans on same-sex marriage, Notre Dame notified its employees it would extend benefits to same-sex spouses.)[19]

She personally believes that the Church's "official stance" on the sinfulness of homosexuality is "outdated." But even if a Catholic believed in that position, the "pastoral social-justice" dimension of Catholicism should take precedence. That's about "extending basic rights to everybody." That might be difficult for some Catholics to accept, she concedes. "But the pastoral side is the more important. You cannot sacrifice the one for the sake of the other."

Focusing only on sexual mores, she adds, "undoes the organic unity" among the various ethical teachings of the church. If a Catholic opposes abortion, how can that same Catholic support capital punishment? She, too, believes that sexual ethics is important but as part of a larger ethical discourse. To do otherwise, "politicizes" Catholicism and is "the kiss of death for a rich, living, healthy tradition."

She believes that Pope Francis, "bless his heart," is promoting this broader understanding, placing sexual ethics in a larger context. While she regrets that the institutional church has consigned women to a "second-class" status because they are denied ordination, she does believe that the pope has made some gestures in the right direction, speaking up for equal pay for women. "He's willing to challenge some things but not others," she concedes. But she adds that the pope at least is "making conversation possible where there was none."

Not that she is content with the status quo. It's time, she says, to revise the church's limiting definition of the role of women. She says Pope John Paul II took the approach of saying, "Yes, we do value women, we just value them as mothers in their specific role." But that view, she insists, is not good enough. "The short answer to that is 'A golden cage is still a cage.' And it doesn't do justice to the full human potential of women. . . . It's time to move beyond this and to reopen the discussion."

Not being part of the conversation at Notre Dame led her to create her own. Along with her academic books, Reydams-Schils wrote *An Anthology of Snakebites: On Women, Love, and Philosophy*. It is a slim volume that imagines a conversation between two women about the sexism informing both our theology and our culture, told through excerpts from major works of literature and philosophy. She jokingly calls the book her "illegitimate child."

The book was written, in part, as a balm to women on her campus and others whose research and teaching deeply engages them in reading and studying what are considered the classics of Western culture. Many of these books are infused with a profound misogyny.

"I read the *Phaedo* when I was about seventeen, and ever since it has both attracted and haunted me," she wrote in 2008. "In Plato's worldview, there is no room for women and children." She became, she writes, "preoccupied with the conditions which the tradition has imposed on women for participating in the philosophical and spiritual life," if they were permitted at all.[20]

"It's just book after book after book"—what she terms "the sheer weight of the tradition. . . . It's not easy to be a woman when you read those books," she says. But she believes that "you cannot walk away" from works that have informed and shaped Western civilization. "And they are masterpieces. That may be the hardest thing to come to terms with: how can these works be masterpieces and yet so terrible in some respects."

Her book includes a feminist commentary on everything from the sin of Adam and Eve, and Eve taking all the blame for succumbing to temptation, to the death of Socrates and his dismissal of his wife, Xantippe, and the story of ill-fated lovers Abelard and Heloise.

Rev. Nicholas Ayo encouraged the book, she says. He was one of two priests whom she befriended during her early years at Notre Dame. They were working at the university while handling pastoral work, so they also knew the challenge of trying to balance the demands of scholarship with their lives outside the academy. She began the book soon after she arrived at Notre Dame. She wrote "a fragment" about Heloise and Abelard and "slipped it under the door" of Ayo's office. He sent the fragment back with a question: "Is there more?" The exchange continued, and the manuscript grew.[21]

The book is experimental, and its commentary, framed as a conversation between two friends, is witty, wistful, and sometimes biting. The two characters have tantalizing backstories, in part based on Reydams-Schils's own life: Marianne is a Catholic academic, Lauren a nonreligious journalist. They meet weekly over coffee at a local café.

Reydams-Schils states firmly that the book is not autobiographical. She also says that all their conversations—about childbirth, being mistakenly perceived as a "loose" woman, falling in love with a gay man, being happily married—are real but occurred in a different context than the book portrays. She does not disclose how closely the stories track her own reality or the lives of others.

In the first chapter of the book, Marianne has a vision of a woman being "stoned" to death by shelves of great books crashing down on her. In her vision, the woman slowly rises, dusts off the books, and puts them back on their shelves. "Because she restored the books by her own doing and sheer will power, chose to pick them up from the floor, . . . from now on they would no longer have the power to harm her."[22]

When the two women discuss the biblical story of Adam and Eve, the conversation begins with Marianne's comment, "It was his fault too."

"For me the core idea is that Adam was right there," Reydams-Schils says. "That's the traditional iconography. You see the tree, you see them standing on both sides, and you see the snake, you know, leaning over to Eve. So if there is a liability to sin, it's for both human beings."

Marianne blames the story of original sin for the view of women that excludes them from the priesthood, or requires priests to be celibate. The image of the snake seducing Eve, and then Eve seducing Adam, leads to the church's assumption that "there is something wrong with women and sexuality; they contaminate the transcendental experience."

That flawed interpretation, Marianne observes, leads to women's continued second-class status in the church. "In *reality* priests perform rituals that are the core and essence of our faith, the sacraments, and *men* have the *power* of the final say in the Church. We're equal, but some of us are more equal than others. . . . The curse of Genesis, only more cleverly disguised this time."[23]

The other point the book tries to make, Reydams-Schils says, is that events and choices with a potential for disaster also often have the potential for great good. *Snakebites* speculates that original sin had to occur at some point in time in order to endow humanity with free will. It is the potential to sin, she says, that makes us "fully human."

In the chapter on Heloise and Abelard, Reydams-Schils reframes the story and explores an alternative ending, one that could have turned a disastrous love affair into a life-saving one.

The story is famous. In the twelfth century, Pierre Abelard, a distinguished scholar, was engaged as a tutor to Heloise, a brilliant young student. She is seventeen, and he is in his thirties. They fall in love, she becomes pregnant, and things get complicated. Prodded by her guardian, Abelard agrees to marry her, but she resists.

Snakebites cites Heloise's arguments against marriage to Abelard, reminding him that a great philosopher could not risk the distractions of domestic life and crying babies. Marianne and Lauren are appalled by Heloise's belittling of her own sex. Marianne speculates that Heloise also might have feared that marriage would swallow her up, too. She would have lost the freedom she'd enjoyed as his mistress.

They do agree to marry in secret. But due to a misunderstanding, Heloise's guardian has Abelard castrated. That's a boon for him, because he's no longer distracted by lust and can enter a monastery and continue his scholarly life. He insists that Heloise become a nun. She does so, becoming an abbess. But, unlike Abelard, she remains unhappy and unfulfilled.

Marianne praises Heloise, whose love was much more than physical attraction. She refuses to sublimate her passion for Abelard into religious fervor. Marianne wonders what would have happened had the two remained together and grown closer in love and scholarship. "We will never know whether it could have led both of them to another path of religious ascent, whether from the early days of passion, they could have come to live the Song of Songs, as an intertwining of the carnal and the spiritual."[24]

In his *Phaedo*, Plato dismisses Xantippe, Socrates' wife, as a hysterical female, unworthy of witnessing Socrates' heroic death by poison. In *Snakebites*, Reydams-Schils challenges that impression, suggesting that Xantippe is a woman who deeply loves her husband and has a generosity of spirit and an intelligence that the *Phaedo* ignores. She also invents a relationship of support between Socrates' friend Crito and Xantippe, although only Crito was able to engage Socrates in philosophical inquiry, something Socrates denied his wife. As Marianne observed, "Xantippe knew and understood more than she could ever show Socrates, because she was not supposed to."[25]

Reydams-Schils has used the Xantippe excerpts from *Snakebites* in Philosophical Inquiry, an introductory course in her department, since the students often read the *Phaedo* in that course. She was reluctant to use her own book, worried that students would not critique it because they didn't want to offend their teacher. She was pleased that they treated her work in a "thoughtfully critical manner."[26]

After he graduated, one male student even wrote to her to let her know of the book's lasting impact. Four men and women students from that class had "gotten together every Sunday to talk to one another and to engage," she says. "I found that deeply moving."

Beyond the student response, the book provoked little reaction at Notre Dame. "How do Catholics respond to an illegitimate child?" she asks. "Silence." She did learn later that the book was considered a "positive" when she was up for a promotion. Otherwise, she says, "nothing."

It is that feeling that her voice does not count that increases her frustration. There was a time, she says, when she felt she was breaking through. She and colleague Kenneth Garcia were instrumental in expanding a university program to help both Catholic and non-Catholic faculty discuss and comment on various aspects of Catholic teaching—the Catholic Intellectual Traditions Initiative. "We wanted to do justice to the pluralism of the tradition, not just the sort of monolithic view," she says. A "very important" component of the program was a yearlong faculty seminar on one theme.

She recalls being "so pleased" that Notre Dame sponsored a year-long seminar on feminist theology. Her role as a "catalyst" for the seminar was "just so fulfilling," she says. "By all accounts it was very successful." But that seminar turned out to be the last. "The whole project came to an end," she says. "Gone. Wasn't considered important enough. . . . That was the only window in the twenty years that I've been at Notre Dame that I feel I was part of the conversation."

As she turns fifty, Reydams-Schils is considering her options. "Political conviction goes pretty deep," she says. "But faith is something, if true, that permeates your very being. I'm sorry, but I don't want every fiber of my being politicized every moment of the day." She doesn't think she wants to spend the rest of her life on the barricades, she says. That may mean moving to a non-Catholic university or staying where she is and just concentrating on her teaching and research, not trying to influence the larger conversation.

She knows she will always be a Catholic. There is so much she values in her faith, she says. The Catholic doctrine of the Holy Trinity and the "centrality of Christ." The sacraments that "keep the visible world connected to the spiritual world, to the afterlife." The love of God and neighbor.

She appreciates the campus liturgies she attends, a blend of simplicity and seriousness. She takes the liturgy so seriously that in 2012 she wrote a letter to the Catholic magazine *Commonweal* criticizing the changes in the new translation of the prayers Catholics recite during Mass, particularly the revision of the Nicene Creed, which used to refer to Christ as "born of the Virgin Mary." The new translation uses the term, *incarnate of*, which she described as an "abstruse alternative." The term *born of*, she wrote, "connects the Mother of God to all human mothers giving birth. . . . Mary is the sister who walks with women and watches over them as they go through this excruciating, momentous experience. Inadvertently (or not so inadvertently?) the new translation may have picked up a deep strand of repulsion at the female body in the Christian tradition. That would be a particularly inadmissible move for a church that sees itself as the chief advocate for the dignity of human life."[27]

At her campus parish, she says, the congregants opted not to use the revised Nicene Creed and to replace it with the Apostles' Creed, with its older wording.

All three of her children were baptized and made their First Communion. But they were permitted to decide whether they wanted to be confirmed. None of them has opted to do so. Her daughters, now in their twenties, have seen her struggles. They continue to ask her, "Why do you insist on holding on?" She wants her children "to keep the door open" to practicing their faith. She thinks faith may come as her children grow older and experience more of life's challenges.

Her daughters are "feisty feminists," she says. Indeed, they alerted her to the fact that Notre Dame is one of the schools featured in the documentary *The Hunting Ground*, an exposé of the rape culture on the campuses of some of the country's most prestigious schools. "Notre Dame was in good company," she says, noting that Harvard also was included in the film. But she hastens to add that a Catholic school should be better than other colleges.

She says that faculty largely are kept in the dark about sexual assaults on campus, part of the effort at "damage control," but she knows they occur. "I think the whole dating culture, that's where the problem starts. It's where the genders end up stereotyping one another."

Because Notre Dame has all-male dorms, she says, there isn't much conversation across genders. Students don't learn to know each other through "normal" interactions like meeting over coffee or discussing a book. When that happens, she says, "you get the hookup culture . . . reducing each other to the genital zone. . . . You end up reducing sex to intercourse and the erotic to the sexual."

She asks her students not to think of the opposite sex as "dating material" but to learn to be friends. "I try to talk about the basic ethics of dating and gender interaction." Often, she lets the students talk to each other. Do these classroom discussions make a difference? "You know, modest expectations, but you do have a feeling that this could stay with them," she says.

She struggles with her own feminism. "The need to be a feminist throws me back on myself much more than is actually good for my spiritual life," she says, explaining that living such a life "to some extent means being able to let go of the ego."

That sense of being "on the barricade" at Notre Dame, she says, also "keeps you trapped in some sense in a kind of ego discourse—not to mention the price you pay for seeing yourself in the role of victim." In her heart, she says, she is a humanist, concerned that both men and women achieve their "full potential."

On the other hand, she is acutely aware of the injustices only women experience. One that particularly galls her concerns the treatment of women who have out-of-wedlock children with priests who belong to religious orders. These women will get some child support from the church, she says, but only if the woman agrees to "signing away all her rights" to ask for more support in the future "if needs arise." The mother has no way to "challenge" the agreement or to seek any more accountability from the father of her child, she says. When one of her daughters heard her railing about this, she told her, "Mom, this goes against everything you stand for."

Still, she persists in her faith. She sometimes jokes—"although it's not a joke"—that she won't be pushed out of her church. "I'm a Catholic, God damn it, and you're not taking that away from me!"

But she has mixed feelings about the path her daughters have taken. "I mean, it's not as if I cover up the fact that I'm a religious person and that faith matters to me. I talk to them about that." She thinks she's passed on some of her values. "But I wasn't going to make them jump through the hoops. I really feel that they have to make this decision for themselves. . . . Sometimes, some days, I'm sad." But other days, she thinks, "I'm sorry, but I just couldn't put that burden on them."

Our interview consumes several hours, well into lunchtime. She rushes to meet her husband. "The kind of conversation that you and I are now having," she confides, is one that she hasn't had at Notre Dame. "I've been there twenty years, and rarely has anybody . . . asked me what I think."

11

JOSHUNDA SANDERS
Coming Home

When she was growing up in New York City, one of the few predictable elements of Joshunda Victoria Sanders's life was Sunday Mass, in midtown Manhattan at Saint Patrick's Cathedral. She and her mother would take the subway to attend the 10 a.m. Mass there. As a small child, she thought of the cathedral as "a palace or a museum." She remembers the highly polished wooden pews, the light of hundreds of candles, the smell of incense, and the way footsteps echoed off its marble floors. Saint Patrick's she says, was one of the few "constant places" in her life.

The experience of the church and the Mass was "very visceral," she recalls. She remembers returning to the cathedral as an adult years later and being "struck by how moved I was to be back there. It became almost like a second home. . . . The ushers with their green blazers," the wooden tapers for lighting candles, the donation boxes—all were familiar elements in a life where nearly everything else was unpredictable. Weekly Mass, she says, was "quite wonderful. It was the thing that gave my life some structure and some order."

Beneath its soaring ceilings, and the glow of its stained-glass windows, she and her mother were two dark reeds in a sea of white. Her mother was a tall, stocky black woman whose high cheekbones and broad brow betrayed her Cherokee blood. Sanders was a "skinnier miniature version" of her mother, but with braids.

Her mother always wore a black wig, and her purse, worn across her body, would bulge with paper, full of missals and holy cards—"pictures of Jesus with lipstick stains on them because she would kiss them." Securely attached to her bra was a safety pin holding all her Catholic medals. Her mother would insist on sitting in the front row, and, unlike her sedate fellow worshippers, she would sing the conventional Catholic hymns "at the top of her lungs."

It would have been clear to the congregation that the pair was living on the edge, dressed as they were in Salvation Army castoffs. Did the Saint Patrick's worshippers reach out to their need? Not really, Sanders recalls. "I was acutely aware that we were poor black women in a world that favored a white male God and white skin," Sanders wrote.[1]

The Communion wafers they received would often be their breakfast, she recalled in a TED talk in 2013. When they left that neo-Gothic bastion of faith that occupies one city block between Fifth and Madison Avenues, some of the priciest real estate in Manhattan, they would be hungry. They would exit from all its power and glory into a part of the city known for its luxury hotels and stores, sensing the "burning salt scent of the pretzels or that wonderful smell of New York pizza," neither of which they could afford. Hunger, Sanders said, was the "tangible manifestation" of the "vicious cycle" that trapped them both.[2]

One can understand how difficult it was for her, a hungry child, to believe in a God who would sustain her, both spiritually and physically. That Sanders eventually left Catholicism is not surprising. What is remarkable is that she returned. In all her years of growing up and coming to terms with her life and history, she never lost faith in a God who was looking out for her and had a plan for her.

In those intervening years, Sanders was not in revolt against the institutional church. Rather, for the nearly twenty years she was estranged from it, she was a searcher, trying to find a faith that resonated with her own identity. She was surprised to discover that, despite her differences with church leaders on many issues, she felt most comfortable in a venerable Catholic church in a big city. But now the city was Washington, DC, and its prosperous congregation was largely African American.

Sanders is a tall African American woman in her thirties with long, dark hair, dark bronze skin glowing with health, and a dazzling smile. She has an expressive, musical voice, and she laughs often and heartily.

She communicates a tranquility that seems at odds with her wretched childhood. She discusses that childhood matter-of-factly, and with restraint. Yet in her writing, she describes more fully some of the terrors she experienced. Meeting her, one finds it difficult to believe that such unpromising circumstances should have produced a woman of such poise and peace.

She spent most of her childhood in New York City, living alone with Marguerite Sandoval, her mentally ill mother, a woman who converted to Catholicism at age eighteen, an outlier in an African American family of Baptists. Sanders's experience of Catholicism was part and parcel of her experience growing up with Maggie, a mother whose devotion was linked to mental problems that had grown much worse after her twelve-year-old son, José, was struck and killed by a bus in Philadelphia in 1976.

Her mother was bipolar with borderline personality disorder, Sanders says. From the way she describes her, it appears that her mother exhibited classic symptoms of the disorder—an intense fear of abandonment, the tendency to express unpredictable rage, difficulty with relationships.[3] The bipolar aspect of her disease produced dramatic mood shifts.

Maggie had divorced her first husband, with whom she had four children, including José. She was recovering from her son's death when she met Victor Sanders, a civil engineer in the middle of his own divorce proceedings. She was a secretary, and he met her on the first day of his new job. The relationship didn't last long. Joshunda was the result of their brief time together. Her mother perceived her to be a "miracle" child, Sanders wrote, the child who would replace the one she had lost.[4] Sanders's name *Joshunda* was her mother's attempt to feminize *José*.

Her early home was in Chester, in suburban Philadelphia, but mother and daughter moved to New York City when she was six.[5] Undiagnosed and unmedicated, Maggie couldn't hold a job for long or keep a roof over their heads "We were always moving, getting evicted, living in the shelter, living in a welfare hotel or a halfway house."

Growing up, Sanders did not know her father, and her half-siblings were at least a decade older. So the emotionally frail mother and her young child navigated the streets of New York unsupported. Because her mother moved so often, it was difficult for her older siblings to keep track of them.

"One of the characteristics of bipolar disorder is this fanaticism about faith," Sanders says. She prefers to call her mother "extremely devoted" to Catholicism, "hyperreligious in a lot of ways." Nearly every morning, she would rise at 4:30 a.m. to say the rosary and would try to take her young daughter with her to daily Mass at 7:30 a.m. "Of course, that wasn't sustainable for someone who was manic," Sanders says matter-of-factly.

The God of Sanders's childhood was her mother's God. "The stereotypical white dude in the sky," she says. "This is not a God who looks like us. This is not a personal God." This God was a heavenly taskmaster, watching to see whether you sinned or not.

This God was front and center in the devotional films her mother loved to watch. "I know pretty much all the words to *The Ten Commandments*. I watched it over and over with my mother. Two VHS tapes." Her mother's favorite time of year was Easter, when the airwaves were full of religious movies. "*Jesus of Nazareth* would come on, and *Ben-Hur*. . . . There was nothing that could get her to sit still like one of these stories."

Her mother believed that God rewarded those believers "who are good and obedient." But as a child, that notion didn't seem to make a lot of sense to Sanders. "We're always in church and always saying the rosary, and our lives are still crazy."

God always rode along on her mother's roller-coaster of a life. Her mother believed that God would watch out for them. She would interpret finding a five-dollar bill on the street as "a miracle." Sanders was far more skeptical. "Because I was in a caretaking role as a kid, I was more inclined to be pragmatic about things that she thought or described as miracles." In a city of eight million people, someone dropped some money, she would think to herself, but she went along with the program, happy to pocket the bill and accept her mother's claims of divine intervention.

Sometimes Maggie would cherish her daughter and instill her with the notion that her potential was infinite, her talents limitless. "When she was in euphoria, I experienced a freedom that very few little girls get to experience with their moms. She had no doubts about anything," Sanders says. She believed that she would win the lottery, that they would be famous. "To grow up with a woman who most people would just discount and completely dismiss as being completely and utterly crazy who says, 'You're a genius; you can do anything' is an incredibly powerful experience.

"She's not the most reliable narrator, but that's what God is for," Sanders says. She explains that she's always thought of her intuition as the voice of God, and that inner voice would help her decipher her mother's claims. "God for me has always been like my mom's fact checker.

"To grow up in a way where you just never rule anything out is really wonderful—enchanting spiritually but also artistically," she says. Maggie's absolute faith in what was possible was in stark contrast to a society that set "specific expectations and roles for how women of color should be in the world."

But the downsides were profound. Once or twice a year, Maggie would fly into unpredictable rages and threaten her daughter. Maggie's instability twice prompted the intervention of Child Protective Services. When she was five years old, Sanders spent a year in foster care.

As her daughter grew older and more self-sufficient, Maggie would leave her alone for hours at a time. Maggie also was incapable of managing money. After the death of her son, Maggie received a settlement from the bus company. She squandered it, buying wigs and gambling in Atlantic City, where one of Sanders's half-brothers worked. She also rented a "tiny studio apartment" in a pricey neighborhood near Saint Patrick's. Sanders attended Catholic school for the first time, while the money lasted. She made her First Communion in fifth grade at Saint Catherine of Siena parish on Sixty-Eighth Street.

But even before Sanders could finish out the school year, they were back on the streets, bouncing from homeless shelter to subsidized housing, often in the Bronx. "Because it's a really poor congressional district, there's tons of subsidized housing there."

Early on, Sanders found solace and some stability in school and books. When she was three or four she would sit at the kitchen table and try to parse out the words in the *Philadelphia Inquirer*. She felt her poverty most acutely when book fairs were held at her school. She almost never had the money to buy books. She confesses to stealing books at the Doubleday bookstore in Midtown Manhattan. When she discovered the public library, it was "like hitting the jackpot," she says. "Books for free." She would read everything from the Sweet Valley High series to novels by Judy Blume and humor by Erma Bombeck to lots of self-help books. "It was interesting to think about how to have better self-esteem."

Later on there would be the fiction of Stephen King, Sidney Sheldon, Jackie Collins, and Danielle Steele. But she would also read Alice Walker's *The Color Purple*. And when she was twelve years old, she read *The Autobiography of Malcolm X*.

She found "parallels and intersections" between her own life and that of Malcolm X. When he was "really young," she says, Malcolm X had to both "fend for himself and fight for himself. . . . That really resonated with me." She was impressed that Malcolm X was able to center himself when he found a belief structure. "Finding a home in faith allowed him to transform his life."

Despite the instability of her life, Sanders excelled academically and was valedictorian of her sixth-grade class. In the Bronx she had one teacher who noticed she wasn't dressed properly for winter and gave her some suitable clothes. She also encouraged Sanders to apply to a middle school for high-achieving economically disadvantaged students throughout New York City. She gave her the application and suggested that her mother fill it out.

"Of course that wasn't going to happen," Sanders says. But she filled the form out herself and forged her mother's signature, went through the testing and interview process, and got accepted. She spent seventh and eighth grade at De La Salle Academy, one of fewer than two hundred gifted students selected from across New York City.

The school, then located on Manhattan's Upper West Side, was non-denominational, but it had spiritual underpinnings. Its founder and president, Brother Brian Carty, is a member of a Catholic order, the De La Salle Christian Brothers.[6] Sanders calls it "Catholic-inspired." Classes opened with a prayer, and parents were encouraged to look out for the spiritual development of the students, in whatever faith they practiced.

Up until then, she and her mother had not received much help from fellow Catholics. Sanders believes that their itinerant life made it difficult for them to be noticed long enough for people to offer assistance. "We were just kind of in their community and then gone."

Brother Brian discovered that they were living in a shelter and found them temporary housing closer to the school. He helped with their food expenses. He was fond of her mother, who would visit him. When he was working in the office on weekends, he'd invite Sanders to come over and chat. "That was a blessing," she says.

In some ways, Brother Brian replaced the father who was missing in her life. "Where my parents failed," she wrote, "God sent angels to fill the void." She got support from her older sister, Rita, and Rita's husband. And "when they were out of my immediate vicinity, I leaned on Brother Brian Carty."

She was so close to the towering six-feet, four-inch principal that he allowed her to "mess with" his gray hair. "He told me to keep studying when things at home were crazy." He would encourage her to "keep writing" and would cheer her up by telling jokes. He also let her linger on the weekends in the school library, a place where she discovered James Baldwin and the *New York Times*.[7]

But Brother Brian's powers were limited when it came to a larger intervention in her mother's life. "It wasn't really that kind of relationship," Sanders says, adding that bipolar individuals often "don't respond well to medication or advice that they should be medicated." She also surmises that her mother "was pretty attached to the highs and lows of her experience."

Brother Brian was able to help her "strategize" about "ways to leave the city," by getting into boarding school. He encouraged her in the search that eventually led to a scholarship to attend Emma Willard School, an elite girls' academy in Troy, New York, near Albany. Brother Brian knew the headmistress there and advocated for Sanders. What made the school attractive, she says, was that it was not too far away, so her mother could come and visit, but not so close that she'd just pop in. That was a problem, Sanders says. "She'd just show up places."

But that scholarship offer did not materialize until a year after she left De La Salle Academy. In the interim, she was a freshman at Aquinas High School in the Bronx. It was a very low point in her life. She'd lost De La Salle's supportive environment. She had failed to reach her goal: an escape to boarding school. Her mother was literally absent from her life, leaving their apartment by 7 a.m. and not coming home until dark. Living in poverty, she says, makes you feel unprotected. And the routine absence of her mother, particularly in summer when school was out, reinforced that sense.

Not that her mother was much of a safe harbor when she was home. The rages were getting worse. When she was fourteen, her mother threatened to kill her. She'd made threats before, Sanders says, but this time was different. "Her hands were around my throat, and she was not really present in her body the way that a sane person is."

Fearful, Sanders ran away to her best friend's house. Sander's mother demanded she return and called the police. New York's Child Protective Services got involved, and Sanders faced the stark choice of either leaving home and living in a group home or returning to her mother. Social workers advised her that she couldn't get into boarding school from a group home. Her mentor Brother Brian said that her mother, despite all her flaws, was still her mother and needed her.

So she returned. But during this time of abandonment, and fear, Sanders did something else: She had sex for the first time. "I had this kind of loneliness that always kind of followed me, you know, sort of like a fog. So I sought ways to try and manage that and cope with it or alleviate it." Becoming sexually active, she says, was one way to cope.

Growing up, she says, she had many questions about sexuality. It was a time, in the eighties and nineties, when controversy over AIDS helped propel "an ongoing conversation about sex and sexuality." But that discussion did not extend to her own family. Her mother had never prepared her for sex or discussed how to avoid an unplanned pregnancy.

Sanders kept a journal, using one of her mother's college notebooks for the purpose. It was difficult to hide it. "We didn't have a lot of furniture. I didn't have a dresser drawer. I didn't have a lot of things that I could hide it under, even if I had a dresser." So she kept her journal in her school backpack. And when she was out skating with her boyfriend, her mother discovered it. The journal pages were folded, making them easy to leaf through. It was not hard to find the sections where she discusses sex; they were written in red marker.

Her mother did not react well. She railed that God didn't want this, warned of the risks of teen pregnancy, and accused her daughter of not keeping her promise and lying to her. Early the next morning, a Saturday, she dragged Sanders to her boyfriend's house, confronted the boyfriend and his mother, and read aloud excerpts from the diary, including the account of them having sex on her boyfriend's mother's bed. Then they took the crosstown bus to Planned Parenthood to get a pregnancy test.

In her mind, Sanders was seeing a cascade of worst-case scenarios come to pass. "What could be worse than your mother finding your journal entry and reading it? Oh, I know what could be worse. She could read it aloud to your boyfriend and his mom. . . . What's worse than that is actually being pregnant and needing to figure out what to do. Because if I tell her she'll kill me, and then if I have a baby, then my life is over."

Maggie made quite an impression when she entered the Planned Parenthood office. She stood in the lobby, reciting her rosary very loudly. It was obvious to the entire staff, she says, that "something was not right" with her mother. She clearly was a "fervent Catholic," and yet she'd taken her daughter to Planned Parenthood. They could sense a "disconnect," she says.

When Sanders's pregnancy test was positive, they asked Sanders whether they should tell her mother. "I didn't know it was an option for them not to tell her, and I was like, 'Actually, I would prefer it if you didn't. Since you're asking, please don't, because that would be awful. As you can see . . . the possibilities here are kind of crazy.'"

The next day, Sanders returned for an abortion. It was not a choice she made lightly. "I was so young. And I really was doing the best that I could with what I had. And I didn't have very much. And I couldn't imagine being anchored in a life that was so chaotic and so confusing. Just for me. I mean, I barely wanted to live. Let alone bringing a child into that situation."

And for the first time in her life, there was a real chance for her: By that time, she'd learned that she'd been offered a scholarship to boarding school for the fall. "I felt very deeply guilty, especially because my mother was so faithful and so Catholic," she says. "But I also was really aware that if I was to remain pregnant" there would not have been an exit strategy. "I would have stayed in the Bronx."

But that didn't make the decision easy. "When I went off to boarding school I would celebrate the baby's birthday. I was just really not forgiving of myself . . . in part because I knew it was so central. It was like one of the things you don't do as a Catholic."

As she struggled with the guilt and the pain, she concluded that "this was a sacrifice that I made so that I could be free of my past. . . . You sort of have to pick your shame, right? Especially as a black woman in this culture I feel like there is so much shaming around single mothers. But there's also this shaming around being sexual and having sexuality, expressing your sexuality for whatever reason you do that. And so I felt like, one way or the other, it was going to be shameful. Shameful that I was pregnant in the first place, regardless of how old I was. Shameful because I had a kid and I was just fourteen."

She never told her mother about the abortion. The only ones who knew were her best friend and her boyfriend. The experience taught her the limits of her mother's worldview. Relying solely on faith was not sufficient "to help me cope with the sort of emotional and physical challenges that I had growing up with my mother," she says, "grappling with loneliness and those kinds of things."

Sanders refused to routinely accompany her mother to Sunday mass. "I just decided that I couldn't. . . . I wasn't getting what my mother got from her experience at Mass." She says that she "appreciated" that Mass was the way her mother brought order into their lives, "but I felt like it wasn't enough. I didn't feel like the Virgin Mary could be my mother. I needed a real-life mother. Ditto for God as my Father. Or Jesus as my Savior. . . . That began for me a long wilderness of turning away from the faith," she says.

Having to deal with her mother's vision of Catholicism was particularly difficult because it was a facet of her mental illness. "Part of borderline personality disorder means that you're meshing your personality," she says. Her mother had difficulties perceiving her daughter as separate from her. She "really did feel like we were the same person in some ways." Part of separating from her was refusing to go to weekly Mass with her.

The separation became more complete when Sanders began her sophomore year at Emma, where she spent the last three years of high school. The school traces its academic roots to 1814, when Emma Willard founded a precursor of the Troy facility, the Middlebury Female Seminary. The Troy school is younger; its stone buildings were built in the early twentieth century. Emma is set on 137 acres.[8] The school's imposing stone structures were built in the Jacobean Revival style that makes them look faintly Medieval.[9] The school declares its mission is to foster "in each young woman a love of learning, the habits of an intellectual life, and the character, moral strength, and qualities of leadership to serve and shape her world."[10]

"You're in this beautiful place," Sanders says. "All your needs are taken care of. That was the first time I'd ever experienced that." For the first time, she wrote, she encountered God in nature. "God was evident to me in the bucolic beauty of my new surroundings."[11]

At Emma, her mind was opened to world religions, an experience that "really expanded" her outlook, she says. "Wow, like, it's one God . . . but there are so many different ways to think about what that looks like." She explored Buddhism, Taoism, and Confucianism.

Sanders doesn't believe that she ever doubted the existence of God. "Okay, there is a creator force in the world that is looking out for me." She says the kindness of Brother Brian, her experience at De La Salle, "all those things show me evidence of divine intervention." What she wasn't sure about was how, "if at all, Catholicism fit into" that belief.

For Sanders, one parent was omnipresent, Maggie's spirit almost seeping into her daughter's. Yet her father was not present at all. When she was a junior in high school, her mother casually suggested that her father "would love" to hear from her. The remark was "totally out of the blue," Sanders says. She had spent years wondering about him, whether he was still alive, where he might be. As it turned out, she says, all the time she'd been fantasizing, her father was living nearby, in New Jersey.

Her father had never married her mother, and he was reluctant to meet his child, now a teenager. But Sanders pursued him. She wrote to him; he ignored it. But she was persistent. "I had been told that I was charming like my mom, so I believed I could convince him I was worthy of being his daughter," she wrote.[12] Her persistence paid off. She met him for the first time when he attended her high school graduation.

That summer he took her on a "road trip" to Ohio to meet her grandmother Betty. They also stopped in Niagara Falls, "because he used to work in Upstate New York," she says. She fell in love with Niagara Falls.

He warned her: "Don't stand too close. The water is toxic. There's all kinds of stuff in it. You'll grow another finger."

"Thanks, Dad," she says with a laugh. "He was just very sardonic," adding that one of her therapists thought her father might have had Asperger's syndrome, a psychological disorder characterized by limited social skills and eccentric behavior.[13] Her father, she says, was "pretty reclusive" and "didn't really seem to respect religion." He behaved, Sanders surmises, "like a really high-functioning autistic person."

After Emma, Sanders had settled on Vassar College. It was among the dozen or schools she had applied to. It made sense to go there, she had decided. She had worked in the Emma alumnae office and had noticed how many grads went on to Vassar. And the school, based in Poughkeepsie, was close enough to New York to make it easy to get to the city. Vassar was offering a very healthy scholarship as well.

Her mother and father took her to Vassar. It was the only time she was in a car with both of them, and it was "pretty painful," she recalls. Her father was driving and "blasting" the rapper Big Pun while her mother fumed in the back seat. Her mother complained that the music was too loud, he was driving too fast. He threatened to stop the car and make her walk to Poughkeepsie.

But in its own way the experience gave her comfort. "If I ever had any question about whether or not I was supposed to be born," she says, seeing her parents together quashed those doubts. That two people so fundamentally unsuited to one another got together even for a short-term relationship must have been the work of Providence, she believes. They must have been brought together to ensure her conception.

But if she thought that Vassar would be "the next iteration" of her Emma experience, she was mistaken. "I became really aware of the gap between me and my contemporaries," she says. Emma had been very sheltering, but Vassar presented more obstacles. She faced some financial pressures, trying to work to pay bills that weren't covered by scholarships. She had troubles with her mother showing up on campus and a boyfriend's infidelity. She was even struggling academically.

She'd always done well in her English classes. "I'm able to write, and it loves me back, and it's my thing to do in the world." But as an English major at Vassar, the road had become rocky. "There weren't many black English majors." One black professor advised her to choose another profession.

A white professor refused to believe that she'd written a paper on Shakespeare's *A Midsummer Night's Dream*. He told her he doubted her authorship because "it was significantly better" than anything she'd produced for his class. That was because the previous course work on *Canterbury Tales* and *Beowulf* hadn't inspired her the way Shakespeare did, she says.

So she was skeptical when she started Frank Bergon's class. Bergon's grandparents were Basque, and he wore his hair in a white afro. He was born in Nevada but grew up on a ranch in the San Joaquin Valley. He wrote essays and novels, many of them about Basque Americans in the

West.[14] "He wrote about cowboys," Sanders sniffs. "I felt like we couldn't be more different. . . . What is this old white dude going to teach me about writing?" She usually came late to his class, often hungover. It was a low point for her. "I felt really tired, and I didn't want to try anymore."

Bergon knew that Sanders aspired to be in senior comp, an elective class that permits a few seniors to do a creative-writing project as their thesis. He pulled her aside one day and warned her that she might not make it into the class. "Look," he told her, "I know that's what you want, but you're not going to get there the way that you're going right now." He told her he could advise her on what she needed to do to "get better" but that the choice was hers. Bergon told her she needed to come to class on time and develop a "better attitude."

Sanders's initial reaction was to resist. "I was like, 'Are you kidding me? Gimme a break, dude. Do you know what my life is like? Come on!'

"I had never been in a situation where I behaved that way with a professor before, and I had never been in a situation where I had a professor talk to me like that." But the encounter led her to respect him, and "so I got my act together. He made an effort. I'm going to make an effort." She got into senior comp, earning an A on her thesis. "We stayed friends."

Her participation in a Vassar program tutoring inmates at Green Haven prison also had a good effect. That experience, she says, "helped me put my life in perspective." Writing about the program "put me on the college wires" and led to freelance writing assignments that eventually earned her a journalism fellowship after college.

Her reporting work took her to newspapers in Seattle, San Francisco, and Austin. Sanders found success and stability. God was more elusive. "I was more of a seeker," she says. She met a Santera, a priestess of the faith of the Yoruba people, or Santeria, a religion that originated in Southwest Africa and includes Caribbean and Catholic influences.[15] "I investigated that for a little while," Sanders says.

When she lived in Oakland, she attended a church of Religious Science. "I started reading Ernest Holmes," she says. Holmes founded the Religious Science movement and in 1922 published *The Science of the Mind.* Holmes blended the teachings of religion and philosophy and developed a belief system based on the existence of God present within each individual. [16]

In Austin Sanders was the religion reporter. In Texas, a newcomer often gets asked, "Do you have a home church?" Sanders felt that, as a black woman, she was expected to join a church, but it wasn't easy.

Catholicism permits a worshipper to be quiet and meditate, she says. But "the black church tradition is very loud and extemporaneous and gregarious." When she was a small child, she'd welcomed all that emotion. She was exposed to black services after she'd been temporarily placed in foster care when she was a small child, after her mother had either deliberately or accidentally burned her with a straightening comb. "I screamed bloody murder," she says, leading to the intervention of the authorities.

Her foster mother took her to services at an African American church. "I just remember being so taken by it. I thought it was so fun." Sanders was particularly impressed when some congregants "fainted" because they were overcome by the spirit. She pretended to faint. She was thinking, "Yeah, that's great. Let's just fall out."

The adults were not amused, but she continued to prefer the black religious experience. "Yeah, this is what it should be like. You should be completely bowled over by emotion and your experience." In contrast, Catholicism seemed "so dry." But as a grown adult, the emotive aspect of black faith seemed overwhelming. Worshipping in this fashion, she says, "took a lot out of me."

As a reporter "I did fall quite in love with Judaism." What appealed to her, she says, was that the Jewish tradition allowed for questions "and room for doubt. . . . Judaism is not reliant on you believing in God. It's really just sort of a way of life."

Sanders ultimately stopping going to church on Sundays and deflected the question by saying that as a religion reporter she had to be open to all denominations. Not going to church, she says, may also have been "a way of rebelling against my mom. Because her whole life, the drum she beat relentlessly was, 'You should go to Mass'—specifically, 'You should go to Mass with me. Because I feel lonely when you're not with me, and I see all these other mothers with their daughters.'"

Running, not religion, helped her recover from her father's sudden death. "He would not be in touch for a long time, and then he'd feel guilty, and he'd either call me at the newspaper or e-mail me," she says.

She treasures one e-mail with the subject line "Remorse." The message contained just a few words: "I miss you. Love, Dad."

It was Earth Day in April 2010 when she got a call from someone she didn't know. She had been assigned to cover an Earth Day event in Austin. One of her father's sisters called her and told her, "Your father has passed away," explaining that he had hung himself and they didn't know how long the body had been in the garage before it had been discovered.

Running helped her recover from the "shock" of her father's death, she says. "It became for me a kind of replacement for going to church." The trail she ran on in Austin became her church. "It turns out that running 26.2 miles, and training body and soul to do it, is useful for heartbreak," she wrote. "It does not mend anything, your muscles are all broken, and that becomes the point. Everything is weary and strained and exhausted like your heart."[17]

But running couldn't help her cope with the loss of her mother. She was diagnosed with cervical cancer in September 2011, with the family quickly learning that it was inoperable. Her mother died at the beginning of 2012, "six days before my birthday." In the aftermath of her mother's illness and death, Sanders says, "I quit everything. I quit therapy. I quit newspapers. I just kind of hung out with my dog. I didn't even really run anymore. I was pretty withdrawn."

It took her about a year to find her bearings again. She found a job as a speechwriter in Washington, DC, and moved there at the end of 2013. It was close to Christmas, and she went looking for a church on Christmas Eve. She discovered the Basilica of the National Shrine of the Immaculate Conception. "It's so beautiful, and it's not that far from where I lived."

The church, begun in 1920, was not fully complete until 1959.[18] It's considered a unique structure, with a distinctly American feel, a combination of the Romanesque and Byzantine architectural styles.[19] Marble, mosaics, and stained-glass windows combine to give worshippers a sense of awe.

Christmas Eve Mass was packed; Sanders couldn't get a seat. But her visit sparked a desire for Mass, and the weekend after Christmas she discovered Saint Augustine's, which calls itself the "mother church" of Washington's African American Catholics. The parish was founded before the Civil War by emancipated black Catholics who were not welcome in white Catholic parishes. One of the largest parishes in the city, its diverse congregation includes many upper- and middle-class black Catholics.[20] The Gothic Revival church is an imposing stone building, more than a hundred years old.[21] The church's stained-glass windows depict a brown-skinned Holy Family and saints who are people of color.

"I immediately felt at home there," Sanders says. At the end of the service, Rev. Paul Dressler, who would become one of her favorite priests, welcomed newcomers to the parish. He told them, "There are no orphans in God's family. If you're visiting or you've recently come to the area, we would love it if you became a member."

His welcome, Sanders concedes, was pretty standard fare. "But being a recent adult orphan, I felt like, 'Wow, he's talking to me.' It just sort of all came together." Helping the transition along was the fact that the institutional church also was changing. The year before, the stern Pope Benedict XVI had resigned and was succeeded by the far sunnier Pope Francis. "It seemed like a good time to come back," she says.

But the return to Catholicism was more visceral than intellectual. After her mother's death, Sanders realized that the two of them "didn't really share a lot." A lot of her childhood really was about absence—her mother's absence when she left her alone, their lack of food, money, and stability. She probed her memory. "What did we have? What did we share?" They must have "shared something," she says, "because the grief is immense, and the love is there."

Their experience together was "centered around Mass and church and this place—not really a physical place, sort of a spiritual location. So I felt, 'If I go back to church, I'm sure that I can meet her there.'"

Sanders belongs to Saint Augustine's choir, one of its younger members. On Sundays, you can find her gathered around the altar with the choir, dressed in long white choir robes with African designs on the cuffs and collars. The choir sways rhythmically to the music, accompanied by piano, electric guitar, and drums. The congregation applauds after every hymn. The service is far warmer than an average Catholic service. Sanders often beams as she sings.

She terms herself a "church lady," but she is far from typical. She views her sexual orientation as fluid. Identifying herself as someone open to questioning her sexuality "along a continuum" was not something she felt safe doing when she lived with her mother, she says.

Sanders believes that God does not "form the desires of our heart in order to condemn them as sinful. I think that institutions do that. I think that doctrines do that . . . as a form of control."

Sanders concedes that the institutional church continues to be prescriptive about many ethical issues, offering "very specific rules" about "divorce, adultery, and fornication." There was a time, she says, when such teachings "frustrated" her. But she says she's now more frustrated by how women religious are treated. "Not even necessarily that they can't be priests but more that there is this dismissal of their legacy in the church." The work they do, she says, often is invisible.

For a long time, too, Sanders struggled with the role of women in any church. "What use did God have for women in general, and, specifically, what use did he have for black women?" Peruse most faith literature, she says, and only two women—-and models—stand out: the Virgin Mary and Mary Magdalene. Neither quite fits, she says.

The Virgin gave birth to Jesus, and that won't happen again, she says. And Mary Magdalene is a figure "who is broken, who is healed and forgiven for her brokenness." There is an element of her story that is attractive, she says, and Mary Magdalene played an important role in the Resurrection story, a role she would have loved to have had. She "went to the tomb and discovered it was empty." But those two models were insufficient, she says. "I couldn't figure out what was so great" about being a woman, particularly a black woman.

She found what she was looking for in the writing of Alice Walker. Walker's *In Search of Our Mothers' Gardens: Womanist Prose* defined the term *womanism*. Walker explores and celebrates the role of black women in achieving justice for all who are marginalized. Womanism connects women and faith and a narrative of "justice and fairness" that includes not only gender but also race and class, Sanders says. Womanism helped "inform my identity" and "changed the way I thought about God."

But Sanders is not a full-blown activist, rallying for church reform. "I don't actually have any expectations for the evolution of the church. I view it as a container for my feelings about God and community" and an avenue for being of service to the world beyond writing and volunteering or charity, she says.

"I still have the grief and the sadness and the heaviness of my past, but I also feel that I have the promise of this really wonderful community." Singing in the choir, she says, "is its own prayer and release and unburdening in a lot of ways."

Her return to Catholicism reminds her of a famous scene from the film adaptation of Walker's *The Color Purple*. The novel is set in a small Southern town between 1910 and 1940. Shug Avery, the daughter of a preacher, has become a jazz singer and has long given up the staid ways of her community and her preacher father. She's singing at a "juke" joint down the road from her father's church. She hears the choir sing, and she starts to sing the same hymn and walk toward the church.

"It's a prodigal moment," Sanders says. Shug eventually enters the church and is embraced by her father. "That's pretty much how I felt when I got to Saint Augustine's."

The choir looks out for her, she says. "It's the first time I've been around middle-class and upper-middle-class African Americans, so many of them old enough to be my mom or dad. And they don't let me forget it," she says with a laugh. "So it's a very nurturing place."

When she was a journalist, Sanders wrote about what happens to girls who have unstable childhoods. They often fall into alcoholism, drug addiction, and prostitution. They are victims of sexual abuse and violence. When she considers her own childhood, she sees the hand of God. "I've always had that sense that God is looking out for me."

AFTERWORD

For Our Daughters

I wrote this book for one reason: To learn whether it was possible for a woman to be both a feminist and a Catholic. I did not have a hypothesis. I only knew that in my own life, it was becoming more and more difficult to bridge that divide. My plan, if you can call it that, was to seek out women with Catholic backgrounds, interesting stories, and connections to the church that were, or had been, profound.

From a variety of sources, I found them. Some are women of considerable media fame; others are established scholars; still others are advocates who have taken on the institutional church in very direct and public ways.

Their stories taught me these lessons:

Faith in God and the core values of Catholicism do not depend on unwavering obedience to an institutional church that denies the potential of roughly half of the human race.

Faith is bigger than the clerics who, at best, don't know what to make of women and, at worst, think we are inferior and not deserving of power.

Rebellion can be a very positive position and sometimes one that brings us closer to the dictates of our conscience.

Change in the church is possible, but it will not depend on even a moderately progressive pope, such as Pope Francis, but on a movement driven by the laity.

And, lastly, *Catholic feminist* is not an oxymoron.

That may be some comfort to me personally, but it doesn't solve the problem. The current status of women raises real challenges for the institutional church. Over the last twenty-five years, women have left the church in far greater numbers than they have in the past. In 1987, 52 percent of Catholic women attended weekly Mass, compared to 35 percent of Catholic men. By 2011, however, attendance by Catholic women had fallen sharply, to 31 percent, roughly equal to the attendance of Catholic men.

In 1987, nearly 60 percent of Catholic women ranked their Catholicism among the most important facets of their life. By 2011, only about a third of Catholic women—35 percent—placed that premium on their faith. Catholic men, whose priorities had not changed much over the same period, actually slightly outranked Catholic women on this indicator of commitment.[1]

An equally telling statistic is the number of the traditional Catholic church weddings. In 1965 there were more than 355,000 such weddings; by 2014 that number had dropped by nearly 60 percent. "Catholics are more often choosing civil ceremonies at country clubs, the beach, or other sites," writes Georgetown University researcher Mark M. Gray.[2] Gray added that fewer Catholics are marrying to begin with. Nevertheless, since women typically drive wedding planning, that statistic also hints at young women's declining interest in Catholicism.

Most of the women I interviewed have kept their ties to the church, some more formally than others. But what of their daughters? They have not. In all, five of the six adult daughters of the women I profiled no longer are practicing Catholics. As mothers, we understand. As Gretchen Reydams-Schils put it, "Some days I'm sad." But other days, she says, "I'm sorry. I just couldn't put that burden on them."

But what does that mean for the institutional church? Yes, there will be women Catholics, but the women who remain are more likely to be singing from the same hymnbook as conservative church leaders, more likely to accept authority, more accepting of second-class status in the church, less motivated to challenge the institution to do better, to *be* better.

A church that loses our daughters will be much poorer, denied their intelligence, their passion, their values, and their commitment to social justice, equity, and fairness.

If that happens, the institutional church will never fulfill its promise.

So I dedicate this book not only to my own nonpracticing daughter but to all our daughters with this hope: Don't give up on Catholicism just yet. Make it work for you. Fight for it. Faith is a gift, even when it is wrapped inside a box marked, *For men only*.

RESOURCES

In writing this book I met people and learned about organizations and media outlets that readers might find helpful. They include the following:

Call To Action "educates, inspires, and activates Catholics to act for justice and build inclusive communities through a lens of antiracism and antioppression principles." Its primary issues are justice for church workers, lay engagement, LGBT justice, racial justice, and women and girls' equality. Call To Action has chapters in many states and holds an annual conference for members. It also offers online courses and webinars on church reform and other issues. http://cta-usa.org/.

Catholics for Choice serves "as a voice for Catholics who believe that the Catholic tradition supports a woman's moral and legal right to follow her conscience in matters of sexuality and reproductive health." It publishes *Conscience*, a news journal of Catholic opinion. http://www.catholicsforchoice.org/.

DignityUSA "works for respect and justice for people of all sexual orientations, genders, and gender identities—especially gay, lesbian, bisexual, and transgender persons—in the Catholic Church and the world through education, advocacy, and support." A national organization with chapters throughout the country, Dignity holds periodic regional meetings and biennial national conventions. https://www.dignityusa.org/.

Fortunate Families "serves as a resource and networking ministry with Catholic parents of lesbian, gay, bisexual, and transgender children." https://fortunatefamilies.com/.

Interfaith Voices is a radio program carried by many public radio stations throughout the country. It is hosted by Maureen Fiedler, a progressive woman religious, and features topical discussions on faith and ethics. http://www.interfaithradio.org/.

National Catholic Reporter is an excellent source of news about the church and the Vatican. It also offers a biweekly newspaper to paid subscribers. http://ncronline.org/.

NETWORK is a Catholic social-justice lobby that advocates for federal policies benefitting the poor and marginalized and promoting human rights and equality. http://www.Networklobby.org.

Saint Augustine's Catholic Church is the mother church of African American Catholics in Washington, DC. It also is one of the most welcoming churches I have ever attended. Its congregation is racially diverse, and its gospel choir has performed for the White House. http://saintaugustine-dc.org/.

SNAP—the Survivors Network of those Abused by Priests, is the world's oldest and largest support group for clergy-abuse victims. SNAP was founded in 1988 and has more than twenty-two thousand members. SNAP is a volunteer self-help organization whose mission is to protect the vulnerable and heal the wounded. http://snapnetwork.org.

WATER—Women's Alliance for Theology, Ethics, and Ritual describes itself as a "global network, an educational and spiritual space, a center for dialogue on feminism, faith, and justice." It "seeks to connect activists, religious leaders, students, scholars, and allies who are using feminist religious values to create social change." It offers monthly rituals and hosts retreats and lectures. Many events can be attended remotely. http://www.waterwomensalliance.org/.

Women's Ordination Conference advocates for the full equality of women in the institutional church, including the deaconate, priesthood, and higher church offices. It holds national conferences. http://www.womensordination.org/.

NOTES

1. INTRODUCTION

1. Margaret Harvey, "Discrimination in the Church," *The Way: Contemporary Christian Spirituality* 3, no. 1, (January 1976): 48.

2. Rachel Donadio and Nicholas Kulish, "A Statement Rocks Rome, Then Sends Shockwaves around the World," *New York Times*, February 12, 2013, http://www.nytimes.com/2013/02/12/world/europe/pope-benedict-xvi-says-he-will-retire.html?ref=topics.

3. Joshua J. McElwee, "Cardinals Elect Pope Francis, Argentinean Jesuit Jorge Mario Bergoglio," *National Catholic Reporter*, March 13, 2013, http://ncronline.org/news/vatican/cardinals-elect-pope-francis-argentinean-jesuit-jorge-mario-bergoglio.

4. Cindy Wooden, Catholic News Service, "Church Needs Women's Voices, Input, Experiences, Pope Tells Religious," *National Catholic Reporter*, May 18, 2015, http://ncronline.org/blogs/francis-chronicles/church-needs-womens-voices-input-experiences-pope-tells-religious.

5. Ines San Martin, "Pope Calls for Female Empowerment, But Not at the Expense of Their Family Role," Crux, February 7, 2015, http://www.cruxnow.com/church/2015/02/07/pope-calls-for-female-empowerment-but-not-at-the-expense-of-their-family-role/.

6. "2014–2015 Synods of Bishops on the Family," United States Conference of Catholic Bishops, accessed December 1, 2015, http://www.usccb.org/issues-and-action/marriage-and-family/2014-2015-synods-of-bishops-on-the-family.cfm#basic.

7. Pope Francis, "Amoris Laetitia," April 8, 2016, accessed April 9, 2016, 190, http://w2.vatican.va/content/francesco/en/apost_exhortations/documents/papa-francesco_esortazione-ap_20160319_amoris-laetitia.html.

8. Ibid., 44.

9. Ibid., 153.

10. Ibid., 154.

11. Ibid., 154.

12. Joshua J. McElwee, "US Sister-Auditor: Synod Shows Cultural Divide between Bishops, Laypeople," *National Catholic Reporter*, October 19, 2015, http://ncronline.org/news/vatican/us-sister-auditor-synod-shows-cultural-divide-between-bishops-laypeople.

13. Wilson Andrews and Thomas Kaplan, "Where the Candidates Stand on 2016's Biggest Issues," *New York Times*, December 15, 2015, http://www.nytimes.com/interactive/2016/us/elections/candidates-on-the-issues.html.

14. "What is Dignity?" DignityUSA website, accessed March 26, 2016, https://www.dignityusa.org/article/what-dignity.

15. John W. O'Malley, "The Style of Vatican II, *America Magazine* (February 24, 2003), http://americamagazine.org/issue/423/article/style-vatican-ii.

16. "Vatican II, an Extraordinary Moment in the Church," *Fairfield County Catholic*, October 11, 2012, http://www.bridgeportdiocese.com/index.php/fcc/article/vatican_ii_an_extraordinary_moment_in_the_church.

17. "The Jews and Vatican II," *America Magazine* (November 30, 1963), http://americamagazine.org/issue/100/jews-and-vatican-ii.

18. O'Malley, "Style of Vatican II."

19. Sidney Callahan, foreword to *Turning Point: The Inside Story of the Papal Birth Control Commission*, by Robert McClory (New York: Crossroad Publishing Company, 1995), viii–ix.

20. Pope Paul VI, *Humanae Vitae*, July 25, 1968, 8, http://w2.vatican.va/content/paul-vi/en/encyclicals/documents/hf_p-vi_enc_25071968_humanae-vitae.html.

21. Richard A. McCormick, "*Humanae Vitae* 25 Years Later," *America Magazine* (July 17, 1993), http://americamagazine.org/issue/100/humanae-vitae-25-years-later.

22. "Do You Hear the Cry of the Poor? Liberation Theology Today: A U.S. Catholic Interview with Michael Lee," *U.S. Catholic* 75, no. 3 (March 10, 2010): 18–21, http://www.uscatholic.org/culture/social-justice/2010/01/do-you-hear-cry-poor-liberation-theology-today.

23. "John Paul II, The Millennial Pope," interview with Roberto Suro, PBS *Frontline*, September 1999, http://www.pbs.org/wgbh/pages/frontline/shows/pope/interviews/suro.html.

24. Jim Yardley and Simon Romero, "Pope's Focus on Poor Revives Scorned Theology," *New York Times*, May 23, 2015, http://www.nytimes.com/2015/05/24/world/europe/popes-focus-on-poor-revives-scorned-theology.html.

25. Alice Walker, *In Search of Our Mothers' Gardens: Womanist Prose* (New York: Open Road Media, 2011), 81–82.

26. Maureen Fiedler and Linda Rabben, eds., *Rome Has Spoken: A Guide to Forgotten Papal Statements and How They Changed through the Centuries* (New York: Crossroad Publishing Company, 1998), 24.

2. MY STORY

1. Mary McCarthy, *Memories of a Catholic Girlhood*, 4th ed. (New York: Vintage Books, 2004), 21.

2. Mary Jo Lamphear, "Mercy Complex Designated Brighton Landmark," *Historic Brighton News* 3, no. 1 (Summer 2002): 2–4, http://www.historicbrighton.org/newsletters/HBNsummer2002.pdf.

3. Carol Morello and Ted Mellnik, "Washington: A World Apart," *Washington Post*, November 9, 2013, http://www.washingtonpost.com/sf/local/2013/11/09/washington-a-world-apart/.

4. "Arlington Diocese to Allow Altar Girls," *Connection Newspapers*, March 28, 2006, http://www.connectionnewspapers.com/news/2006/mar/28/arlington-diocese-to-allow-altar-girls/.

5. Michelle Boorstein, "Arlington Diocese Parishioners Question Need for Fidelity Oath," *Washington Post*, July 11, 2012, http://www.washingtonpost.com/local/sunday-school-teachers-balk-at-oath-agreeing-to-all-church-teachings/2012/07/11/gJQAcAvGeW_story.html.

6. "The True Story of the Inquisition," Institute of Catholic Culture, accessed August 29, 2015, http://www.instituteofcatholicculture.org/the-true-story-of-the-inquisition/.

7. Michael Lee Pope, "Birth-Control Center Finds Home in T.C.," *Alexandria Gazette Packet*, 1, 8, March 11, 2010, http://connectionarchives.com/PDF/2010/031010/Alexandria.pdf.

8. Tim Spector, "What Twins Reveal about the Science of Faith," *Popular Science*, August 8, 2013, http://www.popsci.com/science/article/2013-08/what-twins-reveal-about-god-gene.

9. Madeleine Blais, *The Heart Is an Instrument: Portraits in Journalism* (Amherst: The University of Massachusetts Press, 1992), 341.

3. FRANCES KISSLING

1. This and other direct quotations throughout the book, unless otherwise attributed, are from personal interviews with the author.

2. "History," The New School, accessed January 4, 2016, http://www.newschool.edu/about/history/.

3. Richard Perez-Pena, "'70 Abortion Law: New York Said Yes, Stunning the Nation," *New York Times*, April 9, 2000, http://www.nytimes.com/2000/04/09/nyregion/70-abortion-law-new-york-said-yes-stunning-the-nation.html.

4. Ellen Goodman, "The Endless Game of Family Planning Ping-Pong," *Boston Globe*, January 30, 2009, A-17, http://www.boston.com/bostonglobe/editorial_opinion/oped/articles/2009/01/30/the_endless_game_of_family_planning_ping_pong/.

5. Recounted in Patricia Miller, *Good Catholics: The Battle Over Abortion in the Catholic Church* (Berkeley: University of California Press, 2014), 110–11.

6. Frances Kissling, "Ending the Abortion War: A Modest Proposal," *Christian Century* 107, no. 6 (February 21, 1990): 180–84, archived text available online at http://www.catholicsforchoice.org/news/op-eds/1990s/19900221endingtheabortionwaramodestproposal.asp.

7. Frances Kissling, "The Place for Individual Conscience," *Journal of Medical Ethics* 21, issue supplement 2 (October 2001), http://jme.bmj.com/content/27/suppl_2/ii24.full.

8. Patricia Lefevere, "Vatican Revokes UNICEF Gift in Reproductive Rights Dispute," *National Catholic Reporter*, November 22, 1996, http://natcath.org/NCR_Online/archives2/1996d/112296/112296g.htm.

9. Frances Kissling, "Church and State at the United Nations," *USA Today*, November 1, 2001, http://www.catholicsforchoice.org/news/op-eds/2001/22011101churchandstateattheun.asp.

10. David Burke, "After 25 Years, a Catholic Warrior Steps Aside," Religion News Service, February 22, 2007, http://www.catholicsforchoice.org/news/inthenews/After25YearsaCatholicWarriorStepsAside.asp.

11. Ann Friedman, "A Pain, and Proud of It: Frances Kissling Retires after 25 Years at CFFC," *In These Times* (March 23, 2007), http://inthesetimes.com/article/3088/a_pain_and_proud_of_it.

4. SHARON MacISAAC McKENNA

1. Emma Green, "Sisters of Sion: The Nuns Who Opened Their Doors for Europe's Jews," *The Atlantic* (October 11, 2012), http://www.theatlantic.com/international/archive/2012/10/sisters-of-sion-the-nuns-who-opened-their-doors-for-europes-jews/263525/.

2. Pope Paul VI, *Declaration of the Relationship of the Church to Non-Christian Religions*, October 28, 1965, http://www.vatican.va/archive/hist_councils/ii_vatican_council/documents/vat-ii_decl_19651028_nostra-aetate_en.html.

3. Grant Goodbrand, *Therafields: The Rise and Fall of Lea Hindley-Smith's Psychoanalytic Commune* (Toronto: ECW Press, 2010), 1.

4. Lindsay Scotton, "Therafields Is for Sale," *Toronto Star*, October 16, 1982, F1.

5. Goodbrand, Therafields, 71.

6. United Press International, "Commune Seen Replacing Parish," *Washington Post*, September 15, 1970, A10.

7. "Frequently Requested Church Statistics," Center for Applied Research in the Apostolate, Georgetown University, accessed April 12, 2014, http://cara.georgetown.edu/caraservices/requestedchurchstats.html.

8. Sharon MacIsaac McKenna, "The History of CTP," January 1996, http://ctp.net/PDFs/History.pdf.

9. Pope Paul VI, *Declaration of the Relationship of the Church* .

10. Pope Paul VI, *Declaration on Religious Freedom*, December 7, 1965, http://www.vatican.va/archive/hist_councils/ii_vatican_council/documents/vat-ii_decl_19651207_dignitatis-humanae_en.html.

11. Goodbrand, *Therafields*, 247–49.

12. Ibid., 65.

13. Ibid., 199.

14. Michael McAteer, "A Catholic 'Maverick' Decides to Move On," *Toronto Star*, May 10, 1986, L10.

5. SISTER SIMONE CAMPBELL

1. Sister Simone Campbell, *A Nun on the Bus: How All of Us Can Create Hope, Change, and Community*, with David Gibson, Kindle edition (New York: HarperCollins ebooks, 2014), 26–27.

2. Mary Daly, *The Church and the Second Sex*, 3rd ed. (Boston: Beacon Press, 1985), 9.

3. Edward Maron, "An Interview with Mary Daly," *U.S. Catholic* 34, no. 5 (September 1968): 21, http://www.uscatholic.org/articles/201309/mary-daly-and-second-sex-27774.

4. Margalit Fox, "Mary Daly, a Leader in Feminist Theology, Dies at 81," *New York Times*, January 6, 2010, http://www.nytimes.com/2010/01/07/education/07daly.html?_r=0.

5. "History," NETWORK website, accessed August 25, 2105, http://www.networklobby.org/about-us/history.

6. "Congregation for the Doctrine of the Faith," Vatican website, accessed October 24, 2015, http://www.vatican.va/roman_curia/congregations/cfaith/documents/rc_con_cfaith_pro_14071997_en.html.

7. "About LCWR," Leadership Conference of Women Religious, accessed July 4, 2015, https://lcwr.org/about.

8. "Doctrinal Assessment of the Leadership Conference of Women Religious," Congregation for the Doctrine of the Faith, April 18, 2012, http://www.vatican.va/roman_curia/congregations/cfaith/documents/rc_con_cfaith_doc_20120418_assessment-lcwr_en.html.

9. Laurie Goodstein, "Vatican Reprimands a Group of U.S. Nuns and Plans Changes," *New York Times*, April 18, 2012, http://www.nytimes.com/2012/04/19/us/vatican-reprimands-us-nuns-group.html?_r=0.

10. Eyder Peralta, "Sister Simone Campbell: Vatican Reprimand 'Like a Sock in the Stomach,'" *The Two-Way*, NPR, April 19, 2012, http://www.npr.org/sections/thetwo-way/2012/04/19/150986066/sister-simone-campbell-vatican-reprimand-like-a-sock-in-the-stomach.

11. Dennis Coday, "Thousands of Nuns Support Health Care Reform," *National Catholic Reporter*, March 17, 2010, http://ncronline.org/blogs/ncr-today/thousands-catholic-sisters-support-health-care-reform.

12. Ibid.

13. "Vatican Criticizes Nuns' Stance on Social Issues," interview with Melissa Block, *All Things Considered*, NPR, April 19, 2012, http://www.npr.org/2012/04/19/150984872/vatican-criticizes-nuns-stance-on-social-issues.

14. Campbell, *Nun on the Bus*, preface.

15. Simone Campbell, "We 'Nuns on the Bus' Don't Like Paul Ryan's Idea of Catholic Values," *Guardian*, September 28, 2012, http://www.theguardian.com/commentisfree/2012/sep/28/nuns-on-the-bus-paul-ryan-catholic.

16. Rosalind S. Helderman, "House Approves Ryan Budget Plan to Cut Spending, Taxes," *Washington Post*, March 29, 2012. http://www.washingtonpost.com/blogs/2chambers/post/house-approves-ryan-budget-plan-to-cut-spending-taxes/2012/03/29/gIQAdUXQjS_blog.html.

17. Michael Sean Winters, "USCCB Tackles Paul Ryan," *National Catholic Reporter*, April 18, 2012, http://ncronline.org/blogs/distinctly-catholic/usccb-tackles-paul-ryan.

18. Archbishop William E. Lori, "Opening Remarks for Domestic Religious Freedom," United States Conference of Catholic Bishops, June 13, 2012, http://www.usccb.org/issues-and-action/religious-liberty/opening-remarks-for-domestic-religious-freedom.cfm.

19. Laurie Goodstein, "Nuns, Rebuked by Rome, Plan Road Trip to Spotlight Social Issues," *New York Times*, June 5, 2012, http://www.nytimes.com/2012/06/06/us/us-nuns-bus-tour-to-spotlight-social-issues.html?_r=1.

20. "History of the United Methodist Building," The General Board of Church and Society, accessed August 29, 2014, http://umc-gbcs.org/about-us/the-united-methodist-building#historic.

21. David Gibson, Religion News Service, "New 'Nuns on the Bus' Tour to Highlight Pope Francis' US visit and Agenda," *Washington Post*, August 26, 2015, http://www.washingtonpost.com/national/religion/new-nuns-on-the-bus-tour-to-highlight-pope-francis-us-visit-and-agenda/2015/08/26/116628de-4c0d-11e5-80c2-106ea7fb80d4_story.html.

22. Cathy Lynn Grossman, "Pope Francis to Keep Vatican Reins Tight on U.S. Nuns," *USA Today*, April 15, 2013, http://www.usatoday.com/story/news/world/2013/04/15/pope-francis-nuns-sisters-lcwr-vatican/2084617/.

23. Sister Simone Campbell, "Finally, Affirmation for Nuns," *Time*, April 17, 2015, http://time.com/3825914/sister-simone-campbell-finally-affirmation-for-nuns/.

24. Campbell, *Nun on the Bus*, 8.

25. Richard Lee Colvin, "Idealistic Lay Group Is Legacy of Nuns' Split with Church in 1970," *Los Angeles Times*, April 3, 1993, http://articles.latimes.com/1993-04-03/local/me-18589_1_immaculate-heart-community.

26. Campbell, *Nun on the Bus*, 12.

27. Ibid., 14.

28. Teresa Watanabe, "Sisters Still Standing Up; Speaking Out," *Los Angeles Times*, November 16, 2002, http://articles.latimes.com/2002/nov/16/local/me-relignuns16.

29. Sisters of Social Service, "Celebrating 85 Years in California," *Social Impact* (Fall 2011), http://www.sistersofsocialservice.com/userfiles/File/Fall_2011_Social_Impact_Newsletter.pdf.

30. Sisters of Social Service, "Sisters of Social Service Celebrate 85th Anniversary," press release, November 21, 2011, http://www.sistersofsocialservice.com/userfiles/file/Celebrating85Years-LA..pdf.

31. Carolos Castaneda, "Bay Area Marks 25 Years since Loma Prieta Earthquake: Watch Coverage from 1989," CBS San Francisco, October 15, 2014,

http://sanfrancisco.cbslocal.com/2014/10/15/bay-area-marks-25-years-since-loma-prieta-earthquake-watch-coverage-from-1989/.

32. Sister Simone Campbell, "2014 Ware Lecture," Unitarian Universalist Association, accessed July 3, 2015, http://www.uua.org/economic/ga/295423.shtml.

33. Campbell, *Nun on the Bus*, 110.

34. Ibid., 108–9.

6. MARIANNE DUDDY-BURKE

1. Marianne Duddy-Burke, "15 Years in the Lives of a Catholic Lesbian Couple," op-ed, *Huffington Post*, September 19, 2013, http://www.huffingtonpost.com/marianne-t-duddyburke/15-years-in-the-lives-of-a-catholic-lesbian-couple_b_3935903.html.

2. "About Our Parish," Saint Bartholomew's Church, accessed July 4, 2014, http://www.stbartseb.com/about.html.

3. "School History," Mount Saint Mary's Academy, accessed October 3, 2015, http://www.mountsaintmary.org/page.cfm?p=362.

4. Wellesley College, *1978–1979 Bulletin of Wellesley College* 68, no. 1 (1978): 10, http://repository.wellesley.edu/cgi/viewcontent.cgi?article=1076&context=catalogs.

5. Heather Stevenson and Kiki Zeldes, "Write a Chapter and Change the World: How the Boston Women's Health Book Collective Transformed Women's Health Then—and Now," abstract, *American Journal of Public Health* 98, no. 10 (October 2008), http://www.ncbi.nlm.nih.gov/pmc/articles/PMC2636468/.

6. Sarah Warn, "Cris Williamson's 'The Changer and The Changed,'" AfterEllen.com, May 5, 2005, http://www.afterellen.com/back-in-the-day-cris-williamsons-the-changer-and-the-changed/05/2005/.

7. Sharon Henderson Callahan, "Shifting Images of Church Invite New Leadership Frames," *Journal of Religious Leadership* 1, no. 1, (Spring 2002): 55–64, http://arl-jrl.org/Volumes/CallahanSP02.pdf.

8. Alan Sipress, "Catholic Gays Claim Diocese Ignores Them," *Boston Globe*, August 29, 1982, 21.

9. Jaweed Kaleem, "Roman Missal Changes to Mass Rejected by Majority of Catholic Priests, Survey Shows," *Huffington Post*, April 8, 2014, http://www.huffingtonpost.com/2014/04/08/roman-missal-mass-survey_n_5114138.html.

7. DIANA L. HAYES

1. Rachel L. Swarns, "272 Slaves Were Sold to Save Georgetown. What Does It Owe Their Descendants?" *New York Times*, April 16, 2016.

2. Acts 9:1–9 (New American Bible, Revised Edition).

3. Diana L. Hayes, "Church and Culture: A Black Catholic Womanist Perspective," in *The Labor of God: An Ignatian View of Church and Culture*, edited by William J. O'Brien, 71–72 (Washington: Georgetown University Press, 1991), https://repository.library.georgetown.edu/bitstream/handle/10822/551473/labor-of-god_1.pdf?sequence=4&isAllowed=y.

4. Diana L. Hayes, *Standing in the Shoes My Mother Made: A Womanist Theology* (Minneapolis: Fortress Press, 2011), 3.

5. Diana L. Hayes, "Doorway to Conversion and Theology," *National Catholic Reporter*, October 4, 2002, http://www.natcath.org/NCR_Online/archives/100402/100402h.htm.

6. "Buffalo Remembers Infamous Blizzard of '77," *USA Today*, June 1, 2002, http://usatoday30.usatoday.com/weather/wbufbliz.htm.

7. "1978: The Year of the Three Popes," EWTN, Global Catholic Network, accessed February 21, 2015, https://www.ewtn.com/jp2/papal3/1978.htm.

8. Anne Neville, "Buffalo Native, Now Renowned Theologian, Will Give First Women Wisdom Lecture," *Buffalo News*, April 26, 2014, http://www.buffalonews.com/life-arts/religion/buffalo-native-now-renowned-theologian-will-give-first-women-wisdom-lecture-20140426.

9. Diana L. Hayes, *Trouble Don't Last Always: Soul Prayers* (Collegeville, MN: The Liturgical Press, 1995), 5.

10. Hayes, "Doorway to Conversion."

11. Hayes, *Standing in the Shoes*, 9.

12. Hayes, "Doorway to Conversion."

13. Hayes, *Trouble*, 6.

14. Genesis 16:1–16 (NAB).

15. Genesis 21:1–21 (NAB).

16. Diana L. Hayes, *Hagar's Daughters: Womanist Ways of Being in the World* (Mahwah, NJ: Paulist Press, 1995), 6.

8. TERESA DELGADO

1. Teresa Delgado, "Colgate Love Stories: Pascal Kabemba '85 and Teresa Delgado '88," Colgate University, accessed August 21, 2015, http://news.colgate.edu/scene/2015/02/colgate-love-stories-4.html.

2. "Mission and Vision," Union Theological Seminary, accessed August 31, 2015, https://utsnyc.edu/about/mission-vision/.

3. "How Does Union Change the World?" Union Theological Seminary, accessed August 31, 2015, https://utsnyc.edu/about/.

4. R. Sam Garrett, "The Political Status of Puerto Rico," Congressional Research Service, June 7, 2011, https://www.fas.org/sgp/crs/row/RL32933.pdf.

5. Teresa Delgado, "This Is My Body . . . Given for You: Theological Anthropology *Latina/Mente*," in *Frontiers in Catholic Feminist Theology: Shoulder to Shoulder*, edited by Susan Abraham and Elena Procario-Foley (Minneapolis: Fortress Press, 2009), 40.

6. Associated Press, "Pope Approves Martyrdom Declaration for Oscar Romero, Slain Salvadoran Archbishop," *New York Times*, February 3, 2015. http://www.nytimes.com/aponline/2015/02/03/world/europe/ap-eu-rel-vatican-romero.html?_r=0.

7. Delgado, "This Is My Body," 40.

8. Teresa Delgado, letter to the editor, *The Ionian*, April 2, 2014, http://www.ioniannews.com/opinion/letters_to_editor/article_5069004e-ba76-11e3-89a2-0017a43b2370.html.

9. Ibid.

10. Teresa Delgado, "'Dead in the Water . . . Again': Life, Liberty, and the Pursuit of Happiness in the Twenty-First Century," in *Theological Perspectives for Life, Liberty, and the Pursuit of Happiness*," edited by Ada Maria Isasi-Diaz et al. (New York: Palgrave MacMillan, 2013), 63.

11. Ibid., 65.

12. Ibid., 67.

9. BARBARA BLAINE

1. "Jesuit Tradition and Mission," Saint Louis University website, accessed May 23, 2015, http://www.slu.edu/x844.xml.

2. "Survivor of Sexual Abuse Inspires Others to Speak Up," StoryCorps series, WBEZ radio, August 1, 2014, http://www.wbez.org/series/storycorps/survivor-sexual-abuse-inspires-others-speak-110590.

3. Bill Frogameni, "Toledo Native Barbara Blaine Crusades against Sexual Abuse in the Catholic Church," *Toledo City Paper*, April 29, 2004, http://www.bishop-accountability.org/news2004_01_06/2004_04_29_Frogameni_ToledoNative.htm.

4. Robin Erb, "Bishop Offers Abuse Apology; Blair Cites Victims' Suffering from Acts of Ex-priest," *Toledo Blade*, March 14, 2005, A1, archived online

at http://www.toledoblade.com/Religion/2005/03/14/Bishop-offers-abuse-apology.html.

5. Zoe Ryan, "Vatican Moved Quickly to Punish Gumbleton," *National Catholic Reporter*, November 5, 2011, http://ncronline.org/news/accountability/vatican-moved-quickly-punish-gumbleton.

6. Madeleine Baran, "Betrayed by Silence: An MPR Radio Documentary," Minnesota Public Radio, July 14, 2014, http://minnesota.publicradio.org/collections/catholic-church/betrayed-by-silence/documentary/.

7. "2002 Women of the Year," *Ms. Magazine* (Winter 2002), http://www.msmagazine.com/dec02/womenoftheyear.asp.

8. "Ms. 2002 Women of the Year Awards Ceremony," *Ms. Magazine* (Winter 2002), http://www.msmagazine.com/dec02/woty_roundup.asp.

10. GRETCHEN REYDAMS-SCHILS

1. Paul D. Newpower, M. M., and Stephen T. DeMott, M.M., "The Pope in Central America: What Did His Trip Accomplish?" *St. Anthony Messenger* (June 1983), http://www.americancatholic.org/Features/JohnPaulII/3-CentralAmerica-1983.asp.

2. "John Paul II, The Millennial Pope," interview with Roberto Suro, PBS *Frontline*, September 1999, http://www.pbs.org/wgbh/pages/frontline/shows/pope/interviews/suro.html.

3. "This Is Notre Dame, 2015–16," University of Notre Dame website, accessed January 21, 2016, https://www.nd.edu/assets/docs/this-is-notre-dame-2015-16.pdf.

4. Charles Rice, "Right to Life," *Observer*, September 13, 1974, 6, http://www.archives.nd.edu/Observer/1974-09-13_v09_012.pdf.

5. Arthur Jones, "Death of Notre Dame's Hesburgh Closes an Era," *National Catholic Reporter*, February 27, 2015, http://ncronline.org/news/death-notre-dames-hesburgh-closes-era.

6. "1973–1976: Founding a Civil Rights Center," The Center for Civil and Human Rights, accessed August 1, 2015, http://humanrights.nd.edu/the-center/history/founding-a-civil-rights-center/.

7. "A Plan of God," Focolare Movement, accessed August 1, 2015, http://www.focolare.org/en/movimento-dei-focolari/progetto/.

8. The Catholic University of Leuven is the Dutch-speaking institution. The Catholic University of Louvain is the French-speaking institution.

9. Mario Cuomo, "Religious Belief and Public Morality: A Catholic Governor's Perspective," lecture delivered September 13, 1984, University of Notre Dame Archives, http://archives.nd.edu/research/texts/cuomo.htm.

10. E. J. Dionne, "Religion's Reach and the Tide of Change," *Notre Dame Magazine* (Summer 2008), http://magazine.nd.edu/news/1189-religion-s-reach-and-the-tide-of-change/.

11. Associated Press, "Mario Cuomo Won No Friends," September 14, 1984, LexisNexis.

12. Dirk Johnson, "Invitation to Obama Stirs Up Notre Dame," *New York Times*, April 5, 2009, http://www.nytimes.com/2009/04/06/us/06notredame.html.

13. Michael D. Shear, "Obama Addresses Abortion Protests in Commencement Speech at Notre Dame," *Washington Post*, May 18, 2009, http://www.washingtonpost.com/wp-dyn/content/article/2009/05/17/AR2009051701622.html.

14. Michael Archbold "Special Report: A Decade after Bishops' Policy, Catholic Commencement Scandals Make Sudden Return," Cardinal Newman Society, May 7, 2014, http://www.cardinalnewmansociety.org/CatholicEducationDaily/DetailsPage/tabid/102/ArticleID/3255/SPECIAL-REPORT-A-Decade-after-Bishops%E2%80%99-Policy-Catholic-Commencement-Scandals-Make-Sudden-Return.aspx.

15. "Letters about the Obama Visit," *Notre Dame Magazine* (Summer 2009), http://magazine.nd.edu/news/11845-letters-about-the-obama-visit/.

16. Emma Green, "Notre Dame's Moral Dilemma over Birth Control," *The Atlantic* (January 7, 2014), http://www.theatlantic.com/national/archive/2014/01/notre-dame-s-moral-dilemma-over-birth-control/282864/.

17. Benjamin Rossi and Kathryn Pogin, "Letter of Inquiry and Petition for Action: Students Take On Notre Dame over the Birth Control Benefit," RH Reality Check website, September 6, 2012, http://rhrealitycheck.org/article/2012/09/06/letter-inquiry-petition-action-why-exactly-does-university-notre-dame-oppose-cont/.

18. Margaret Fosmoe, "Notre Dame Faculty Members Demand Apology from Jenky," April 24, 2012, http://articles.southbendtribune.com/2012-04-24/news/31395577_1_peoria-bishop-catholic-newman-centers-auxiliary-bishop.

19. Margaret Fosmoe, "Notre Dame, Saint Mary's Extend Benefits to Same-Sex Spouses," *South Bend Tribune*, October 9, 2014, http://www.southbendtribune.com/news/notre-dame-saint-mary-s-extend-benefits-to-same-sex/article_63d706f6-4fbf-11e4-a9d8-001a4bcf6878.html.

20. Gretchen Reydams-Schils, "The Dignity of Women," University of Notre Dame, Forum on Gender Issues in the Classroom, 2008, http://www3.nd.edu/~adinega/WAL/WAL.teachingforum.html.

21. Gretchen J. Reydams-Schils, *An Anthology of Snakebites: On Women, Love, and Philosophy* (New York: Seven Bridges Press, 2001), x.

22. Ibid., 10.

23. Ibid., 12–13, emphasis original.

24. Ibid., 35.

25. Ibid., 50.

26. Reydams Schils, "Dignity of Women."

27. Gretchen Reydams-Schils, letter to the editor, *Commonweal* (February 24, 2012), Lexis-Nexis.

11. JOSHUNDA SANDERS

1. Joshunda Victoria Sanders, "Seducing God," in *Beyond Belief: The Secret Lives of Women in Extreme Religions*, Kindle edition, edited by Susan Tive and Cami Ostman (Berkeley: Seal Press, 2013), 63.

2. Joshunda Sanders, "Remapping the Mental Urban Landscape with Memoir," TedCity2.0 2013 conference video, September 2013, http://www.tedcity2.org/talks/remapping-the-mental-urban-landscape-with-memoir/.

3. "What Is Borderline Personality Disorder?" National Institute of Mental Health, accessed February 15, 2009, http://www.nimh.nih.gov/health/topics/borderline-personality-disorder/index.shtml.

4. Joshunda Sanders, "Running through Madness," Joshunda (blog), May 20, 2015, http://joshunda.com/2015/05/20/running-through-madness/.

5. Sanders, "Remapping the Mental Urban Landscape."

6. Jenny Anderson, "Tough as Nails, but Always Ready for a Bearhug," *New York Times*, October 24, 2010, http://www.nytimes.com/2010/10/25/nyregion/25brother.html?pagewanted=all&_r=0.

7. Joshunda Sanders, "Father Time," Joshunda Victoria Sanders (blog), accessed February 16, 2015, http://jvictoriasanders.com/post/52863590953/father-time.

8. "About Emma: Fast Facts," Emma Willard School, accessed October 3, 2015, http://www.emmawillard.org/about-emma/fast-facts.

9. "Emma Willard School," National Park Service, US Department of Interior, March 30, 1998, http://www.nps.gov/nr/travel/pwwmh/ny17.htm.

10. "About Emma, Mission," Emma Willard School, accessed October 3, 2015, http://www.emmawillard.org/about-emma/mission.

11. Sanders, "Seducing God," 68.

12. Sanders, "Father Time."

13. "Asperger's Syndrome," WebMD, accessed June 22, 2015, http://www.webmd.com/brain/autism/mental-health-aspergers-syndrome.

14. "Biography," Frank Bergon (blog), accessed October 3, 2015, http://frankbergon.com/biography.

15. "Why Is It Called Santeria?" About Santeria, accessed March 7, 2015, http://www.aboutsanteria.com/santeriacutea.html.

16. "About Ernest Holmes," Science of Mind Archives, accessed March 7, 2015, http://www.scienceofmindarchives.org/about-the-archives/about-ernest-holmes.

17. Sanders, "Running through Madness."

18. "Historic Highlights," Basilica of the National Shrine of the Immaculate Conception, accessed October 3, 2015, http://www.nationalshrine.com/site/c. osJRKVPBJnH/b.4764143/k.F4E0/Historic_Highlights.htm.

19. "Architecture," Basilica of the National Shrine of the Immaculate Conception, accessed October 3, 2015, http://www.nationalshrine.com/site/c. osJRKVPBJnH/b.4764147/k.9FF6/Architecture.htm.

20. "Our History Since 1858," Saint Augustine Catholic Church, accessed October 3, 2015, http://saintaugustine-dc.org/about-us/history/.

21. "St. Augustine's Roman Catholic Church," MacDonald and Mack Architects, accessed October 3, 2015, http://www.mmarchltd.com/saint-augustine-church.html.

AFTERWORD

1. William V. D'Antonio, Michelle Dillon, and Mary L. Gautier, *American Catholics in Transition* (Lanham, MD: Rowman and Littlefield, 2013), 90–91.

2. Mark M. Gray, "When the Pope Visits," Nineteen Sixty-Four, research blog, Center for Applied Research in the Apostolate, August 20, 2015, 5, http://nineteensixty-four.blogspot.com/2015/08/when-pope-visits.html.

BIBLIOGRAPHY

Abraham, Susan, and Elena Procario-Foley, eds. *Frontiers in Catholic Feminist Theology: Shoulder to Shoulder*. Mineapolis: Fortress Press, 2009.

America Magazine. "The Jews and Vatican II." (November 30, 1963). http://americamagazine.org/issue/100/jews-and-vatican-ii.

Blais, Madeleine. *The Heart Is an Instrument: Portraits in Journalism*. Amherst: The University of Massachusetts Press, 1992.

Bonavoglia, Angela. *Good Catholic Girls: How Women Are Leading the Fight to Change the Church*. New York: HarperCollins Publishers, 2005.

Callahan, Sharon Henderson. "Shifting Images of Church Invite New Leadership Frames." *Journal of Religious Leadership* 1, no. 1, (Spring 2002): 55–64. http://arl-jrl.org/Volumes/CallahanSP02.pdf.

Callahan, Sidney. Foreword to *Turning Point: The Inside Story of the Papal Birth Control Commission*, by Robert McClory, viii–ix. New York: Crossroad Publishing Company, 1995.

Campbell, Sister Simone. *A Nun on the Bus: How All of Us Can Create Hope, Change, and Community*. With David Gibson. Kindle edition. New York: HarperOne, 2014.

Daly, Mary. *The Church and the Second Sex*. 3rd. ed. Boston: Beacon Press, 1985.

D'Antonio, William V., Michelle Dillon, and Mary L. Gautier. *American Catholics in Transition*. Lanham, MD: Rowman & Littlefield, 2013.

Delgado, Teresa. "'Dead in the Water . . . Again': Life, Liberty, and the Pursuit of Happiness in the Twenty-First Century." In *Theological Perspectives for Life, Liberty, and the Pursuit of Happiness*," edited by Ada Maria Isasi-Diaz et al., 61–69. New York: Palgrave MacMillan, 2013.

———. "This Is My Body . . . Given for You: Theological Anthropology *Latina/Mente*." In *Frontiers in Catholic Feminist Theology: Shoulder to Shoulder*, edited by Susan Abraham and Elena Procario-Foley, 25–48. Minneapolis: Fortress Press, 2009.

Dionne, E. J. "Religion's Reach and the Tide of Change." *Notre Dame Magazine* (Summer 2008). http://magazine.nd.edu/news/1189-religion-s-reach-and-the-tide-of-change/.

Fiedler, Maureen, and Linda Rabben, eds. *Rome Has Spoken: A Guide to Forgotten Papal Statements and How They Changed through the Centuries*. New York: The Crossroad Publishing Company, 1998.

Frankfort, Ellen. *Rosie: The Investigation of a Wrongful Death*. With Frances Kissling. New York: The Dial Press, 1978.

Friedman, Ann. "A Pain, and Proud of It: Frances Kissling Retires after 25 Years at CFFC." *In These Times* (March 23, 2007). http://inthesetimes.com/article/3088/a_pain_and_proud_of_it.

Garrett, R. Sam. "The Political Status of Puerto Rico." Congressional Research Service, June 7, 2011. https://www.fas.org/sgp/crs/row/RL32933.pdf.

Goodbrand, Grant. *Therafields: The Rise and Fall of Lea Hindley-Smith's Psychoanalytic Commune*. Toronto: ECW Press, 2010.

Green, Emma. "Notre Dame's Moral Dilemma Over Birth Control." *The Atlantic* (January 7, 2014). http://www.theatlantic.com/national/archive/2014/01/notre-dame-s-moral-dilemma-over-birth-control/282864/.

Hancock, Rev. E. Lee, ed. *The Book of Women's Sermons: Hearing God in Each Other's Voices*. New York: The Berkley Publishing Group, 2000.

Harvey, Margaret. "Discrimination in the Church." *The Way: Contemporary Christian Spirituality* 3, no. 1, (January 1976): 48–56.

Hayes, Diana L. "Church and Culture: A Black Catholic Womanist Perspective." In *The Labor of God: An Ignatian View of Church and Culture*, edited by William J. O'Brien, 65–87. Washington: Georgetown University Press, 1991. https://repository.library.georgetown.edu/bitstream/handle/10822/551473/labor-of-god_1.pdf?sequence=4&isAllowed=y.

———. *Hagar's Daughters: Womanist Ways of Being in the World*. Mahwah, NJ: Paulist Press, 1995.

———. *Standing in the Shoes My Mother Made: A Womanist Theology*. Minneapolis: Fortress Press, 2011.

———. *Trouble Don't Last Always: Soul Prayers*. Collegeville, MN: The Liturgical Press, 1995.

Isasi-Díaz, Ada María, Mary McClintock Fulkerson, and Rosemary P. Carbine, eds. *Theological Perspectives for Life, Liberty, and the Pursuit of Happiness: Public Intellectuals for the Twenty-First Century*. New York: Palgrave Macmillan, 2013.

Kazantzakis, Nikos. *Christ Recrucified*. Translated by Jonathan Griffin. 2nd ed. London: Faber and Faber Limited, 1962.

Kissling, Frances. "Ending the Abortion War: A Modest Proposal." *Christian Century* 107, no. 6 (February 21, 1990): 180–84. Archived text available online at http://www.catholicsforchoice.org/news/op-eds/1990s/19900221endingtheabortionwaramodestproposal.asp.

———. "The Place for Individual Conscience." *Journal of Medical Ethics* 21, issue supplement 2 (October 2001). http://jme.bmj.com/content/27/suppl_2/ii24.full.

MacIsaac, Sharon. *Freud and Original Sin*. New York: Paulist Press, 1974.

Maron, Edward. "An Interview with Mary Daly." *U.S. Catholic* 34, no. 5 (September 1968): 21–24. http://www.uscatholic.org/articles/201309/mary-daly-and-second-sex-27774.

McCarthy, Mary. *Memories of a Catholic Girlhood*. 4th ed. New York: Vintage, 2004.

McClory, Robert. *Turning Point: The Inside Story of the Papal Birth Control Commission, and How "Humane Vitae" Changed the Life of Patty Crowley and the Future of the Church*. New York: The Crossroad Publiishing Company, 1995.

McCormick, Richard A. "*Humanae Vitae* 25 Years Later." *America Magazine* (July 17, 1993). http://americamagazine.org/issue/100/humanae-vitae-25-years-later.

McEnroy, Carmel Elizabeth. *Guests in the House: The Women of Vatican II*. New York: The Crossroad Publishing Company, 1996.

Miller, Patricia. *Good Catholics: The Battle Over Abortion in the Catholic Church*. Berkeley: University of California Press, 2014.

Newpower, Paul D., M. M., and Stephen T. DeMott, M.M. "The Pope in Central America: What Did His Trip Accomplish?" *St. Anthony Messenger* (June 1983). http://www.americancatholic.org/Features/JohnPaulII/3-CentralAmerica-1983.asp.

Notre Dame Magazine. "Letters about the Obama visit" (Summer 2009). http://magazine.nd.edu/news/11845-letters-about-the-obama-visit/.

O'Malley, John W. "The Style of Vatican II." *America Magazine* (February 24, 2003). http://americamagazine.org/issue/423/article/style-vatican-ii.

Pope Francis, *Amoris Laetitia*, April 8, 2016, http://w2.vatican.va/content/francesco/en/apost_exhortations/documents/papa-francesco_esortazione-ap_20160319_amoris-laetitia.html.

Pope Paul VI. *Humanae Vitae.* July 25, 1968. http://w2.vatican.va/content/paul-vi/en/encyclicals/documents/hf_p-vi_enc_25071968_humanae-vitae.html.

Reydams-Schils, Gretchen. *An Anthology of Snakebites: On Women, Love, and Philosophy.* New York: Seven Bridges Press, 2001.

———. Letter to the editor. *Commonweal* (February 24, 2012). Lexis-Nexis.

Sanders, Joshunda Victoria. "Seducing God." In *Beyond Belief: The Secret Lives of Women in Extreme Religions*, Kindle edition, edited by Susan Tive and Cami Ostman, 62–74. Berkeley: Seal Press, 2013.

Spector, Tim. "What Twins Reveal about the Science of Faith." *Popular Science* (August 8, 2013). http://www.popsci.com/science/article/2013-08/what-twins-reveal-about-god-gene.

Stevenson, Heather, and Kiki Zeldes. "Write a Chapter and Change the World: How the Boston Women's Health Book Collective Transformed Women's' Health Then—and Now." Abstract. *American Journal of Public Health* 98, no. 10 (October 2008): 174–45. http://www.ncbi.nlm.nih.gov/pmc/articles/PMC2636468/.

Tive, Susan, and Cami Ostman, eds. *Beyond Belief: The Secret Lives of Women in Extreme Religions.* Berkeley: Seal Press, 2013.

Troester, Rosalie Riegle, comp. and ed. *Voices from the Catholic Worker.* Philadelphia: Temple University Press, 1993.

U.S. Catholic. "Do You Hear the Cry of the Poor? Liberation Theology Today: A U.S. Catholic Interview with Michael Lee," 75, no. 3 (March 10, 2010): 18–21. http://www.uscatholic.org/culture/social-justice/2010/01/do-you-hear-cry-poor-liberation-theology-today.

Walker, Alice. *The Color Purple.* 1st Harvest Edition. New York: Houghton Mifflin Harcourt Publishing Company, 2003.

———. *In Search of Our Mothers' Gardens: Womanist Prose.* New York: Open Road Media, 2011.

Wellesley College. *1978–1979 Bulletin of Wellesley College* 68, no. 1 (1978). http://repository.wellesley.edu/cgi/viewcontent.cgi?article=1076&context=catalogs.

INDEX

abortion, 25, 29–31, 34, 35, 36, 56, 58, 68, 78, 144, 148, 167–168; Church opposition, 4, 19, 20, 25–26, 33, 34, 35, 57, 116, 118; morality of, 29–30, 31, 32, 33, 35, 36, 150; politics of, 3, 58, 147, 149; pro-choice Catholics, 4, 26, 32, 33; Roe v. Wade, 18, 29. *See also* Catholics for Choice; contraception; Kissling, Frances

Affordable Care Act, 58; contraception coverage, 20, 21, 59, 61, 148–149

African American Catholicism, 5, 9, 88, 95, 96–98, 101, 103, 104, 160, 161, 172, 173, 176, 182; and feminism, 9, 102–103. *See also* Hayes, Diana L.; womanism

Aquinas, Thomas, 44

Ayo, Nicholas, 152

Baum, Gregory, 7, 17, 42–43, 44, 45, 47, 49, 52. *See also* MacIsaac McKenna, Sharon

birth control. *See* contraception

Blaine, Barbara, 6, 123–139; Catholic Worker movement, 124, 130–131, 134, 138; Jamaica, work in, 123, 129–130, 130; sexual abuse, personal experience, 124–125, 126–129, 132–133, 135, 139; Survivors Network of those Abused by Priests, 125, 133–134, 135, 136, 137–139

Blais, Madeleine, vii, 23

Brown, Coleman, 110, 112

Campbell, Simone, 5, 10, 55–68; 2012 Democratic National Convention, 56, 61; Affordable Care Act, support for, 58, 59, 61; Leadership Conference of Women Religious, 57, 58, 61; NETWORK, 56–60, 61, 62, 64, 67; Nuns on the Bus, 58–60; Ryan Budget, opposition to, 59, 60, 61; Sisters of Social Service, 63–64

Catholics for Choice, 4, 26, 31, 32, 35, 36, 38, 181; abortion, position on, 33; Vatican, conflict with, 32–33, 33–34, 35. *See also* Kissling, Frances

Catholics for a Free Choice. *See* Catholics for Choice

Catholic University of America, 95, 98, 99, 100

Catholic University of Louvain, 5, 99, 100, 101

Carty, Brian, 164–165, 166, 169

Center for Health, Ethics and Social Policy, 4, 36. *See also* Kissling, Frances

The Church and the Second Sex, 55–56

Cone, James, 97

Congregation for the Doctrine of the Faith, 57

contraception, 3, 4, 19, 20, 29, 31, 34, 36, 52, 58, 67, 78, 116, 118; abortion, prevention of, 19, 34; and Affordable Care Act, 20, 21, 148–149; *Humanae Vitae*, 7–8

Day, Dorothy, 112, 130
Delgado, Teresa, 5, 105–121; Iona College, 105, 116–117, 118, 119, 120; Latina perspective on theology, 106, 114–115, 119; liberation theology, 106, 115; rape, personal experience, 105, 106, 108, 109; womanism, 106, 112, 115, 119
DignityUSA, 5, 71, 82, 83, 84–85, 181; Dignity/Boston, 81. *See also* Duddy-Burke, Marianne
Dressler, Paul, 174
Duddy-Burke, Marianne, 5, 71–86; adoption, personal experience, 83; lesbian and Catholic, personal experience, 71, 77–78, 78–80, 82, 83; DignityUSA, 71, 81, 82, 83, 84–85; women priests, 82, 84

Eschmann Theodore, Ignatius, 44

feminism, 6, 9, 30, 33, 36, 56, 109, 146, 151, 155, 156, 182; African-American Catholic women, experience of, 9, 101–102; conflict with Catholicism, 2, 3, 4, 55–56, 57, 101, 117, 156, 177, 178. *See also* ordination of women; womanism
Flynn, Harry, 136
Freud, Sigmund, 4, 40, 47

Georgetown University, 5, 100, 101, 178; Jesuit ownership of slaves, 87. *See also* Hayes, Diana L.
Gumbleton, Thomas, 135–136. *See also* Blaine, Barbara
Gutiérrez, Gustavo, 8

Humanae Vitae, 7–8
Harvey, Margaret, 1
Hayes, Diana L., 5, 87–104; chondromalacia, personal experience, 94; Georgetown University, work at, 87, 100–101; *Hagar's Daughters*, 88, 102–103; womanist theology, 9, 88, 97, 101–102

Hesburgh, Theodore, 143–144
Hindley-Smith, Lea, 44–45, 50–51. *See also* MacIsaac McKenna, Sharon; Therafields
Hubbard, Howard, 98–99

Jenkins, John I., 148, 149

Kissling, Frances, 4, 25–38; abortion clinics, work at, 29–30; abortion rights, 26, 35; and adoption, 83; Catholics for Choice, work at, 31–35, 36, 38

LGBT issues, 5, 20, 36, 61, 88, 148, 181, 182; Church response, 71, 71–72, 79, 81, 85–86; gay and lesbian Catholics, experiences of, 18, 19, 77–78, 80, 81–82, 82–83, 83. *See also* DignityUSA; Duddy-Burke, Marianne
liberation theology, 8, 97, 100, 106, 115, 130, 145; papal views on, 8, 141

MacIsaac McKenna, Sharon, 4, 9, 39–53; Freud, research on, 40, 47; Sisters of Our Lady of Sion, 41–42, 46, 51; Therafields, time at, 44–45, 46, 48, 50–51
Magdalene, Mary, 175
McCarthy, Mary, 13–14
Medicaid, 60, 61; abortion funding, 30

National Catholic Reporter, 3, 34, 124, 182
NETWORK, 5, 56–57; Vatican censure, 57. *See also* Campbell, Simone
New York Times, 32, 36, 59, 165

ordination of women, 2, 9, 10, 52–53, 58, 65–67, 76, 82, 84, 111, 150, 183

Peter, Carl, 97
Plato, 142, 151, 154
Pope Benedict XVI, 1, 8, 104, 174
Pope Francis, 2, 3, 4, 8, 10, 36, 61–62, 62, 68, 72, 86, 104, 120, 138, 174, 177; *Amoris Laetitia*, 3; approach to women, 2, 10, 61, 104, 120, 150; tone, 7, 174; U.S. visit, 61

Pope John XXIII, 6, 7, 16, 44, 72
Pope John Paul II, 8, 35, 93, 99, 151;
    liberation theology, response to, 8, 141
Pope Paul VI, 7, 63, 93

Reydams-Schils, Gretchen, 6, 10,
    141–157, 178; *An Anthology of
    Snakebites: On Women, Love, and
    Philosophy*, 151, 151–154; European
    Catholicism, 142, 144–145, 146, 149;
    Notre Dame, time at, 142, 143, 144,
    147–149, 151, 154, 156, 157
*Rosie: The Investigation of a Wrongful
    Death*, 30. *See also* Medicaid
Ryan, Paul, 59, 60, 61

Sanders, Joshunda, 6, 159–176; abortion,
    personal experience, 166–168; Brother
    Brian Carty, 164–165, 166; mother's
    mental illness, 161–162, 162–163,
    165–166, 166–167, 168; Saint
    Augustine's Church, 173–174, 174,
    176
Second Vatican Council, 4, 9, 39, 42, 44,
    63, 66; backlash, 7–8, 49, 52, 145;
    reforms, 6–7, 44, 49, 56, 76, 94, 96,
    126
sexual abuse by priests, 6, 20, 133–134,
    135, 136, 137; Church response, 125,
    132, 132–133, 135, 139; trauma of
    victims, 124–125, 125, 139. *See also*
    Blaine, Barbara; Survivors Network of
    those Abused by Priests
social justice, 3, 5, 17, 33, 37, 56, 58, 62,
    68, 121, 123, 124, 131, 134, 145, 178,
    182; Church de-emphasis of, 9, 62,

148, 150
synod, 2–3
Survivors Network of those Abused by
    Priests (SNAP), 6, 125, 133–134, 135,
    136, 137–139, 182. *See also* Blaine,
    Barbara; sexual abuse by priests

Therafields, 44–45, 45, 46, 48, 50–51. *See
    also* Hindley-Smith, Lea; MacIsaac
    McKenna, Sharon
Tremblay, Nellis, 93, 94, 95

United Nations, 29, 33–34, 125, 139
United States Conference of Catholic
    Bishops, 3, 84, 98, 136; To Live in
    Christ Jesus, letter, 81
University of Toronto, 16, 43; Saint
    Michael's College, 17, 43, 45, 52

Vatican, 1, 4, 26, 39, 42, 52, 67, 84, 85, 87;
    conflict with Catholic women, 5,
    33–34, 57–58, 58, 61–62; and gay and
    lesbian Catholics, 71, 86; sexual abuse,
    response to, 135–136
Vatican II. *See* Second Vatican Council
Virgin Mary, 17–18, 103, 110, 114, 155,
    168, 175

Walker, Alice, 9, 164, 175, 176
Warren, Chet, 124, 126–129, 132–133,
    133, 135. *See also* sexual abuse by
    priests
womanism, 9, 101–102, 106, 120, 175;
    womanist theology, 5, 9, 88, 97,
    102–103, 106–107, 112, 115. *See also*
    Delgado, Teresa; Hayes, Diana L

ABOUT THE AUTHOR

Celia Viggo Wexler is an award-winning former journalist and nonfiction author. She graduated summa cum laude from the University of Toronto, where she earned the prestigious Governor General's Medal in English Literature. She earned a graduate degree in journalism from Point Park University, Pittsburgh. Her work has appeared in *The New York Times*, *The Washington Post*, *Columbia Journalism Review*, and *The Nation*.

Wexler's first book, *Out of the News: Former Journalists Discuss a Profession in Crisis*, won a national award for excellence from the Society of Professional Journalists, one of the oldest and largest journalism organizations in the country.

She has worked as a public-interest lobbyist since 1996, first as vice president of advocacy for the good-government group Common Cause and then as senior Washington representative for the Union of Concerned Scientists. She lives in Alexandria, Virginia, with her husband, Richard. She has one daughter, Valerie.